Edgar Powell

The Rising in East Anglia in 1381

With an Appendix Containing the Suffolk Poll Tax Lists for that Year

Edgar Powell

The Rising in East Anglia in 1381
With an Appendix Containing the Suffolk Poll Tax Lists for that Year

ISBN/EAN: 9783744767675

Printed in Europe, USA, Canada, Australia, Japan

Cover: Foto ©ninafisch / pixelio.de

More available books at **www.hansebooks.com**

THE
RISING IN EAST ANGLIA
IN
1381.

London: C. J. CLAY AND SONS,
CAMBRIDGE UNIVERSITY PRESS WAREHOUSE,
AVE MARIA LANE.
Glasgow: 263, ARGYLE STREET.

Leipzig: F. A. BROCKHAUS.
New York: MACMILLAN AND CO.

THE

RISING IN EAST ANGLIA

IN

1381

WITH AN APPENDIX CONTAINING

THE SUFFOLK POLL TAX LISTS
FOR THAT YEAR.

BY

EDGAR POWELL, B.A.

CAMBRIDGE:
AT THE UNIVERSITY PRESS.
1896

[All Rights reserved.]

Cambridge:
PRINTED BY J. AND C. F. CLAY,
AT THE UNIVERSITY PRESS.

PREFACE.

DURING a search among the archives at the Public Record Office, in connection with a work of a genealogical and topographical nature relating to the County of Suffolk, I discovered that there were many unpublished records in existence which throw a considerable amount of fresh light on that very interesting crisis of our social history known as the Peasants' Rising in 1381.

After a careful perusal of these and a search through the more likely classes of MSS. at the Museum and elsewhere, I embodied the results of my work in a paper, treating of the Rising in Suffolk only, which I read before the Royal Historical Society in 1894.

A further search has enabled me to extend the narrative so as to embrace the incidents of the revolt, as far as I have been able to trace them, in the counties of Norfolk, Suffolk and Cambridgeshire, and thus to render the account both more complete and more interesting.

The hope that such a compilation may be of some use to historians and others interested in this period of English History must be my apology for offering it to the public.

In the first appendix will be found transcripts of a series of documents, which I think can hardly fail to be of interest to students of fourteenth-century history, namely the lists of the inhabitants of the villages and towns in Suffolk, made by the collectors of the Poll Tax of 1381.

The special and distinct importance of such documents lies in the fact that they give so much detailed information as to the condition and occupations of the inhabitants of the country villages, from the wealthy manorial lord, such as he whose household is enumerated at Stowlangtoft, down to the humblest serf on his manor.

It is to be regretted that so many of these records have perished; those given here, which refer only to some fifty places, are all that are now extant for a county which contained not far short of five hundred parishes.

The final return of the results of the Poll Tax of 1381 gives a census of the population of the various counties in England, and this return, together with that of the Poll Tax of 1377, will be found given in a tabular form.

The second appendix contains transcripts from various authorities cited.

E. POWELL.

December, 1895.

TABLE OF CONTENTS.

	PAGE
PREFACE	v
INTRODUCTION	1
AN ACCOUNT OF THE RISING IN SUFFOLK	9
,, ,, ,, NORFOLK	26
,, ,, ,, CAMBRIDGESHIRE	41
GENERAL REMARKS ON THE RISING IN EAST ANGLIA	57

APPENDIX I.

Analysis of the population of the Hundred of Thingo in 1381   67

SUFFOLK POLL TAX LISTS.

	PAGE		PAGE
Barrow	67	Harleston	98
Benacre	116	Hawsted	74
Bregg	117	Hengrave	75
Brockley	69	Hinderclay	105
Bulchamp	117	Horningsheath Magna	76
Buxhall	92	Horningsheath Parva	77
Buxlow	115	Ickworth	78
Chevington	70	Ixworth Thorpe	106
Combes	99	Kessingland	115
Dagworth	97	Knattishall	104
Euston	103	Lackford	79
Fakenham Magna	102	Langham	107
Finborough Magna	91	Mildenhall	85
Flempton	71	Nowton	80
Fornham All Saints	72	Old Newton	95
Gipping Newton	97	Onehouse	98
Hadleigh	111	Reed	69
Hargrave	73	Risby	82

CONTENTS.

	PAGE		PAGE
Saxham Magna	80	West Creting	94
Saxham Parva	81	Westley	83
Shelland	98	Wetherden	95
Stowlangtoft	109	Whepsted	84
Stowmarket	89	Wordwell	110
Thorney	101		
Thwaite	114	Unidentified (2)	117, 119

Table showing population of England as returned in 1377 and 1381 120
Table showing clerical population of England and Wales, 1381   123

Appendix II.

Transcripts of various Indictments 126
Extracts from Assize Roll 103 136
Transcripts from Cottonian MS. Claudius A. XII . . . 138
Escheator's Inquisition as to the property of Thomas Sampson   143

Index 147

INTRODUCTION.

THOUGH much of the subsequent improvement in the conditions of life among the rural population of England was doubtless originally due to the ravages of the Black Death in 1348 and 1361, yet the more immediate effect of that catastrophe, during the complete disorganisation of all social relations which followed in its wake, was rather to check for the time being the process of amelioration which had been going on.

In the country districts the sudden sweeping away of nearly one-half of the population had rendered the supply of agricultural labour exceedingly scarce, and the inevitable demand for higher wages had at once followed. The stubborn refusal, however, on the part of the landowners to pay the higher rate necessary under the new conditions of life, and the equally stubborn refusal on the part of the labourers to work at the old, had brought the business of agriculture almost to a standstill. Alarmed at the gravity of the situation the Legislature stepped in and limited by statute the legal wages to be received by labourers, artisans, and servants, and by punitive measures against those who gave or received any higher, endeavoured to force down wages to the now impossible rates which had ruled before the plague. This legislation, though practically a failure for the object for which it was designed, had the effect of exasperating to the last degree a large class of the community, and by extorting from them great sums in fines subjected their respect for law and order almost to the breaking strain. Notwithstanding the rigour of the statutes, the condition of the labourers at this time appears to have been one of considerable prosperity, and one in which, to judge from the description given in the Vision of Piers the Plowman in

1377[1], the standard of comfort was fairly high. They had thus arrived as a class at a condition in which oppression and continued extortion were well calculated to produce dangerous results.

When, indeed, we consider how large was the class which these statutes affected, and the great severity with which they curtailed personal liberty—even going the length of the revolting. cruelty of branding the foreheads of those who infringed them with an F for falsity[2]—we can only wonder, not so much at the outbreak of an insurrection, as that it should have been so long delayed.

A glance at the Poll Tax schedules for the hundred of Thingo (see Appendix, p. 67), where the inhabitants are arranged in classes as labourers, artificers, and servants (a terminology similar to that of the statutes), will show that out of a total of 870 names, no less than 808 came under the three classes aimed at by the statutes; and I think we may fairly infer some such proportion would hold good throughout the country districts, at all events in East Anglia. The amount of money wrung by these means from the above-mentioned classes was very large, for we find application made to Parliament for powers to utilise the sums coming in under the statutes, for paying the taxes due from a community, and other general purposes.

Already do we find that in self-defence the working-classes had begun to form confederate clubs, the prototypes of our modern trades-unions, whose object was to resist with a strong hand the claims for customary labour due from the holders of servile lands, which it appears the landlords owing to the scarcity of labourers were now trying to enforce to the utmost.

In the struggle that eventually ensued we do not find that the working-classes were left to fight alone, for Walsingham's description of the insurgents as 'discaligati ribaldi,' though doubtless true to a large extent, is far from being

---

[1] Vision of William concerning Piers the Plowman, Passus vi. (Ed. Skeat, 1874).
[2] This penalty could be enforced if the prosecuting party wished it. It was, however, ordered that the branding-iron should be kept in custody of the sheriff. (See Statute 34 Ed. III.)

exhaustive. When we find such names as Richard Talmache de Bentley, John Talmache, Esq., Sir Thomas Cornerd, Knt., Thomas Monchesey of Edwardstone, James de Bedyngfield, Sir Roger Bacon, Knt., Thomas de Gissing, and others, all names of well-known county families, among the active leaders of revolt, we must admit that the popular party had obtained the active support and sympathy of a considerable proportion of the country gentry.

A genuine sympathy for the working-classes, combined with the strong aversion which they held, in common with them, to the payment of the Poll Tax, may possibly account for some of the better class giving their active assistance to the revolutionary party, but the movement was distinctly against their interests as a class. Some indeed may have felt the full force of the complaint, re-echoed in the Vision of Piers the Plowman, 'Væ terræ ubi puer rex est,' and have hoped that had success crowned their efforts some change for the better governance of the realm might have been brought about.

The awful mortality during the Black Death had also, by severing so much of the tradition of the past, given scope for the growth of new ideas and aspirations, which, under the impetus given them by the genius of the great reformer, spread far and wide through the land. Indeed, the keen criticisms of Church and State poured forth by travelling priests such as John Balle—himself, it is said, a disciple of Wiclif—found an eager audience among the working-classes, and, being carried through the length and breadth of the country, left men's minds unsettled and expectant in every department of life.

Nor were these social problems which called for solution within the realm the only trouble with which the nation was at this time confronted.

On the northern border the savage incursions of the Scots had devastated the land, so that indeed no return for the Poll Tax appears to have been possible for the county of Northumberland, and the townsmen of Penrith state that, for the same reason, they were 'adeo depauperati,' that they could only furnish seventy-five shillings to the collectors, while the return of population for Cumberland, given as 11,800 in 1377, is returned in 1381 as only 4,700.

Nor were matters very much better on the southern shores of the island, where the frequent descents made on the coast by the French checked all industry and kept the inhabitants in a state of continual alarm.

Distracted thus on all hands by difficulty and danger, the country, after providing tax after tax without any apparent benefit accruing, was called on by the Parliament which met at Northampton in November 1380, to provide still further for the expenses of a military expedition on the other side of the Channel. This was done by means of a Poll Tax, to fully collect which the ordinary methods appear to have failed, and the rigorous means thereupon introduced to enforce payment at once fanned into open flame the long smouldering discontent which overspread the country.

This tax, which forms so important a factor in the subject before us, was to be charged at the rate of three groats, or twelve pence, on every lay person male and female of the age of fifteen years, beggars only excepted. Though the sum total for each township was to be as many shillings as it contained residents over the age of fifteen years, it was also arranged that the richer members of each community should pay more than the poorer, within the limits that no one should pay more than sixty groats, or less than one groat, for himself and his wife; and no one could be charged except in the township within which ' he and his wife and children dwelt, or where he was domiciled if in service.' The proceeds of the tax were to be paid into the Treasury in two sums, viz.: two-thirds were due in January 1380, and the remainder in the following June [Rot. Parl. III. 90].

The procedure of the collection of the tax appears to have been as follows. The collectors acting on the authority of Letters Patent dated December 7, 1380, set to work at once, and it seems for the most part collected the entire subsidy of three groats per head at one collection, of which amount they paid over two-thirds into the Treasury, furnishing at the same time an account of what the population in each county amounted to, and of the money due. These accounts, where extant, are preserved among the Exchequer Lay Subsidies, and are arranged under counties as 'views of accounts.' Though this collection was made with much difficulty and delay, it does not appear to have met with any organised resistance. But the amount collected was regarded as very unsatisfactory.

On February 22, the king, with the advice of his council, issued a writ to the Barons of the Exchequer[1] in which he states that the two-thirds already received had fallen so far short of the amount anticipated as to be quite inadequate for carrying out the ordinances made by Parliament for the safety of the realm and support of the army abroad, and ordered them, since he understood that the tax had been already wholly levied[2], to instruct the collectors to pay in at once all the sums levied, and all they could still levy, on April 21, instead of in June as originally ordered, in order thus to avoid any mischief that might happen to the realm and army through lack of funds.

When the disappointing nature of the results to be obtained from the tax were fully realised, it became evident that something was very wrong, and severe measures were deemed necessary to rectify matters[3]. Accordingly on March 16, we find[4] that the king, having satisfactory evidence in his possession that the collectors had been guilty of gross negligence and favouritism in the performance of their duties, commissioned a staff of inspectors for each district named, armed with large authority and powers of imprisonment, to travel from place to place, scrutinising carefully the lists of inhabitants, and forcibly compelling payment from those who had evaded it before. This commission was however limited to the following districts,

Norfolk	Hunts	Notts and Derbyshire	Canterbury	Somerset
Suffolk	Herts	Devon and Cornwall	Northants	(West Riding (Yorks)
Cambs	Essex	Kent	Gloucestershire	

[1] Q. R. Memoranda Roll, 4 Ric. II., Brevia, m. xxv.

[2] L. T. R. Enrolled Accounts (Subs.) No. 13; under 'Villa Leycester,' 'quod collectores idem subsidium integre levaverunt et collegerunt ut rex intellexit.'

[3] The total amount which finally reached the Treasury for the Lay Poll Tax of 1381 appears to have been £41825. 14s. 3d. Lay Subsidies, Divers Counties, $\frac{243}{13}$. P.R.O.

[4] L. T. R. Orig., 4 Ric. II. m. 12 and 13.

Some of the appointments under this commission do not seem to have been made till May, so perhaps no steps were taken till after the time appointed to the collectors for making their final payments[1].

It appears that it was the action taken under this second commission, regarded as it possibly may have been by the people rather in the light of an attempt to extort a fresh tax without the authority of Parliament, that was the more immediate cause of the outbreak.

Henry Knighton relates that the person who suggested this latter course to the king was a certain John Leg whose name appears as 'serviens ad arma regis' in the second commission, for the county of Kent, and no doubt the same person whose death at the hands of the London mob is related by Walsingham.

The enrolled accounts of this Poll Tax seem generally to give the population in the several counties at a higher figure than the first returns of the collectors, and in the districts affected by the second commission this increase is very noticeable indeed; but when we come to compare these totals with those given in the enrolled accounts for the 4d. Poll Tax of 1377 a most remarkable diminution of the population appears[2].

It will be best to give in a tabular form the results of the three returns mentioned above, for the counties of Norfolk and Suffolk.

—	First returns made by collectors 1381	L.T.R. enrolled account 1381	L.T.R. enrolled account 1377
Norfolk . . .	58,714	66,719	88,797
Norwich . . .	3,268	3,833	3,925
Lynn . . .	1,757	1,824	3,127
Yarmouth . . .	no separate return	no separate return	1,941
Suffolk . . .	31,734	44,635	58,610
Bury . . .	no separate return	1,334	2,445
Ipswich . . .	963	963	1,507

[1] The account of one of the inspectors, Thomas Sayvill, who was sent to Notts and Derbyshire, is extant. He left London on April 30, 1381, and returned on August 4, and his expenses were 1s. 6d. per day for the ninety-six days he was away. Exch. Q. R. Misc. $\frac{2}{16}$.

[2] See Appendix, p. 121.

INTRODUCTION. 7

A Poll Tax was also laid on the clergy at this time[1], charged on the higher grades at twenty groats, and on the inferior clergy, over the age of sixteen at three groats, which was to be paid in two sums, on February 22, 1381, and June 24 following.

The large discrepancy between the returns of the population in 1377 and 1381 is to be accounted for, not, I think, on the supposition that the population had necessarily decreased, though that may possibly have been the case, so much as that in order to evade the Poll Tax collector, a large portion of the inhabitants of the towns and villages had left their homes and taken to a roving life in the woods and wastes of the country. The fact that no one could be legally charged except at the place where he dwelt, may have encouraged a process, which if it went on on a large scale, would certainly have facilitated the work of the leaders of the popular party in collecting their large bands of malcontents. The possibility too of bodies of men being able to move from place to place, without being suspected of any motive ulterior to the evasion of the tax, may perhaps account, partially at any rate, for the country being taken so much by surprise, and so completely at a disadvantage, when the outbreak came.

The following accounts of the proceedings in Suffolk and Norfolk during the rising in 1381 are chiefly compiled from the legal records of the proceedings taken against the rioters after order was restored. These are to be found on the Coram Rege Rolls of the period, and in the Antient Indictments referring to these counties[2]. From the latter class unfortunately all the Indictments taken at Bury St Edmunds, it is stated, were handed over to Sir Thomas Morieux; and thus a very large and interesting portion of the records for Suffolk have been lost from the series. This gap has however been filled to a certain extent, by the account given of the transactions at Bury and Mildenhall by John Gosford, almoner at that time to the Abbey of Bury, and afterwards Prior. A

---

[1] See Appendix, p. 123.
[2] Both these classes of documents are in the Public Record Office. Bundle 128 of the Antient Indictments contains those referring to Suffolk and Norfolk, and for the latter county appears to be complete.

fifteenth-century transcript of his work is preserved in a volume of the Cottonian MSS. in the British Museum, marked Claudius, A. XII. On folio 81 of this volume begins the 'Registrum hostlarie Sancti Edmundi factum sive compilatum per fratrem Andream Astone de diversis evidenciis anno mccccxxvj^{to} in quo continentur diversa subscripta sub hac forma'; and on folio 126b begins the account from which I have drawn: it is headed thus—' Electio domini Johannis Tymworth in abbatem cum actibus provisoris et insurrectione comunitatis cum dampnis horribilibus et malefactis perpetratis priori conventui et monasterio Sancti Edmundi per insurrectores de Bury prout scribitur per J. Gosford.'

Of that part of this MS. which refers to the riots in 1381 I have given a full transcript in Appendix II., p. 139.

CHAPTER I.

AN ACCOUNT OF THE RISING IN SUFFOLK.

THE principal leader of the popular party in Suffolk, and, indeed, it appears a chief mover and leading spirit in the insurrection throughout the counties of Norfolk, Suffolk, and Cambridgeshire, was a certain John Wrawe, of Sudbury, described on the Coram Rege Rolls as a 'capellanus' or chaplain.

Thomas of Walsingham, who gives a long account of this period, tells us that Wrawe had been in London immediately before the outbreak in Suffolk, and in close intercourse with Wat Tyler, the Kentish leader. Judging from subsequent events, we may infer that they then finally decided that the time for action had arrived, and arranged that the outbreak should be simultaneous, as far as possible, in the districts over which their organisation extended. After his final consultation with Tyler, Wrawe returned immediately to Suffolk, and in the town of Sudbury on Wednesday, June 12, 1381, gave the first signal for revolt.

The opening scene in the terrible tragedy which ensued during the month of June was laid at the little village of Liston in Essex, which lies not far from the town of Long Melford, and close on the borders of Suffolk.

To this spot on the 12th Wrawe directed his forces, being it seems already in command of a large body of countrymen, drawn chiefly from the counties of Norfolk, Suffolk, Herts, and Essex. Immediately on his arrival he dispatched emissaries to the neighbouring town of Sudbury, some three miles distant, commanding all men of that town forthwith to repair to him at Liston. Joined by such reinforcements as arrived, the mob marched with one accord to the manor house of Overhall. This they assailed with great fury and completely wrecked, breaking in, we are told, both doors and windows, and destroying the tiles on the roof.

In choosing the object for his first attack, Wrawe was no doubt guided by a knowledge of what would best give the popular discontent unanimous expression. This appears more clearly when we find that the owner of this manor of Overhall was Richard Lyons, a man who had obtained considerable, though unenviable, notoriety during the reign of Edward the Third. In the Parliament of 1379–80 he appears to have sat for Essex, but had previously been a farmer of subsidies and money-lender to the king, in which capacity he fell foul of the Parliament in 1376, and having been impeached for various extensive frauds and peculations was deprived of his lands and goods. These, however, he managed eventually to regain, though, as was supposed at the time, chiefly through the instrumentality of Alice Perrers, the king's mistress. We can thus see why popular feeling may well have been so strong against him as to induce Wrawe to select his house for the first attack. Lyons himself, indeed, according to Henry Knighton's account, fell a victim to the popular fury in London. He certainly died on June 14, 1381, for it is by means of his Inquisition post-mortem that he can be identified as the owner of Overhall at Liston.

Stow, in his Chronicle, states that Richard Lyons was a lapidary and wine-merchant of London, and Grafton's Chronicle relates that he once had Wat Tyler dwelling with him, presumably as apprentice, 'and on a tyme did beate him,' so that in procuring his death we are led to infer that Tyler was paying off an old grudge.

On the following day, Thursday, June 13, being the feast of Corpus Christi, the mob proceeded to Cavendish, a village about six miles to the north-east of Sudbury, and John Wrawe is again their leader. The attack here was directed on the parish church, but not with any idea it would seem of harming the edifice. They appear even to have taken the trouble to procure the keys, through the felonious practices, we are told, of Ralph Somerton, dyer of Sudbury, who thereupon admitted John Wrawe and his crowd of followers into the church, and led them to the belfry, where they had been informed the goods of 'John de Cavendish, late Justice of our Lord the King,' had been hidden away. These they at once seized, taking away from the church tower, as we are told, a 'Jakke of Velvet,' price 26s. 8d., a silver candlestick worth seven pounds, and other articles of value, which spoil Wrawe was called upon to divide among his followers.

The fact that the king's justice should have found it necessary to remove his valuables to the church for safe custody, would seem to indicate that he knew himself to be obnoxious to the people, and felt strongly the growing discontent of the times.

After pillaging the church tower at Cavendish, Wrawe, wishing to fortify his band for their all-important expedition to Bury, led them at once to Melford Green, where, we are told, they repaired to the tavern of one Onewene to refresh themselves, and, as the roll quaintly tells us, 'adinvicem biberunt unam pipam vini rubei,' of the price of seven marks, 3s. 4d., which amount was, however, faithfully paid to the taverner from the spoils already taken. After a short halt they again set forth, this time taking the road to Bury St Edmunds, which they reached the same day, though probably late in the evening, the distance from Melford being about seventeen miles. Arrived here, Wrawe lost no time in issuing a proclamation to the men of Bury, which one regrets much has not been fully recorded. Its main point, however, at all events from a legal point of view, seems to have been a summons to the townsmen to meet him and his band in the Southgate of Bury, and to act with them in all things, on pain of instant decapitation if they gainsaid him. (Coram Rege Roll, 484, Rex 26.)

The next morning (Friday, June 14) the mob, under the command of John Wrawe, Robert Tavell, of Lavenham, and John Talmache, Esquire, directed their attack on the house of John de Cambridge, the prior of the abbey, which they succeeded in breaking into and despoiled of its contents. Meanwhile a detachment had been dispatched by John

Wrawe to Thetford under the command of Geoffrey Parfay, vicar of All Saints, Sudbury, together with his chaplain Thomas, and one Adam Bray, of Sudbury; Thos. Monchesey, of Edwardstone, Esquire, junior, being also mentioned as one of the party. On their arrival there they summoned the mayor, Simon Barbour, and the chief burgesses before them, and levied blackmail on the town to the extent of forty marks of gold, threatening that if the money was not paid down at once, they would send to Bury and fetch John Wrawe and all his band, who would burn their town about them.

From this incident we see the great terror which the name of Wrawe inspired, for from the Norfolk indictments referring to the same matter we learn that the whole band who came to Thetford consisted of only seventeen men, a force which one can hardly suppose the mayor and corporation could have failed in giving a good account of had not the name of Wrawe completely overawed the town.

On the same day, we learn from the Coram Rege Roll, Sir Thomas Cornerd, Knight, took advantage of the occasion to go over to Stansfield, near Bury, and entering the house of one John Rokwood[1] there, took from him the sum of five marks, using threats similar to those Parfay had so successfully employed at Thetford. Wrawe states that Cornerd's little expedition was made without any authority from him, though he did not scruple to benefit by it; for it appears Cornerd was only allowed to keep 40s. 'pro labore suo' out of the money taken, the rest falling to Wrawe, to whom it is also recorded the money taken at Thetford, with the exception of 4l., was duly handed over.

Wrawe and his band at Bury, having wrecked the house of the prior, proceeded to that of John de Cavendish in the same town, which they subjected to similar treatment. Of the spoil taken hence it is noted that Robert Tavell got possession of a remarkable sword, described as 'unum gladium argento harnesiatum et deauratum et perre[2],' of the value of a hundred marks. While his house was thus being

[1] A Johannes de Rokwood was escheator for Norfolk and Suffolk in 1375. Rymer iii. 1044.
[2] 'Perre' probably from the French, meaning set with stones.

ransacked at Bury St Edmunds, John de Cavendish himself had had the misfortune to fall into the hands of another band of rioters in the neighbourhood of Lakenheath, a parish lying in the fens beyond Mildenhall, some twenty miles to the north-west of Bury. Owing to the fact that the indictments taken at Bury have been lost from the series, I have not been able to find a detailed account of Cavendish's capture and death; a list, however, of 104 of the malefactors is preserved[1], and in some cases the different parts they took in this tragedy have been duly noted against their names. Also from the Placita Coronæ, at Mildenhall, on June 27[2], we learn, on the authority of John de Pole, late 'camerarius' to John de Cavendish, who there accused John Poter, of Somerton, of abetting the murder, that it took place in the parish of Lakenheath, and on June 14. We may suppose that the justice was travelling on his round of duty in the district, but with too weak an escort, and being surprised by a band of rioters was compelled to fly for his life. Chief among his pursuers were Stephen Martyn and Richard Rond, who, as the scribe has noted, followed him 'usque ad mortem.' Perhaps thinking of Ely as a refuge he directed his steps for the river, hoping that by boat his chance of escape thither would be considerably enhanced, or that, could he even manage to put that barrier between himself and his pursuers he might yet manage to elude them.

At the water's edge, however, his object was cruelly frustrated, and that too by a woman, for against the name of Katharine Gamen, of Lakenheath, stands the following note—'liberavit batellam de terra, perquod dictus Johannes de Cavendish non potuit evadere mortem.' From which we may gather that, seeing the pursuit, and divining the object the unhappy man was straining every nerve to obtain, she rushed for the boat, and by pushing it off into mid-stream rendered escape in that direction impossible. The final scene in the tragedy probably followed immediately. The justice was soon seized by one John Pedder, of Fordham, and on the

---

[1] The list contains the names of those whose indictments were taken at Bury St Edmunds.
[2] See Appendix, p. 126.

arrival of the mob was beheaded forthwith, one Matthew Miller, we are told, performing the horrid office of executioner. Cavendish's head was then carried back by the mob to Bury, and placed over the pillory there.

It has been often stated that the murder of John de Cavendish was committed by the insurgents in revenge for the death of Wat Tyler, who is said by some to have been finally dispatched by the justice's younger son. This I think can hardly have been the reason, as, on examining the evidences of the dates, it appears that Tyler's death did not take place till after that of Cavendish.

The real clue to the justice's unpopularity among the peasant class is, I think, given on the rolls of Parliament, where it appears he was granted extra salary as a justice for enforcing the Statutes of Labourers in the counties of Suffolk and Essex.

He was, as we have seen, a resident in the county, and he died seized of the manor of Overhall at Cavendish and a small estate there. He was also chancellor of the University of Cambridge, an office now held by his lineal descendant.

On the same day (June 14) we have an instance of what would seem to be an attempt to right some grievous private wrong with the aid of the rioters. For we find Simon, the vicar of Mildenhall [1], was arrested on charge of having, with some others, insulted Ralph Attwyk, the Cambridgeshire escheator, at his house at Newmarket, and threatened to behead him unless he gave up the daughter of Ralph de Walsham, of Mildenhall, who had lately been carried off [2].

In order to understand correctly the action in Bury and the district during this period, it will be necessary to take a short review of the interesting events which had occurred in connection with the town and monastery during the two years previous to the rising.

On December 30, 1378 [3], had died, at his house at Elmswell, John Brynkele, abbot of the monastery, and after

[1] From the Tanner MSS. at Norwich 'Symon Domynyk' appears to have been Vicar from 1375–1408.
[2] Assize Roll 103, m. 5 d.
[3] So given on Coram Rege Roll, 476, Rex 1, but Gosford gives the date 1379.

his burial in St Mary's Chapel the prior and convent, having obtained leave of the king, proceeded according to custom to elect his successor. After some delay their choice fell upon one John Tymworth, then occupying the position of sub-prior, who with great difficulty was prevailed on to accept the post.

It was now necessary to obtain the pope's confirmation to make the election valid, so Tymworth, having been forbidden by the king to leave the country, sent off two monks of his house to Rome to obtain the needful documents. These men left Bury on February 10, and arrived at Rome on April 4 following, occupying a little more than seven weeks in the journey. Arrived here, they were very kindly received and entertained by the pope, but when it came to talking of the business of their mission, they met with nothing but fair words and endless delay. The reason for this treatment they soon found out, namely, that the pope had granted the abbacy to a provisor, one Edmund Brounfeld, a Bury monk, who had been in residence at Rome as procurator-general for the order of Benedictines in England, and who, having obtained by express messenger the news of the abbot's death, was now well on his way back to England with his credentials and bulls from the pope.

When the news of Brounfeld's return to England reached his adherents among the monks at Bury, their first move was made at a chapter-meeting in the abbey[1], when one of them got up and endeavoured to read the papal bulls appointing their leader abbot. The prior, finding the documents lengthy, asked to have them to peruse at leisure, which being refused, he moved to adjourn the meeting for divine service, whereupon arose a fracas in the chapter-house, in which the prior, according to Gosford's account, was somewhat roughly handled. Eventually the provisor's party, defying the prior's authority, left the abbey without leave and went out to the parochial churches in the town, there relating their grievances to the populace, and alleging that the prior and his party had attacked them with murderous intent in the chapter-

---

[1] See Appendix, p. 138.

house and cruelly ill-used them. Thus by enlisting on their side the sympathies of the good people of Bury, who were always, it would seem, glad enough of an opportunity to testify their antipathy to the monastery, they managed to persuade them to take an active part on the provisor's side in the quarrel which ensued.

Reinforced by the Bury populace, among whom we may note the names of Thomas Halesworth, Robert Westbron, John Clakke, John Smyth, parson of Stansfield, and Walter, parson of Ixworth, they returned to the abbey, and, having forced their way into the building, succeeded in reading the bulls from the steps of the high altar. On the third day after this Brounfeld himself, who had been hiding at the Carmelites' house in Ipswich, arrived on the scene, and, with the help of the townspeople and of his own party among the monks, was eventually installed as abbot, and the day following celebrated mass with mitre and staff.

Of the monks within the abbey we learn that forty-two were on the side of the prior and seventeen on that of Brounfeld, and between these two parties continual strife ensued, and most unseemly conduct is graphically related by Gosford as going on within the precincts.

News of these transactions, however, soon reached the king, who at once dispatched his officers to bring Brounfeld to London, where he was tried and condemned under the Statute against provisors, and sent prisoner to the Tower[1]. Many of the leaders among the townsfolk were also tried and condemned for the share they had taken in the late riots, and were finally severally bound over in large sums of money from entering the abbey precincts or in any way molesting or interfering with the prior or his dependants.

Actual violence between the town and monastery was thus for a time forcibly suppressed, but the ill-feeling between them continued as strong as ever, and only waited for a suitable opportunity to again break out into open hostilities. Great, then, must have been the consternation within the

---

[1] Brounfeld appears to have been confined also at Corfe Castle, and at Nottingham.

monastery when, in the summer of 1381, the collection of the poll tax threw the whole county into open insurrection.

It would seem that news of the approach of the rioters from the south under John Wrawe was brought to the prior, John de Cambridge, some time during the afternoon of June 13, 1381. Knowing, it would seem, that any effective defence of the monastery was out of the question, and feeling that the temper of the townsfolk rendered his position an exceedingly dangerous one, he decided to leave the monastery, and, waiting till nightfall, fled under cover of darkness to the house of a certain faithful servant of the monastery at Mildenhall, a town some twelve miles to the north-west, where he hoped to be able to remain in hiding till law and order could be again restored. Here he passed the night and the following day, June 14, in great anxiety and suspense, which we can well imagine became almost insupportable, as late in the day the rioters from Lakenheath were probably pouring through the town on their way to Bury, bearing with them the gory head of his old friend the justice.

Towards evening, we learn, it became evident to the prior that to remain concealed much longer in Mildenhall would be impossible, and, feeling that if he could only make good his escape to Ely he would be at least in comparative safety, he resolved to make the attempt to fly thither. to Ely

Waiting till dusk he set out on the journey, meaning to take a boat and proceed by water; on arriving, however, at the place where he hoped to embark, he found himself confronted by a band of rioters, who not only refused to allow him to enter the boat, but were with difficulty restrained from attacking him with their swords. Having at length got clear of these men, and after experiencing two or three very unpleasant encounters with roving bands in the neighbourhood, the prior and his guide directed their flight towards Newmarket, where they managed to conceal themselves for a while in a wood about three miles from the town. Leaving the prior in hiding, his guide set out, ostensibly, to obtain provisions, but having returned to Mildenhall, as Gosford relates, he traitorously betrayed his master and informed the rioters there, of whom a large portion were from Bury, of the prior's whereabouts. On learning this the mob at once set out towards Newmarket, and a cordon having been formed round the wood, some of their number, amid cries of 'Where lurks the traitor?' advanced to seize the unhappy man, whom having made prisoner they conducted to Newmarket. Here, we are told, they all night long most blasphemously mocked him; kneeling before him they cried 'Hail, master!' and striking him with their hands cried to him, 'Prophesy who smote thee.' At break of day on Saturday, June 15, the rioters led their victim back to Mildenhall, where they were joined by a large conflux of people, probably being the mob under John Wrawe, lately arrived from Bury, who on the appearance of the prior raised a great cry of 'Kill the traitor!' 'Kill the traitor!' Having led him about a mile from the town to a place known as Mildenhall Heath, the leaders commanded the prior to dismount. Here a council was held by the men from Bury, in which Halesworth and Denham took a leading part[1], by which the prior was condemned to instant execution; which sentence, after allowing him the privilege of confession to a monk of Mildenhall, was forthwith carried out, his head being severed from his body at a single blow. The headless corpse, we are told by Gosford, lay unburied on Mildenhall Heath till the Thursday following, none of the monks daring to take it away for fear of the men of Bury, who held both him and them in the greatest hatred.

After the murder of the prior his head was placed on the point of a lance and carried by the mob to Bury, where it was met by an excited rabble of the populace with cries of 'See the traitor's head!' 'Happy the day that sees our wish accomplished!'

A ghastly sort of play was then enacted with the head of the prior and that of John de Cavendish, which had been brought to Bury the night before, in mockery of the great friendship which had existed between them in life; after which the two heads were placed over the pillory, where they remained till the arrival of the Earl of Suffolk, some eight

---

[1] Coram Rege Roll 484, Rex 26.

days afterwards. The reasons for the great detestation in which the prior was held were, according to Walsingham, not far to seek, as he had assiduously striven for the rights of the monastery against the townsmen of Bury. He appears on the same authority to have been a man of great intelligence and cultivated taste, besides being an excellent musician.

His death cannot, perhaps, be looked upon as having been a special object of, or directly compassed by, John Wrawe and his bands of countrymen, but rather as brought about by the men of Bury, led by Thomas Halesworth, Esq., and Geoffrey Denham, Esq. (described on the Coram Rege Roll as servants of the prior), in settlement of a long-standing quarrel. Indeed Wrawe in his evidence makes a point of saying that had it not been for Denham and Halesworth the prior would never have been slain. Wrawe was, however, present at the execution on Mildenhall Heath, having probably found himself unable to withhold his support.

Their thirst for blood having been thoroughly excited, the mob proceeded next to the monastery and demanded the person of a monk named Walter de Totyngton. A search on the Coram Rege Rolls [Coram Rege Roll 476, Rex 5] shows that this Walter de Totyngton, alias Walter Colman, was tried for the part he had taken in the election of Brounfeld, and that it was he who dispatched an express to Rome to tell Brounfeld of the abbot's death and advise him to take immediate action. He thus appears as a strong partisan of the provisor, whose cause the men of Bury had warmly espoused, so that it seems curious they should now seek his life; unless, indeed, the fact that the king had seen fit to pardon him may have altered their feelings towards him. Be that as it may, when the mob arrived at the monastery Brother Walter was nowhere to be found. Not to be thus baulked, they next demand John de Lakenheath, the Custos Baroniæ, who, scorning to fly, boldly proclaimed himself and was handed over to the mob, who dragged him with great violence to the market-place; where his head, having been barbarously hacked off with eight blows, was placed with the others on the pillory.

This done, the whole mob, 'illa maledicta comitiva,' as

Gosford calls them, were returning again to the monastery to demand two more monks for execution, when a report went round that Walter de Totyngton, against whom they had especial spite, was in hiding at Rougham, on which they at once diverted their course thither. After passing, however, through the east gate, they espied, on looking back, a monk standing in the bell tower above; concluding that he was the man they were in search of, the mob again surged back to the monastery, and entering the building rushed through the presbytery to the bell tower in pursuit of their victim. Meanwhile the aforesaid two monks, who had learnt that the mob intended their execution, owing to the excitement caused by the man in the belfry were, we are told, completely forgotten, and after expecting instant death for three hours and more before the high altar, found themselves no further molested; thus, as Gosford remarks, 'Dei clementiâ non humanâ industriâ,' escaping the sacrilegious hands of the rioters.

The next day, being Sunday, witnessed yet another execution, after which the townsmen went to the monastery and demanded that all deeds and muniments which at all concerned them should be given up, threatening that if their request was not complied with they would bring the whole rout of insurgents to slay all the monks and extirpate the monastery. On Monday accordingly, at a meeting in the Guildhall, the documents were handed over by the monks, and an agreement was made between the subprior, who acted as president for the time being, and the convent on the one hand, and the townsmen on the other, to the effect that when Edmund Brounfeld should enjoy the abbacy, he and the convent should grant to the town not only their ancient liberties, but also some further concessions which they would subsequently ask. In pledge of fulfilment the convent had to give up their valuable jewels and relics to the custody of the town, and a brother of Brounfeld's had to become surety that the provisor would perform his part of the covenant. This agreement was made by the townsmen, thinking that Brounfeld would succeed to the abbey at once, as they heard that the Essex mob in London had compelled the king to set him at liberty.

Events, however, not turning out as they expected, we learn that the townsmen, fearing the king's hand, returned both the jewels and documents to the monastery. The town was nevertheless condemned to pay a fine of 2,000 marks, of which the king had 1,000*l.* and the abbey 500 marks for the injuries they had received.

While these events had been occurring in Bury and the district, the other parts of the county had been faring equally badly. On June 14 we find mention in the indictments of depredations going on at the house of William Gerard, of Watlesfield, by a band under Adam Rogges, bailiff of Aldham. On the 15th a more important outbreak is recorded of a large body under James de Bedyngfield, a man, I take it, of good social position and a younger son of Sir Peter de Bedyngfield[1], who marched to the house of William Rous, of Denington, chief constable of the hundred of Hoxne, and compelled him under threats of instant decapitation to give them ten archers belonging to the said hundred, de Bedyngfield undertaking to pay them at the rate of 6*d.* per day[2]. The next day they advanced to Gislingham, and there pillaged the house and 'lifted' the cattle of Edmund de Lakenheath, a man of large property.

This Edmund de Lakenheath, whose name appears as one of the justices before whom the rioters were tried, was pursued by the insurgents with relentless vigour; for we find that on the feast of Corpus Christi his house at Gislingham had been attacked, his court rolls burnt, and his goods taken; as well as similar attacks made on his property at Herringswell, Lakenheath, and Stoke juxta Clare. So keen indeed was the pursuit after him that, despairing of safety on land, he was compelled to seek refuge on the high seas, but here also misfortune pursued him, for his boat, we read, was very soon captured and himself taken prisoner by the French admiral who was cruising off the coast. From the French he obtained his liberty only on payment of a ransom of 500 marks, which, together with the damage done to his property, made

---

[1] See pedigree of family, Add. MSS. 19117, Brit. Mus.
[2] See Appendix, p. 130.

de Lakenheath's losses amount in all to the sum of 1,000*l*. (Coram Rege Roll, 488, 35 [1]). It is, however, stated in the indictments that James de Bedyngfield restored to de Lakenheath the property taken from him at Stoke.

On Saturday, the 15th, it appears troubles began in the Ipswich district, Thomas Sampson, of Harksted—also it would seem a man of good social position[2]—who was the chief leader in this part of the county, having chosen this day to put forth his manifesto to the people of Ipswich and the adjoining hundreds, commanding them on pain of death to join his band on the Sunday morning following. His appeal seems to have been responded to with alacrity, and Melton, a village which appears on the map about twelve miles to the north-east, being their destination, a large body of men under Sampson forthwith set out thither. Arrived here they attacked and plundered the house of William Fraunces[3], a man whom Richard Talmache de Bentley and his band had, it appears, seized in Ipswich, where he was soon after beheaded, John Battisford, parson of Bucklesham, we are told, taking a leading part at the execution.

What may have been the reason for especial antipathy in this case I have not been able to discover.

The mob in these parts do not appear to have been as scrupulous as to taking personal property as some of the chroniclers note of the London mob. In the case of W. Fraunces, the Coram Rege Roll (487, Rex 14) gives a list of the spoils taken—to wit, gold and pieces of silver, spoons, cups of wood (ciphi de macer), belts, rings, domestic utensils and vessels of pewter, as well as beer, corn, and beasts. In the town of Ipswich itself the houses of John Gerard, John Cobat, John the rector of St Stephen's, and of the archdeacon of Suffolk fell a prey to the mob. The second may be sufficiently explained, perhaps, by the fact that John Cobat's name appears as one of the poll-tax collectors. He sat in the Par-

---

[1] The date given here for this attack on de Lakenheath is Corpus Christi day, 5 Ric. II. [1382]. I think, however, from several considerations that this was a slip on the part of the scribe, and should have been written 4 Ric. II. [1381].

[2] His property lay at Kersey, Harksted, and Freston and was of considerable amount. See Appendix, p. 143.

[3] See Appendix, p. 127.

liament of 1377 for the town, and was no doubt a well-to-do man, the goods taken from him being valued at 100*l*. The office of archdeacon of Suffolk was at this time held by the Cardinal of St Angelo at Rome, a fact which, together with others of a like nature, had been prominently brought forward by the Commons for complaint in the Good Parliament of 1376. So that it is possible that the attack in this instance was intended by the mob to testify pointedly their dislike to these infringements of the Statutes of Provisors.

At Culpho again, on the 16th, the house of Roger de Wolfreston, formerly escheator for the county, was despoiled of goods, the cattle and horses to the value of 100 marks being driven off. Sampson seems to have continued his depredations for some little time, outrages by the mob under him being noted at Bramfield, Barking, and Needham, and as they marched, as the roll has it, 'from village to village throughout the hundreds of Bosmere and Claydon.' He seems, however, to have managed to elude the grasp of the law till July 23, when he was captured and shortly afterwards condemned to death, but was pardoned finally by the king, and his goods, which had been forfeited, were restored to him[1].

On Monday, June 17, Bergholt appears as the scene of violence. A band under Thomas Fletcher of that place having forcibly compelled William Atte Heath, bailiff of the manor, to give up to them all the court rolls and extents of the manor in his possession, publicly burnt them in front of the church, thereby, we are informed, disinheriting the Lady Margaret de Sutton and John de Sutton, her husband[2]. Proceeding hence to Stratford, a village close by, they attacked Roger the parson there, threatening to take his life unless he gave them gold. This apparently he was unable to produce, and the mob eventually had to content themselves with a meagre 26*s*. 8*d*. extracted by the fear of death from

---

[1] Sampson's name occurs on the list, preserved on the Rolls of Parliament, of those excluded from the general pardon. The Coram Rege Roll, however, states that he was pardoned by the king at the prayer of his lady mother. (No. 487, Rex 14 d.)

[2] John de Sutton, M.P. for Suffolk in 1377.

his unfortunate chaplain, John Attebrook. At Mettingham, however, on the following day, a band under Walter Coselere, who, like many of the leaders who were unlucky enough to be taken, eventually paid the penalty with his head, managed to secure a very much larger booty. In this case the attack was on Mettingham Castle, which seems to have belonged at this time to John Plays and Roger de Boys, Chivalers, into which the mob forced their way and succeeded in securing goods and arms to the value of 1,000*l*., besides 40*l*. in money; nor did they omit to carry away all court rolls, extents, and surveys upon which they could lay their hands. Under this date we also find mention of sums of money collected for the tax being taken from the house of William Marsh, of Soterley, one of the collectors.

Again, on the 19th, a second attack was made on Mettingham Castle by a large body of men under another John Wrawe, described as parson of Ringsfield Church, no doubt attracted thither by the large booty which had been taken thence on the previous day. This time, however, they only managed to get 40*l*. in gold and silver and 20*l*. worth of goods. Under this date also an attack on a manor belonging to the Countess of Norfolk at Walton is related, and the destruction of all the court rolls and manorial documents there.

In the eastern parts of the county we read of serious riots on the 18th at Lowestoft, chiefly, as appears from the indictments, under the guidance of one Richard Ressh, a foreigner from Holland; while in the Beccles district John Wrawe, of Ringsfield, leads an attack on the house of Hugh Fastolf at Bradwell, from which some 400*l*. worth of goods were carried off by the rioters. Also at Beccles itself the murder of one Geoffrey Southgate is recorded, who was dragged from his house by the rioters and slain in the presence of John Wrawe, clerk, even though he held the king's protection in his hands.

The latest date of acts of violence in Suffolk which I have met with is June 28, on which day John Reynolds, of Bawdsey, seized the court rolls of the manors of Hollesley and Bawdsey on the east coast, and broke into the houses of

George Glanvyle and Clement Brethenham there. John Northern, also of Bawdsey, on the same day attacked the manor house at Hollesley belonging to William of Ufford, Earl of Suffolk, who was then at Bury trying rioters in his official capacity, and took and burnt all his court rolls.

The indictments which refer to West Suffolk having been lost, it is impossible to say exactly how long the rioting went on, but in all probability the worst of it was well over by June 20, and on the 23rd Gosford tells us the Earl of Suffolk arrived in Bury, having been dispatched thither by the king, with a body of 500 lances to quell the revolt.

It would seem he found but little difficulty or opposition in pacifying the district, for after the short space of only four days we find him engaged in hearing the pleas of the Crown at Mildenhall, and at other towns during the following week. In the records of these proceedings the frequent occurrence of the word 'decollatus' shows the severity with which punishment was meted out. The principal leader, John Wrawe, chaplain of Sudbury, was tried in London and condemned to be hung, drawn, and quartered. He appears to have turned approver, but was not allowed on that account to escape his doom (Coram Rege Roll, 484, Rex 26).

In the eastern parts of the county lawlessness, it would seem, perhaps prevailed rather longer than in the western, but the arrival of the king in Essex with a large force, and the severe measures taken, soon awed the insurgents into at least comparative tranquillity[1].

[1] That the county remained for some time in a very unsettled state is likely enough, and we find what seems rather a serious outbreak going on in the summer of 1383 at Hollesley. On this occasion we are told Walter son of Walter Manton of Wrotham, William Skrevenor 'manens in Marleford' and Roger Powel of Eyk endeavoured to raise a "new insurrection," and collecting a body of some 100 or so men attacked the house of George Glanvill of Hollesley and compelled him and Matilda his wife to pay a fine of 10*l.*, besides looting their premises. The houses of John the rector of Parham and several others were similarly treated during the outbreak, which however only lasted for three days. (Gaol Delivery Roll, 164, m. 33.)

CHAPTER II.

AN ACCOUNT OF THE RISING IN NORFOLK.

THE insurrection, though commencing slightly later in Norfolk than it did in Suffolk, nevertheless appears to have spread with similar fury and rapidity, and to have affected every part of the county. According to the presentment of the Metford Jury the principal leaders of the insurgents in this county were Sir Roger Bacon Knight, Thomas, son of Thomas de Gyssing Knight, John Chacchevache[1], 'qui se facit vocari' John de Montenay de Bokenham, and Geoffrey Lister of Felmingham[2].

Sir Roger Bacon, Knight and Chivaler, who took a very leading part in the Norfolk rising, is described on the Coram Rege Roll[3] as of Baconsthorpe; and there seems to be good reason to suppose that he was uncle to the James de Bedyngfield, mentioned as one of the leaders in Suffolk[4].

Thomas de Gyssing Knight, it may be noted, sat in the Parliament of 1380 for the county of Norfolk, and his son's sphere of activity seems to have been in the south-western parts of the county.

The rôle played by John de Montenay does not seem to have been one of great importance; while that of Geoffrey Lister was perhaps the most active of any. The name of the last-mentioned leader is still to be seen on the Poll Tax roll

[1] Cf. Blomefield's Norf. I. 382 and 385.
[2] See Appendix, p. 132.
[3] Coram Rege Roll 483, Rex 19.
[4] Cf. Davy's Suffolk Collections, 'Bedingfield' Pedigree. Add. MSS. in Brit. Mus.

for 1379 as a resident at Felmingham, and he is there described as a 'lestere' or dyer¹. He has however been erroneously described by Walsingham as 'John Lister of Norwich,' and by Froissart as 'William Lister of Stanford.' Capgrave, however, though he calls him 'Jekk Lister²' has given us his place of residence correctly as Felmingham.

A John Lister of Binham does indeed appear as taking a minor part in the proceedings, and is mentioned as being in company with Geoffrey Lister on June 21, which may possibly account for Walsingham's confusion of the names. It is noted on the Indictments³ that Geoffrey Lister was slain by the Bishop, which is the fate accorded to this leader both by Capgrave and Walsingham.

From the information given us in the indictments, it appears that the action which first brought the revolutionary leaders within reach of the law, was that of sending their agents to ride systematically through the various hundreds of the county, in their final efforts to induce the people to join the revolt. Some measure of this kind was no doubt necessary, before the appeal to arms, in order to apprize the supporters of the cause, of the date finally fixed for the general uprising; and had been doubtless anxiously awaited throughout the county. The carrying out of the above important task appears to have been intrusted chiefly to John Gentilhomme and Richard Filmond, both of Buxton, who are described in one of the indictments as "principal instigators of revolt throughout the whole county," and as being employed on June 14 in riding from village to village throughout the county⁴, making proclamations in Lister's name for all men to rise in arms. They also appear engaged on the same work on June the 17th and even as late as the 21st.

It does not appear that any very serious outbreak took place in this county before the 17th, which was the date of the great meeting on Mushold Heath near Norwich.

On the 16th indeed we find mention of an isolated attack

---

¹ Norfolk Lay Subsidies, $\frac{149}{5}$, P.R.O.
² The corruption of Jeff into Jekk is not difficult to understand.
³ Ant. Indictments 129. Norf. Hundreds of Blofield, Walsham, Taverham.
⁴ Ant. Indict. 128. Norf. South Erpingham Hundred.

on a manor house of the Duke of Lancaster's at Methwold, and the burning of his court rolls there, by a band of rioters under William, son of William de Metfield, of Brandon Ferry. We may note also the great hatred at once evinced against the Tax Collectors in a message sent by John Coventry, bowyer of Lynn, on June 16th to Nicholas de Massingham, Justice of the Peace, and collector under the second commission, informing him, that unless 10*l.* were forwarded forthwith to Lynn, he might shortly expect a visit from a band of the insurgents.

On June 17, however, at Norwich, the insurgents opened their campaign under Sir Roger Bacon and Geoffrey Lister in grim earnest. In answer to the numerous proclamations which had been made throughout the various hundreds of the county, and which appear to have been generally put forth in Lister's name, a large concourse of countrymen assembled on that day on Mushold Heath, close by Norwich. The place of rendezvous was doubtless well known, and was evidently largely attended from all quarters; many no doubt coming thither with the same object as that attributed on the indictments to Symon Cook and Henry Sherman, of Walsingham parva, who, we are told, rode over to the Mushold meeting on the 17th in order to try and induce Lister, who occupied a leading position on the occasion[1], to advance into their district with fire and sword. Great alarm naturally spread at once through the city at the increasing numbers and threatening attitude of so large a muster in its immediate vicinity; and such measures as were possible were forthwith taken for arming the citizens

[1] The Jury of the Hundred of Fourhow say that the chief leaders of the rebel party at the Mushold meeting on the 17th, were Roger Bacon Chivaler, Richard Felmond of Buxton, John Gentilome of Buxton, John Wattes, Geoffrey Lister, Thomas Skeet, William Kybyte, John de Trunche, and Thomas Sampson. (Ant. Indictments, No. 128, Norfolk.) The last named must not be confused with the Suffolk leader of the same name. The Sampson here named was beheaded; his goods amounted to 20*l.* William Kybyte is described on the Escheator's Roll as "de Wirsted" and his goods are there given as worth 60*s.*; while Lister's goods and chattels were only valued at 33*s.* 9*d.*, for which Henry Bettes of Felmingham, and Agnes, formerly the wife of Geoffrey Lister, had to answer. The record for Skeet is illegible. (Escheator's Inquis. Norf. and Suff. 5–6 Ric. II., Series I. File 1168.)

and appointing guards to defend the gates should the bands under Bacon and Lister advance to the attack [1].

The leader within the walls, to whom the defence of the city had been intrusted, was a certain Sir Robert Salle, a man of considerable note and great personal prowess, and who, though not of gentle blood, had been knighted by Edward III., and who appears also to have sat in the Parliament of 1378 for the county of Norfolk.

From the account given by Froissart [2] we learn that the insurgents first sent in an imperious demand that Sir Robert Salle should come out and speak with them, threatening that if he did not do so they would storm and burn the city.

In compliance with this Sir Robert rode out alone to Mushold Heath to meet the insurgent leaders, who soon made known to him the object of the interview, namely, to persuade him to turn traitor, throw in his lot with them, and join their insurrection as leader. This course he at once, and scornfully, rejected; but on endeavouring to regain the saddle, in order to return to the city, he unluckily missed his stirrup, owing to his horse becoming restive. At sight of this mishap a dastardly cry was at once raised to fall upon and slay him. On this Sir Robert at once let his horse go, and, drawing the beautiful Bordeaux blade which he carried, laid about him with terrible effect "que c'estoit grand' beauté de le veoir." Though his great personal strength enabled him to lay no less than twelve of his antagonists low, the odds proved too great, and at length he fell, borne down by the multitude of his assailants. The spot where he died we learn from the indictments was close by the Hospital of St Mary Magdalen,—a building which stood about one mile to the north-east of the Magdalen gates of the city [3],— slain by the hands of Henry Royse of Dilham, Adam Martyn, and many others [4].

Though one must admire the gallantry and bravery of Sir Robert's conduct in thus venturing alone among the

---

[1] Cf. Blomfield's Norf. III. 106.
[2] Froissart's Chronicles, vol. II. chap. 77 (Ed. Lyons, 1559).
[3] Blomfield's Norf. IV. 440.
[4] See Appendix, p. 132.

rebels, one can hardly commend it for wisdom, unless we suppose that, distrusting the forces within the town, and his means of defence, the course he pursued, though well nigh desperate, appeared to him the only one which afforded a chance of saving the city from attack and pillage.

It would seem that during the confusion and alarm caused by the fall of their chief, or possibly owing to some treachery, the citizens of Norwich suffered the insurgents to effect an entrance into the city; for the Coram Rege Roll (No. 483, Rex 19) tells us that on this day Sir Roger Bacon at the head of the rebel bands had marched into the city "with pennons flying and in warlike array."

In the scenes of rapine and bloodshed which ensued Reginald de Eccles, Justice of the Peace, was perhaps the most distinguished victim, who, we are told, having been seized in his lodgings at the manor of the Abbot of St Benedict de Hulm in Heigham, by Thomas Aslak cordwainer of Norwich, and Adam Pulter of Heigham, and others, was dragged to the pillory and there barbarously stabbed in the abdomen with a dagger, and finally beheaded. His goods and chattels to the value of one hundred marks were at once seized and confiscated by the rioters, of whom one Thomas Atte Church of Felthorp is noted as having made off with the Justice's furred gown. The house of Sir Robert Salle was also wrecked and two hundred pounds worth of goods carried off; while from that of Henry Lomyner, a wealthy citizen and one who had represented the city in Parliament in 1378, various goods and chattels[1] to the value of 1000 marks were taken away by the mob.

A similar fate befel the houses in the city belonging to John de Freston, Archdeacon of Norwich; and of Walter de Bixton, one of the tax collectors for the city, who had also been its representative in the first three Parliaments of this reign.

From the account given by Blomfield it appears that the townspeople were compelled by the rioters to pay large sums of money to save their city from further destruction, till, on

[1] Among these were a "pokett of Wad" valued at 100s., a furred gown worth 40s., and a barrel of "Astere" valued as 40s.

the arrival of Sir Thomas Morieux, some force, it would seem, was organised which could afford protection from the rioters.

According to the account of the rising given by Thomas of Walsingham, Sir Robert Salle was one of five knights who were captured by the insurgents and detained in their service, but owing it would seem to his severe condemnation of their measures did not long survive, "non diu permansit inter eos," being slain by one of his own bondmen. The other four knights, de Scales, William de Morlee, John de Brewes, and Stephen Hales[1] found favour, we are told, with Lister, who styled himself King of the Commons, and served him on bended knee.

As regards Sir Robert Salle, I am inclined to follow Froissart's account; and whatever of truth there may be in the story as regards the others, there does not seem to be any corroboration for it on the indictments. The name of John de Brewes does indeed occur at Heydon, when all the court rolls of his manor there were committed to the flames by the rioters on the 21st; so that service with the rebels does not appear to have conferred immunity from their violence.

Nor was Norwich and its immediate neighbourhood the only scene of violence on the 17th, for outbreaks are recorded at Rougham and Wyghton, while in the south-western parts of the county,—where William Geldore of Feltwell appears as a leader of some importance, and one who assumed to himself royal power,—we read of the destruction of the house and property of John de Methwold[2] at Langford, and serious disturbances at Suthrey. Of Robert Tewe, another ringleader in these parts, it is related, that he and his companions fell upon and captured Robert de Gravele and laid his head upon the block for execution, "super quendam stipitem ad eum decollandum"; but more merciful counsels prevailing, eventually allowed him to redeem his life by paying 8 marks 16 pence and 28 cows (valued at 10 marks),

---

[1] The name of Stephen Hales occurs as being one of the controllers of the Poll Tax for the county of Norfolk. (L. T. R. orig. 4 Ric. II. m. 34.)

[2] John Methwold is described in the Registers of the Duke of Lancaster (vol. XIV. fol. 117 d in P.R.O.) as "Seneschall of our Court at Castleacre in the county of Norfolk," in this year.

the latter being probably required for commissariat purposes. On the next day, 18th of June, the rioters, under Adam Smith and Henry Stanford, both of Wroxham, advanced on Carrow Priory, close by Norwich, and by threats of violence obtained various deeds and Court rolls from Margaret de Euges the Prioress, which they afterwards burnt in Norwich, in the presence of Lister and John de Trunch. On the same day[1], according to the presentments of the Jury at Yarmouth, made on July 16, Sir Roger Bacon, Geoffrey Lister, William Kybit, John Tronch, John Kik, and others advanced to that town at the head of a large band of insurgents and there by threats of violence compelled the burgesses to surrender to them their Charter of Liberties[2]. Having got possession of the document they cut it in two pieces, one of which was forwarded to John Seynsbury, John Wrawe chaplain, Robt. Garveys, Wm. Coupere, Edmund Hemyng, William Lacy senior, and many others in the county of Suffolk, to show that by their help, consent and advice these matters had been taken in hand.

On the 19th the insurgents attacked and broke open the gaol at Yarmouth and beheaded three wretched prisoners for no other reason, it would seem, than that they happened to be men of Flanders, while John Cook, a felon from Coventry, they at once set at liberty.

The houses in Yarmouth belonging to Hugh Fastolf[3] and William Elys, both of whose names appear as members of Parliament for the borough in 1377, were plundered by the mob. We also read that Edmund Hemyng collected the royal customs at a place called 'Kyrkelerode,' at the port of

---

[1] It is stated in Manship's History, apparently on the authority of some chronological table then in Yarmouth Guildhall, that the "sagittarii" under Lister entered the town on the morrow of St Botolph [18 June], but were repulsed by the townsfolk on the following day with considerable loss.

[2] Charters uniting Kyrkley Road to Yarmouth were granted and repealed many times in this and the preceding reign, and public feeling ran very high on the subject between Yarmouth and Lowestoft. The union enabled the burgesses of Yarmouth to levy tolls at Kyrkley Road and was injurious to Lowestoft interests. See Manship's Hist. of Yarmouth (C. J. Palmer, 1854), vol. I. 335–337. Probably the charter destroyed by the insurgents was one of these.

[3] The name of Hugh Fastolf appears as M.P. for Yarmouth in 1376–77; also as a collector for Norfolk under second commission.

Yarmouth, for the benefit of the insurgents, "juxta proclamationem factam per dictum Rogerum Bakon et socios suos predictos."

From the presentments of the juries of the Hundreds of East and West Flegg, it appears, that Bacon moved northwards on the 19th, and after plundering the house of John Fastolf at Caistor, where we are told that even the lead from the chapel and from the house (de gurgite messuagii) was carried off by the rioters, advanced to Winterton, where in company with John Copping of Norwich, he was present at a similar attack on the house of John Curteys, who was forced to pay a fine of 10 marks to escape instant execution.

It also appears from the Tunsted presentments that Bacon assisted on June 20 at the burning of the Court rolls belonging to the Abbey of St Benedict de Hulm in company with Hervey Copping, Thomas Lomb of Neteshird and others; but after this date his name does not appear, and we hear no more of him till his trial, and imprisonment in the Tower.

It seems that on one occasion, at least, Bacon made use of his position as leader to further his own private ends, for we learn that he seized William Clere in Yarmouth, and carried him off to Sondes Castle, where he forcibly obtained from him an acquittance of the manor of Antingham, which he thereupon entered and held for three days[1].

During the week following the 17th, the insurgents seem to have done what they pleased, violence and plundering being recorded in almost every district; nor do the indictments lead us to suppose that any resistance was offered by those responsible for law and order. Once indeed we hear of a Norfolk man, who being taken to Littleport for execution, was there rescued by the Prior and good men of Ely: and on another occasion, when John Atte Hyll, Chief Constable of the hundred of Hensted, endeavoured, at the risk of his life, to arrest John Qwyntenoye of Haynford and some other rioters. But such instances serve rather to emphasize the hopeless inability of the authorities to deal with the situation.

---

[1] Bacon had previously sold the manor to William de Wechingham, "per cartam et licenciam regis."

The Church, as represented by the larger ecclesiastical establishments, was regarded with very marked ill feeling and antipathy by the common people; and we find here, as elsewhere, that their strongholds were constantly assailed, and their property destroyed during the revolt. Thus we find the manors belonging to the wealthy Abbey of St Edmundsbury were attacked and plundered at Suthrey on the 17th, and at Aylsham on the 22nd. The Priory at Bromholm as well as those at Binham and Carrow were forced to give up their Court rolls and muniments to be publicly burned by the rioters; and the Abbey at West Dereham was attacked and plundered on the 20th by John Marshall, and John Pykerel of Mildenhall with other rioters. Perhaps however the most remarkable onslaught on a religious house recorded in this county, was that made on the Eve of the Feast of the Nativity of St John the Baptist (Sunday, 23 June), on the Abbey of St Benedict de Hulm. Here the insurgents had mustered in force to the number of some 400 armed men; and led on by William de Kymberly, the Abbot's carter, they advanced to the head of the Abbey causeway at dead of night, and endeavoured to storm the building. The Abbot and convent, roughly disturbed at prayer, flew to arms to defend their walls, or as the record runs "ad matutinas[1] tunc existentes servicium divinum metu mortis dimiserunt et ipsos armaverunt," and after fighting for their lives throughout the night, managed, it seems, to successfully resist the attack. It would appear also, from the wording of the indictment, that this attack was aimed to some extent at the Bishop of the diocese[2], whom they probably hoped to catch and slay in the Abbey.

It is curious to note that in these parts we also come across the name of a Walter Tyler, an active leader on the popular side. He is described as "manens in Ketleston,"

---

[1] Matins began at midnight and lasted till 3 a.m.

[2] The indictment contains the following:—' per totam noctem illam obsederunt dominum Abbatem et omnes servientes suos ac etiam dominum Episcopum Norvicensem si in partes illas venisset ad ipsos interficiendos.' (Ant. Indict. No. 128, Norf. Tnusted.) From this I infer that the Bishop had returned to his diocese to quell the revolt before the 23rd of June, and was probably expected to be lodging at the Abbey on the night of the attack.

from which we may perhaps infer that he was not a resident in the district.

The Jury however reported, that he was the first to instigate the rising in the neighbourhood of Walsingham, announcing that John Holkam, 'Justice of our Lord the King,' would be at the house of William the parson of Thursford, and urging that he should at once be seized and slain, a plan which Tyler at the head of a band of rioters, afterwards endeavoured to carry into execution.

The above mentioned John Holkam, and Edmund Gurney of West Lexham, Justice of the Peace, seem to have been particularly obnoxious to the rioters. On the 15th a proclamation had been issued putting a reward of 20s. on their heads, and so keenly were they pursued by Thomas Kenman and others, that on the 18th they fled to sea in a boat, and were pursued by water as far as the port of Burnham[1]. It does not appear that either of them was caught, and though the mob broke into and plundered Gurney's house on the 20th, yet he himself managed to escape in safety; for on the 10th Dec. following we find him, in conjunction with Sir Adam Pope, appointed deputy to enquire into the damage done to the Duke of Lancaster's estates in the county during the rising[2]. Gurney was Steward[3] for the Duchy of Lancaster property in this county and in Suffolk, which fact may perhaps explain the animus shown against him.

From the presentments of the Jury of Holt it appears that Geoffrey Lister was at Thorpe Market on the 21st, and engaged, among other things, in holding some kind of session, at which men brought their complaints before him, and preferred bills against various people, in order, according to the Jury presentments, that vengeance might be taken on them. Here he was joined by John Lister of Binham, and both it seems were present at the burning of the Court rolls of Binham Priory on the same day.

At Lynn we find several tradesmen of the town mentioned as being on the side of the rioters; thus in the list of

[1] See Appendix, p. 135.
[2] Registers of John Duke of Lancaster, in P.R.O., vol. xiv. fol. 120 d.
[3] Ibid. vol. xiii. fol. 159.

ringleaders, among whom John Spanye, soutere and cordwainer "in le gres market," was the chief, we find the names of "Thos Colyn tayllor, Thomas filius Thome Paynot, John Whetewong webster, Henry Cornish glover, Walter Prat glover, —— Pinchebek tayllor, —— Sadelere manens in le Cokrowe juxta Bokenhams Place, John Bokelerplayer" and others taking active part in the insurrection.

A body of rioters under John Spanye seem to have marched from place to place throughout the neighbourhood, collecting money by threats of violence and killing any unhappy Flemings they met with. Thus we find them levying blackmail of Symon de Snyterton on the 19th, and at Berewyke on the same day turning Nicholas Mawpas out of his free tenement and installing one John Coventry a bowyer of Lynn in his place, and on the 22nd surprising Edmund de Reynham[1] in a wood at Rising and fining him 14 quarters of oats as ransom. From an inquisition at East Rudham taken on 15th July it appears that Robt Fleccher of Hunstanton advanced with a company armed with bows and arrows and other weapons to Hecham to make men rise against the peace, "cursing" we are told "our reverend Father Henry Lord Bishop of Norwich" for riding through the county to chastise the rebels on July the 8th[2].

It is interesting to note the influence and power exerted by John Wrawe in Norfolk, for besides the remarkable occurrence mentioned as taking place at Yarmouth, we have two other instances of his authority given on the indictments, which tend to show that it was recognised throughout the county. The first is recorded by the Jury at East Dereham, who relate that certain letters had been sent from Sudbury in Suffolk, on behalf of John Wrawe, to Rodoland Lucas, and others at East Dereham, containing orders as to the disposal of a certain free tenement there[3]. The second is contained in a statement made by the Jury of the Hundred of South Grenhow to the effect that on the 20th of June John Ikesworth and other rioters had attacked and broken into

---

[1] A "controller" for the Poll Tax collection.
[2] See Appendix, p. 135.
[3] See Appendix, p. 133.

the Rectory at Wickmere, "by the command and warrant of John Wrawe," and had by the same authority taken possession of the goods of Thomas de Hengham, the Rector there, to the value of 10*l*. The desire to destroy Court rolls and kindred documents is here as elsewhere a very marked characteristic of the revolt. A determined expedition with this object occurred on the 19th of June under John Taylor of North Woodbarningham. The rioters having arrested John de Bessingham and Thomas Colman at Overstrand compelled them by force of arms to accompany them as they marched to Hanworth, Felbrigg, Barningham, Bessingham, and other places in the district, destroying all the rolls they could lay their hands on. On the same day also John Madour of Southrepps, described as a helper and counsellor of Geoffrey Lister, broke into and plundered a manor belonging to the Duke of Lancaster.

The reign of violence and lawlessness does not appear to have continued for more than a week or so after the Mushold meeting at Norwich on the 17th, though order does not seem to have been altogether restored in the Eastern parts of the county as late as the 28th of June.

The indictments give us no clue to the circumstances, date or place of the final suppression of the revolt, though they mention incidentally, as shown above, that probably the Bishop had arrived in the county before June 23, and show that as late as the 8th of July he was still prosecuting vigorously his work of restoring order and punishing the offenders. We know however that Geoffrey Lister was alive and at Thorpe Market on the 21st, so it seems probable that the affair at North Walsham may have taken place on the 22nd or 23rd of June.

The historian John Capgrave has given us a graphic account of the final collapse of the insurgents at Walsham, and his account, since it explains the silence of the indictments by showing that the rebels offered no resistance to the Bishop on that occasion, would seem most probably to be the true one[1]. Capgrave was indeed a Norfolk man himself

---

[1] Capgrave's account differs considerably from that given by Thomas of Walsingham, who relates that there was a fierce engagement at Walsham, in

—having been born at Lynn in 1393—and was educated at Cambridge, so that he undoubtedly must have had good opportunities of ascertaining the truth.

His account of the suppression of the revolt in Norfolk is as follows[1].

"Afterwards when [the Bishop] came to Icklingham, at a spot where a mill somewhat narrowed the roadway, between Cambridge and Thetford[2], he met lord Thomas de Morley and another a knight named Brewes. And here they delivered up to him the three aforesaid malefactors, Sceth, Trunch and Cubith. For they themselves did not dare to put them to death without special command from the king. But this most excellent man, having the zeal of Phineas in his breast and taking into consideration the peril of the people, led them with him to Wymondham, where, after they had been confessed, he caused them to be beheaded. In the same place many malefactors remained, who, terrified by dread of death, did not dare to proceed further in their insurrection.

"The good pastor coming to the principal city of his diocese, namely to Norwich, saw and bewailed the destruction of houses and places made by the aforesaid furious people while they were thus excited. For in his absence, one of their principal leaders, Jekke Litster, and a large multitude associated with him, entered the city against the will of the citizens and committed many horrid deeds, especially in the destruction of houses and places in which certain nobles lived who were friends of the law or of the king....

"But this Henry, a good bishop and pastor, who seeing the wolf, fled not, but exposed himself to danger, enquired of the citizens where the head of all the evil and of all this infamy might be found. And they said that he was

which an attack on the entrenched position of the rebels, led by the warlike bishop in person, who displayed great prowess on the occasion, was completely successful and was followed by great slaughter of the rebels, as well as the capture and execution of their leader.

[1] Jo. Capgrave's Liber de Illustribus Henricis, Pt. III. cap. 9. Translation by F. C. Hingeston, 1858.

[2] This spot (according to Blomfield's Norf. III. 109) is known as Temple bridge in Icklingham, where the old road from Cambridge to Thetford crossed the Lark. The present road crosses at the mill at Barton Mills.

wandering about the neighbourhood of Walsham Market and Gimingham, where he had the largest number of rustics and ribald fellows. Thereupon the bishop commanded his domestics to transfer themselves to those parts, and with them he himself was always foremost. For the bishop had said to those who were with him 'It is better that one evil and wicked man should die, than that the whole people perish, for they taking license from him, commit assaults and robberies, killing those who are unconscious of crime.'

"And saying this he came to the town called Felmingham where the said ringleader had a mansion. And those who resided there, being questioned where he was, said that on the previous day he was at Thorpe Market, where he had caused it to be publicly proclaimed that all who desired the welfare of the kingdom and of the community should follow him to Walsham; where he intended, as he said, to defend the people against the tyranny of the approaching bishop by military force. And on this all the able-bodied of the adjacent villages had followed him, and were there....And thus hastening on to Walsham he [the bishop] found the openings of the roads blocked with timbers and towers, and other impediments. But by good management of the bishop and of other men who had assembled there, the whole people surrendered, rejoicing that they might withdraw in peace. Jekke Litster himself, leaping over a wall, hid himself in a cornfield. And one of the people perceiving this, announced it to the bishop. The traitor was sought and found; he was captured and beheaded; and, divided into four parts, he was sent through the country to Norwich, Yarmouth, and Lynn, and to the site of his mansion; that rebels and insurgents against the peace might learn by what end they will finish their career."

Sir Roger Bacon, the principal leader, was taken, I think probably before the affair at Walsham, though as to when and where, information is not given. He was tried and condemned, and was imprisoned in the Tower of London. His misdoings are recounted at length on the Coram Rege Roll (483, Rex 19), where it is stated that he was finally pardoned by the king at the prayer of his future queen.

Thomas de Gyssing seems also to have been imprisoned in the Tower for his action during the rising, for on the Claus. Roll is an order to the Constable of the Tower to set free Thomas son of Thomas de Gyssing chivaler, who had been there confined. This order is dated 20th of Nov. 1381 and is made by the advice of the council and consent of the king[1].

No clue is given us as to the fate of John de Monteney, while the ominous word "decollatus," which appears on the indictments over the names of several of the lesser leaders, would seem to show that, at least in the opinion of the judges of assize, considerable severity was deemed necessary to firmly reestablish the reign of law.

[1] Rot. Claus. 5 Ric. II. m. 27.

CHAPTER III.

AN ACCOUNT OF THE RISING IN CAMBRIDGESHIRE.

My chief authority in compiling the following account of the proceedings of the rioters in Cambridgeshire in June 1381, is the Assize Roll No. 103 in the series of those documents now preserved in the Record Office in Fetter Lane. This roll is composed of twelve skins, and contains the records of the trials of the insurgents which came on before the Assizes held at Cambridge, Ely, and various other places in the county, during the month of July following.

It appears that tactics similar to those employed in Norfolk and Suffolk were also made use of in this county in order to induce the people to rise; and we find again here revolutionary agents at work in the county before the general rising in arms. This point is brought out at the trial of Thomas Wroo of Wooditton,—a name, by the way, which also occurs in the Suffolk indictments, in connection with the rising in that county,—who we are told was actively engaged in what we may call "agitation" for a period of six days both before and after the feast of Corpus Christi, threatening men with fire and the sword unless they joined the revolt, and instructing them that it was the command and wish of the king that they should do so. In Cambridgeshire we see again the hand of John Wrawe at work, and can trace his emissaries in the county; and though it may be doubted if the organisation of the rebels was so complete here as in more Easterly districts, yet his influence was no doubt strongly felt.

Nor does it appear that the movement in this county gained to so great an extent the active support of the better class among the inhabitants; for the names of the leaders here do not seem to indicate quite the position and influence which attaches to many of those in Norfolk and Suffolk.

In the trials relating to the rioters in this county, one point, it will be seen, is especially noticeable, and that is the frequency with which it is affirmed by the rebel leaders that their action was taken at the express command of the king. Indeed the Mayor of Cambridge, when brought up for trial, appears to urge the widespread understanding that the king supported the movement, as a plea in extenuation of the part he had taken in the riots. We also find among the Cambridgeshire trials two cases which point clearly to the fact that a close intercourse existed between the rioters in this county and the revolutionary party in London.

The first of these is a case which came on before the assizes at Bottisham on July 1st. The Jury of the hundred of Stane here state that a certain rebel leader of the name of John Greyston of Bottisham, having left Cambridgeshire before the disturbances there began, had gone off to the insurgent bands in London and Kent and stayed in those parts during the murders of the Archbishop of Canterbury and of Robert de Hales. Returning to Bottisham he then became an active instigator of sedition in the neighbourhood, and is stated to have gone through the villages of Burwell, Swaffham, and Wilbraham, and exhibiting a certain protection for his goods granted him previously by the Court of Chancery, declared that he had full authority from the king (plenam potestatem regiam) to raise men and destroy traitors and others whom he would name; and further to have commanded all men to join him under pain of death. By an assiduous use of these means, and with the active help of one Robert of Corby near Rockingham, he appears to have collected a considerable body of men with whose aid, among other things, he attacked a house at Bottisham and obtained money by threats of violence from various people. Greyston however does not appear to have been a person of much position, for on his execution his worldly goods seem to have consisted only of a house and one acre and three roods of land in Bottisham worth 5s. per annum, which were then forfeited to the king.

The second case occurs at the trial of a leader of the name of John Stannford, who similarly went about the county giving out that he had authority from the king, "in quâdam pixide," to destroy traitors[1]. This John Stannford[2], though, it appears, a Cambridgeshire man, is described as a saddler from London, and according to the Jury of the hundreds of Stane, Wycherly, and Armingford, was a leader of some importance in this county, and had been concerned in an attack on the house of William North at Abington on 15th of June.

Though June the 9th is the earliest date given in the Assize roll as an occasion of open violence, yet the outbreak in this case, which took place at the house of Roger Harleston at Cottenham, appears to have been rather of an isolated nature. The rising in its more organised and general form does not appear to have been seriously begun in this county till after the feast of Corpus Christi on June 13th. On the 15th of June indeed rioting and violence appear to have been raging without any check in almost every part of the county; thus at Reach, a village some 10 miles North-East of Cambridge, a band under John Saffrey of Stow juxta Anglesey and Peter le Eyr of Thurlow parva assaulted on this day a house belonging to Thomas de Swaffham and carried off thence goods and chattels to the value of £40. In addition to the spoil taken here, Saffrey, it is added, returned with his cart laden with lead, chairs, and other articles, chiefly of household furniture, which he had stolen from one Thomas Torel, a Poll Tax collector[3]; and as one among many of a similar nature this incident may serve to show how prominently freebooting in their nature were many of these expeditions.

[1] See also Coram Rege Roll 485, Rex 27.
[2] John Staunford's property consisted of two messuages, a garden and 40 acres worth 24s. per annum in Barentoft: Exch. L. T. R., Enrolled Accts. (Escheators), No. 8, m. 26 d. The name of John Stannford Sadler and Nicholas his wife, occur in the Camb. Fines in connection with an estate at Barenton. Pedes Finium, Camb. Arch. Soc. 132. 37.
[3] L. T. R., Enrolled Acct. (Subsidies), No. 13.

On the same day again the house and goods of Henry English, the Sheriff of Cambridgeshire, at Ditton Valence fell a prey to the rioters, while at Chippenham a band under Robert Tavell and William Cobbe of Gazeley[1] attacked the Priory of 'Saint John of Jerusalem in England,' seizing the goods there and driving off the cattle; not to mention such smaller felonies en route as taking £4 from Richard Macworth of Soham, and similar sums from Augustin Kellyng and Gilbert Helgey at Isleham. At the same time also the south-western parts of the county were ablaze with riot and rapine, and perhaps most conspicuously so at the villages of Steeple Morden and Gilden Morden, where lay the Manors of Thomas Haselden, a person against whom the rioters appear to have entertained a bitter hatred.

A search through the registers of John Duke of Lancaster for this period[2] discloses the fact that Thomas Haselden was an important retainer of the Duke's, being also controller of his household, steward of his Manor of Bassingbourn, and lessee of that of Babraham, which facts give us perhaps the clue to the reason for the animus displayed against him. He was also a Justice of the Peace for the county.

The principal leader in this attack appears to have been John Hanchach of Shudy Camps, a landowner of some considerable position and probably the chief organiser of the revolt in this county[3] (cf. Appendix, p. 137).

The local bands of rioters on this occasion appear to have been reinforced by a body of 160 horse who rode over from Cambridge under John Gibonn junior and some of the Bailiffs of the town to take part in the attack. Geoffrey Cobbe[4], a man of considerable estate in Cambridgeshire, also

[1] These men also appear as leaders in the Suffolk riots.
[2] Reg. of Jo. Duke of Lanc. in P.R.O. Vol. XIII. ff. 81, 153, 150 d.
[3] Hanchach owned ¼th of the manor of Linton and other manors, as well as land at Babraham, Abynton parva, Cambridge, Hadenham and elsewhere. Exch. L. T. R., Enrolled Accts. (Escheators), No. 8, m. 27. He was executed at the assizes. His widow Ann petitioned the king for dower for herself and her four children out of her late husband's lands. Ant. Petitions, 5754.
[4] He owned land at Wimpole, Orwell, Croydon, Papworth, and elsewhere, worth 22l. per annum. He was pardoned under the general pardon. Exch. L. T. R., Enrolled Accts. (Escheators), No. 8, m. 26 d. See also Rot. Claus. 5 Ric. II. m. 33–34.

arrived on the scene with a band of his retainers, of whom it is noted on the Assize Roll that they publicly proclaimed that they were acting with a commission from the king (cf. Appendix, p. 137).

The whole band then advanced on Haselden's devoted manors, where they wrecked and totally destroyed the manor-houses and seized on all the moveable property they found, which in order to transform into a more portable form they appear to have sold on the premises; the damage done being reckoned at one thousand pounds sterling. Haselden himself with his retainers was probably with the duke in the North at the time of the attack or no doubt some resistance would have been made.

The Hospital at Shengay, a village some three miles to the North, was also attacked and destroyed by the same band; and on the same day Hanchach is reported to have sacked the Priory of St John of Jerusalem at 'Dokeswurth' (Duxford ?).

On Sunday 16th we still find John Saffrey continuing his depredations, this time at Great and Little Wilbraham, where he destroyed the houses of William Malt and John Rogers, in the former case, we are told, even selling the timber of the house. Nor was any respect shown here for the King's Bailiff, William Margret, from whom, under threats of instant death, Saffrey extracted a fine of 26s.

Again at Little Swaffham we find him forcibly ejecting Simon Andrew the lessee (firmarius) of Thomas de Swaffham from his house there and putting in his place Margaret the widow of John Andrew; though as to any reason for this transaction the assize roll is silent. John Saffrey himself, at the time of the assizes, had eluded the grasp of the law, and he eventually escaped punishment under the general pardon[1].

Thomas de Swaffham's house at Burwell was also plundered on Sunday by John Kempe of Dullingham, who, we are told, rode thither with banner displayed; whilst at Harleston and Arnington the houses of William Bateman and Geoffrey

---

[1] John Saffrey's estate consisted of land at Stow, Quy, and Wimpole, worth 5s. per annum, and goods worth £20. 2s. 6d. which were escheated but restored to him on his receiving the king's pardon. Exch. L. T. R., Enrolled Acct. (Escheators), No. 8, m. 26 d.

Michel were burnt and plundered in like manner. During the riots at Sutton also we learn that the constable of the village, Richard Waltesheff, was compelled by Thomas Barr and others to join them in a pursuit through the country after John Fedeler and John Whyte, two men of Ely, whom they sought to slay.

On June 17th the Court Rolls and documents belonging to Thomas Bishop of Ely at Balsham were seized and burnt by a body of rioters under Thomas Ixning and Thomas Lyncoln of Littleport. In like manner on the previous day those of the Prioress of Iklington had been committed to the flames by James Hog of that place; while on the 15th those belonging to the Prior of Ely at West Wratting had been destroyed in the same way by Robert Randesson and others: and in this county as elsewhere the destruction of these and similar documents appears to have been a leading feature in the plans of the rioters.

On the 18th an expedition from Ely appears to have carried fire and sword in a north-westerly direction, penetrating into Huntingdonshire as far as Ramsey, under Robert Plumer, John son of Nicholas Gunneld,—both of Ely,—and Robert Tavell; the last mentioned being identical with the Robert Tavell of Lavenham, who had taken so prominent a part in the disturbances at Bury St Edmunds on June 14th. Tavell had been admitted into the Ely district over the bridge and causeway at Stuntney, a position which had been seized and occupied by the rebels in force, as appears from the trial of William Combe[1], the rebel leader at that point, who while allowing ingress to Tavell and his band from Suffolk had prevented any men belonging to the king or bishop from passing, and was therefore condemned at the Assizes to be hung.

The above-mentioned expedition to Ramsey on the 18th was, I think, the last of the adventures of Robert Tavell, for on turning to the[2] Escheators roll we find not only that Tavell himself was beheaded at Ramsey, and his horse valued at 30s. escheated to the crown; but that 17 horses, 19 saddles

---

[1] Assize Roll 103, m. 10 d.
[2] L. T. R., Enrolled Accts. (Escheators), No. 8, m. 26 d.

and bridles, 6 swords, and various other properties, lately belonging to Robert Tavell, William Cobbe and many other insurgents, were then in hands of the Abbot of Ramsey, who had to account for them to the king[1]. This circumstance seems to suggest that the abbot had turned his retainers out in force and given the rioters a very different reception to that which they generally met with.

On the 19th an attempt was made by a body of men chiefly, it would seem, belonging to Sutton, to seize the Sacrist of Ely at his manor-house at Wentworth. The attempt however does not appear to have been successful, for the Assize Roll does not mention any violence done to the sacrist, who had probably sought safety in precipitate flight.

While the country districts lay thus at the mercy of the insurgents, who appear to have carried all before them in their career of violence and plunder, the towns of Ely and Cambridge, to which we will now turn to trace the course of events, were faring even worse.

At Ely the outbreak appears to have begun on June 15th under the leadership of Richard de Leycester of Ely, who on that day went through the town proclaiming that all men should rise and join his band, that they might, on behalf of the king (ex parte Regis) and his faithful commons, destroy certain traitors who would be named.

On the day following, being Sunday, Leycester and his band, having forcibly compelled John Shethe, glover, and Thomas Litster, both of Ely, and several others to accompany and support him, marched to the Monastery, where, apparently without any opposition, he boldly mounted up into the pulpit and thence publicly declared on behalf of the king what measures were to be taken against the said traitors[2].

On the Monday morning, the populace being now, it would seem, worked up to the pitch of excitement needful for extremes of violence, proceeded under Leycester's guidance to the Bishop of Ely's gaol, into which they forced an entrance and forthwith set free all the prisoners therein confined.

---

[1] L. T. R., Enrolled Accounts (Escheators), No. 8, m. 26 d.
[2] Assize Roll 103, m. 10.

Aided by the additions thus made to their members, the mob proceeded to wreak their fury on Edmund de Walsingham, a Justice of the Peace for the county. The rioters having once got possession of his person the fate of the unfortunate Justice was not long doubtful. Sentence of death, we are told, was at once passed on him and the wretched man was forthwith dragged off to the block by the infuriated mob; whence after a bloody execution his head was taken away and placed over the town pillory[1]. We note also that Edmund de Walsingham's house at Eversden had been attacked and plundered by a band of rioters under John Peper of Linton on the preceding day.

Both Richard de Leycester, and his coadjutor John Buk of Ely, were eventually arrested; of the latter it is stated that in addition to his other crimes and misdemeanours, he had basely set upon Edmund de Walsingham, as he was hurrying him off to execution, and had stolen his purse containing 42½d. Of this sum, it is noted, Buk appropriated to himself 30½d., having paid out of it 12d. "pro labore suo" to John Deye of Willingham[2], a miscreant whom he had employed as executioner.

Both leaders[3] suffered the extreme penalty of the law, being condemned to be drawn and quartered, and their property was duly escheated to the crown. Buk seems to have repented of his crimes for at his trial being asked who commanded him to take Walsingham's purse answered that he believed he then acted "ex precepto diaboli."

At Ely we come across some evidence as to the position and influence of John Wrawe in Cambridgeshire. A certain chaplain named John Michel had, it appears, been arrested for the part he had taken in the disturbances here, and was

---

[1] Capgrave in his Chronicle says "at Hely they killed a man of Cort thei cleped Edmund Galon for her entent was to kille all the men that lerned ony lawe."

[2] Deye had also taken part in the riots at Cambridge on Saturday. He owned a messuage and 1 rood of land in Willingham and goods valued at £6. 17s. 2d. Exch. L. T. R., Enrolled Accts. (Escheators), No. 8, m. 26 d.

[3] Leycester's property consisted of a tenement with dovecot and two shops in Bochersrowe Ely, and goods valued at 40 marks. That of Buk, of a messuage at Castlepath, 4 shops and other property in Walpolelane, worth £17. 11s. 6d., 2 silver spoons and £4 in money. Exch. L. T. R., Enrolled Accts. (Escheators), No. 8, m. 26 d.

eventually brought up for trial. In the record of the case it is stated that Michel went off from Ely to join Wrawe's band in Suffolk, "exivit de insula Eliensi usque in comitivam Johannis Wrawe capellani capitalis ductoris," and became a "subductor"; but returned to Ely, doubtless as an emissary of Wrawe's, in time to take part in the rioting in this district, where he appears to have assumed the part of a leader of more or less importance, and to have issued revolutionary proclamations in the town.

There can also be little doubt that Tavell, who was acting with Wrawe at Bury, was despatched hither by that leader's orders to take part in the Cambridgeshire insurrection.

We may further note here evidence of the strong feeling which pervaded the people against the performance of customary services and of the determined struggle which was intended against them, which is brought out at the trial of Adam Clymme, who was for his various misdemeanors condemned at the assize at Ely to be hung[1]. Clymme, it appears, had ridden up and down the county armed, during the time of the riots, urging the people to join the movement, and commanding all men, whether bond or free as they valued their heads, to cease the performance of any service or custom that might be due to their lords; except as he might inform them on behalf of the great society (*aliter quam eis informaret ex parte magne societatis*).

Besides this Clymme had also been a leading spirit in destroying the Rolls of the Green Wax and many other valuable documents belonging both to the King and Bishop; and had also openly proclaimed to the people that they should at once behead all men connected with the law.

During the three days from June 15th to 17th the town of Cambridge seems to have been completely at the mercy of the rioters, who did as they pleased without any resistance from constituted authorities.

The first disturbance here noted on the Assize Roll occurred on the 15th (Saturday). The scene in this case was Bridge

---

[1] Adam Clymme's goods escheated to the Crown were valued at £10. 19s. 5d. Exch. L. T. R., Enrolled Accts. (Escheators), No. 8, m. 26, d.

Street, down which rushed an infuriated mob seeking with murderous intent the person of one Roger son of Richard Blankgren, who abode there. His house was forthwith searched and ransacked, but the owner, luckily for him, was not to be found, having taken timely flight to the Church of St Giles hard by, whither the mob exasperated at the escape of their victim at once followed. Here, it seems, they met with some kind of resistance, for we are told that the rioters, who were bent on beheading Blankgren there and then, were prevented from carrying out their bloodthirsty intention by the action of the parishioners there; who we may suppose had hurriedly assembled to offer what protection they could to the life of their fellow citizen. Savage at being thus baulked of their prey the mob returned to Blankgren's house, and by dastardly threats of violence obtained money from his unfortunate wife who, it is related, threw herself on her knees before the leaders and besought to be allowed to purchase peace for herself and husband.

It must be borne in mind that at this time a very bitter feud existed between the University and town of Cambridge, which only in the April preceding had resulted in open violence. The townsmen had on that occasion broken into the University treasury and abstracted many valuable charters and muniments which they committed to the flames; and had then compelled the University officials to execute two deeds relinquishing all right of action, and binding themselves to pay a large sum to the town[1].

Thus it will be seen that when the insurrection broke out in June relations between the town and University were, to say the least of it, exceedingly strained.

It appears that on the evening of Saturday June 15th the townsmen, in answer to a solemn proclamation, assembled in great force at the sound of the St Mary's bells in front of the Guildhall. Here they elected two brothers, James and Thomas de Grantchester, as leaders[2], who in company with

---

[1] Rot. Parl. III. 106 et seq.
[2] These names though given on Rolls of Parliament, do not seem to occur on the Assize Roll,

Simon Hosier[1], John Russel, Thomas Forbishour[2], John Hanchach and others, advanced at the head of the rioters, at about ten o'clock at night, to a savage onslaught on the house of William Bedel.

The house was destroyed and its contents carried off, but their intended victim having escaped them, the leaders issued a command that anyone who met him should forthwith slay him. This man, who is called William Bedel both on the Assize Roll and on the Parliament Rolls, is stated in the account in the Arundel MS.[3] to have been William Wigmore, Bedel of the University, which statement I think is no doubt correct, and at once gives us a clue to the animosity displayed against him.

From the ruins of William Bedel's house the rioters went on to the College and Hospital of Corpus Christi, which since it was unable to offer much resistance they soon entered and completely sacked. Not content indeed with pillaging the goods and chattels and destroying the muniments of the society, the rioters, we are told, carried off even the doors and windows of the building.

Nor did Sunday morning witness any abatement in the fury of the rioters. First, it would seem, a sacrilegious attack was made on the Church of St Mary, into which the mob forced their way during service time, to the great alarm of the priest then celebrating Mass and the parishioners there assembled, and seized a certain chest, full of jewels and "utensilia" which, it is noted, was sold to John Gibonn senior for the sum of 10s. Proceeding thence to the monastery of the Carmelite Brothers, which stood on a site now occupied by Queens' College, the mob, headed by Thomas Forbishour and others, broke into the Church there and took possession of

---

[1] Simon Hosier by timely flight eluded the grasp of the law. His goods, escheated to the Crown, consisted of 22s. 1d. and 10 barrels of honey, of which one had gone bad, the 9 being valued at 53s.; they were all 10 carted up to London to the Keeper of Victuals at the Tower.

[2] Thos. Forbishour was also present at the murder of John de Cavendish, and therefore excluded from pardon. His goods were valued at 26s. 8d.

[3] Arundel MSS. No. 350, fol. 15 b-18. See also Caius' Hist. of Camb. 1574. Vol. I. 96-100.

another chest, stated to have been full of books and valuables[1]. The Arundel MS. above mentioned states that the chests thus taken by the rioters were both of them the property of the University; the one in St Mary's Church being the Common Chest of the University and full of muniments, which were thereupon taken out and publicly burnt in the Market Place, while the beldam Margaret Starre, as she flung to the winds the ashes of priceless documents, cried out "Away with the learning of the clerks, away with it." These statements as to the contents of the chests are borne out by the information given on the Rolls of Parliament[2], from which we also gather that the University was compelled by the rioters to formally give up all the privileges which had ever been granted them by the Crown, and to submit themselves for all future time entirely to the rules and governance of the municipal authorities.

Nor were these scenes of violence, which appear to be more closely connected with the feud betwixt the town and the University, the only outbreaks on this eventful Sunday, for the assize roll lifts the curtain on another scene of violence, devastation and robbery going on at the house of Roger Harleston[3], a Justice of the Peace for the county, and its Parliamentary representative in 1377; the chief leaders in this case being John Noreys, wright, Hugh Candlesby, Thomas Lister and John his son. Harleston, it seems, also possessed a country house at Cottenham. This had been sacked as early as the ninth of June by the rioters under Richard Martyn, and all the goods found there sold.

Yet another outrage occurred on Sunday, this time at the house, in 'le Petycure' and Market Place, belonging to John Blankpayn, a man who appears to have been burgess for Cambridge in Parliament of 1377; and whose position as one of the Poll Tax collectors may, doubtless, help to account for the odium which prompted the attack.

On Monday 17th June the chief interest centres in

---

[1] The jury were ignorant as to the price of these, but estimated their value at £20.
[2] Rot. Parl. III. 108.
[3] Harleston's name occurs as supervisor of Poll Tax collection.

the great attack made by the Mayor, townsmen, and rioters generally on the Priory at Barnwell.

At the Assizes held at Cambridge on July the 3rd, the Prior brings a bill of complaint against Edmund Redmedowe[1], Mayor of Cambridge, in which he states that Redmedowe, as leader of a large body of rioters, came out to Barnwell on June 17th, and broke into the close belonging to the Priory: and further that he and his band pulled down walls and cut down trees to the value of £400, and that besides destroying the pales of the watergate, together with the gates, they carried off fish, sedge, and turf from the premises, causing damage to the said Prior to the value of no less than £2000.

The Prior also states that John Tyteshall, Hugh Candlesby, Robert Barbour, Nich. Wympol, and Richard Martyn were chief leaders in the insurrection.

The issues at this trial are somewhat complicated, owing to what has always proved a fruitful source of quarrel, namely, a dispute about common rights.

The Prior had, it appears, tried to enclose some land on which the commoners of Cambridge asserted that they had always had the right of free pasture, in a place called Estenhall or The Drove[2]. The populace seem to have seized this opportunity for pulling down the palings put up by the Prior in his endeavour to enclose the land in question.

The Mayor being already in custody is brought into court. He pleads not guilty and urges firstly, that it was a well-known thing in Cambridge that the commons of Kent, Essex, Herts and London, had risen in revolt and that the rising was asserted by them to be in accordance with the King's command; also, that on the day in question a large number of men from Cambridge and elsewhere surrounded him and addressed him as follows: "You are the Mayor of this the King's town and governor of our community, if you do not consent to our will and commands in carrying out all that shall be said to you on behalf of the King and his faithful commons, you will be at once beheaded" (statim decapi-

---

[1] Edmund Redmedowe here, but sometimes called Edmund Lister.
[2] Called "le Grenecroft" on the Rolls of Parliament, and in Arundel MS. 350.

tatus cris). The Mayor further states that he thereupon asked to see the King's warrant, but this request would seem to have been regarded by the mob as merely evasive, for the Mayor goes on to say that he was then seized and thereafter acted under compulsion.

Redmedowe is then further required to give in writing the names of those who thus compelled him to act, to which he replied that in the crowd in and around the Guildhall there were more than 1000 men, and that he could not remember more of them than Simon Hosier, Thomas Forbishour, John Russel, and Thomas Lister and John his son.

The explanations of the Mayor, who from his own account seems to have been placed on the horns of a very unpleasant dilemma, were not deemed to be satisfactory, and he was remanded to prison. Whereupon certain trustworthy men of the town of Cambridge point out to the Justices the good character that their Mayor bore, and moreover, that, should he be thus left in prison, the town would have no governor to direct them in that perilous time. These considerations appear so far to have weighed with the Justices that they allowed the Mayor to go out on bail.

The riotous proceedings which had taken place in Cambridge, both in April and June, were eventually investigated before Parliament at Westminster[1], in the December following, where the deeds which had been made under compulsion by the University, were of course quashed, and the functions of the municipality and University, as to the governance of the town, eventually rearranged on a new basis, apparently on the model of Oxford.

To the trial of John Shirle of Nottinghamshire, which took place at Cambridge on July 16th, considerable interest attaches on account of its incidentally throwing some light on the nature of John Balle's preaching, which, if Shirle's statements are to be believed, would seem to have savoured more of politics than religion.

It appears that Shirle, who is described as a vagabond

---

[1] See Cooper's Annals of Camb. I. 122, for a good precis of the information given on the Rolls of Parliament, relating to these affairs.

through diverse counties[1] during the time of the rising, is charged with having made certain statements in a Cambridge tavern, "in quadam taverna in vico de Briggestrete," where many congregated to listen to the news and "frivola" wherewith he regaled his audience. The accusation brought against him was that he had there said that the King's officers and ministers were more worthy of being hung and drawn and of suffering the various other torments inflicted by the law, than John Balle, chaplain, who was condemned to death unjustly and of envy by the said ministers; and that John Balle was indeed an honest and true man who prophecied things useful to the commons of this realm, and who set forth the injuries and oppressions wrought on the people by the king and his ministers; and further, that Shirle had stated that Balle's death[2] would not long go unpunished but in a short time would be avenged both on king and ministers. For making these statements "inter alia verba ruinosa" which he did not attempt to deny, he was hung at Cambridge.

The sudden and unexpected nature of the outbreak and the rapidity with which it spread, seem, here as elsewhere, to have struck terror through the country and paralysed all attempt at resistance. Nowhere indeed do we find any evidence of a serious opposition to the insurgents, till the arrival on the scene of Henry Spenser, Bishop of Norwich.

Capgrave, in his Liber de Illustribus Henricis, tells us that the Bishop had heard of the riots in his diocese when in company with the king near London; and adds, "The pious pastor therefore left London and came as he was bound to succour his people. And first finding certain of this wicked mob at Cambridge he slew some, imprisoned others, and others he sent back to their homes after taking their oath that thenceforth they would never turn out for like purpose[3]."

[1] "Vagabundus per diversos comitatus toto tempore perturbationis gerens mendacia et frivola incommoda de patria in patriam per quod pax domini infringi potuit et populus inquietari." (Assize Roll, 103. m. 5).

[2] Thomas of Walsingham tells us that John Balle was executed at St Albans on July 15, 1381.

[3] Capgrave, De Illustribus Henricis, Part III. Hingeston's Translation.

We gather then that the insurrection, which had reached its height during the 15th, 16th, and 17th of June ceased as suddenly as it began, for the Assize does not record any serious disturbance going on in the county after the 18th of June. The collapse of the revolt here was, no doubt, owing to the advent and prompt measures of the Bishop, who probably arrived on the 18th or 19th.

The assizes, we know, had begun as early as the first of July, which would indicate that peace had been by that time restored on a firm footing in the county.

CHAPTER IV.

GENERAL REMARKS ON THE RISING IN EAST ANGLIA.

ON reviewing the rising generally, in the three counties under consideration, there seems good reason to believe that it was the matured result of a comprehensive plan, carried out by means of a more or less perfect organisation, extending throughout the Eastern Counties. From the fact that one of the rebels, executed at Bury St Edmunds, is described as "Georgius de Dounesby in Com. Linc.," and as having been sent to Bury as the messenger of a great society, it seems probable enough that the organisation extended as far as the Humber[1]. What may have been the precise nature of this organisation does not indeed appear; but it would seem evident that the clubs or societies, which the working classes had already instituted, to enable them jointly to resist the obnoxious claims for labour, must have offered a convenient stock whereon to graft the scion of deliberate rebellion.

During the period immediately preceding the outbreak, the revolutionary agents had been, as we have seen, hard at work; and such men as Filmond in Norfolk, Greyston, Shirle, and others in Cambridgeshire, kept the leaders in the various districts in touch with each other, and also in frequent communication with London.

However we may endeavour to account for it, it is certainly a remarkable fact that the outbreak was practically unopposed, and when the storm burst there was no local force anywhere which made any endeavour to offer protection from its fury.

It is indeed not a little surprising to read of the fall of such a stronghold as Mettingham Castle, a place of great defensive capabilities, having been converted from a Manor

[1] See Appendix, p. 127.

House into a strong moated fortress by Sir John de Norwich only some 40 years previously, and which could doubtless, with very little care, have been made impregnable to any force which the rioters could bring against it; yet it fell, it would seem, an easy prey to their attacks on two occasions.

The absence of any resistance is the more noteworthy when we find there was in existence some kind of force which might have been made available to the authorities, namely the body of archers which is mentioned as existing in the hundred of Hoxne and under the command of the Chief Constable there. As some such body must probably have been provided in every hundred of the county, it seems unaccountable that no effort should have been made to get together some force to oppose the insurgents; unless indeed we suppose that sympathy for the popular cause so permeated the classes from which they were drawn, that no force could be depended on for action in time of emergency.

This indeed taken in conjunction with the fact that many local magnates, with their retainers, were absent on foreign service, appears, in the absence of any more probable supposition, to be the most natural explanation of the fact.

One of the measures which seem to have been generally adopted by the revolutionary leaders in order to get the active support of the common people, was that of giving out that in urging all men to rise in arms they were acting on the command and at the wish of the king. This point was very fully brought out at the Cambridgeshire Assizes, but in other places the same tactics were made use of, and in Hertfordshire, we are even told that the Standard raised by the rioters was emblazoned with the king's arms[1]. So often indeed does the king's name appear that the question naturally rises as to whether there may not have been some foundation in fact for the widespread belief that he himself had encouraged the insurrection.

When we consider the position of the king at this time, and the great power and ambition of the Duke of Lancaster, it seems far from improbable that the idea of guiding the

---

[1] Coram Rege Roll 482, Rex 16.

popular discontent for his own advantage may have presented itself to Richard; as well as the great advantage of securing to himself the support of the people, whose power was now first asserting itself in the political world, as a counterpoise to the influence of his uncle. That he should have overrated that power is probable enough, for the revolutionary leaders themselves, who had perhaps too much of the visionary enthusiast in them, seem to have thought their position far stronger than it was, and did not sufficiently realise that, without military training, mere numbers and enthusiasm must always avail but little.

Were it possible to establish the supposition that the king had been in communication with the leading spirits of the rebellion, a new light would be thrown on several points which at present stand rather in need of elucidation. Among other things it would certainly lend fresh significance and point to the animus displayed against the Duke of Lancaster, and to the persistent malignity with which his agents were attacked, his' manors assailed, and his property destroyed, as we have seen was the case in East Anglia. It would also render the position of the country gentry who favoured the insurrection more easy to understand, for otherwise they must, one would think, have stood to lose rather than gain by having anything to do with the movement. And it would explain, what has always stood rather in need of explanation, the sudden and peculiar ease with which, on the death of Wat Tyler, the rebels transferred their allegiance to the king. And if we suppose that even a strong suspicion had got abroad, that the king was behind the movement, it might well account for hesitation on the part of those in authority in taking prompt measures to suppress it.

It may of course be urged that the king denied emphatically the assertion made by the rioters, that they were acting with his authority and wish, and that he caused notice of his denial to be given in every town and village. But his action here, while it testifies to the widespread belief, was not taken till June 23rd[1], when he must have known that,

[1] Assize Roll 103. m. 1.

however formidable at first, the movement had no backbone in it and was practically crushed. It would have been madness then for him to avow any connection with it.

It is possible enough that the general pardon for the rioters originated from the king, and it is noticeable that two offenders, who were excluded therefrom by Parliament, were saved by the king's action.

That certain reports were current with reference to the Duke of Lancaster having some connection with the movement is evidenced by the king's contradiction of them, given in Rymer; but I have not come across any other evidence in support of this, except that of a rather vague statement made by a Kentish rioter of the name of Cole, which was elicited at his trial. In that county, according to Cole, the revolutionary party, having been informed that the duke had freed all the natives on his estates, entertained the idea of making him king[1], though there is nothing to show that any steps were taken to carry the idea into execution.

I have not met with any evidence to show what ideas of constitutional reconstruction may have been entertained by the leaders in East Anglia, nor any hint to show the existence of such sweeping ideas of reform as are set forth in Jack Straw's reputed confession, as given by Walsingham.

In the counties we are considering the energies of the revolt seem to have been allowed to dissipate themselves in a series of isolated outbreaks, and cohesion to any combined design for offensive and defensive action would appear to have been wanting. The leaders, blinded probably by the immense support which the ostensible objects of the rising commanded throughout the country, failed to recognise the necessity of a more military organisation, and the want of this was the chief cause of their disaster. One cannot but feel that had a commander of real genius risen among them the result might have been very different indeed.

The counties of Norfolk, Suffolk, and Cambridgeshire were at this time among the most thickly populated in the kingdom, and the rising in these counties was probably, in

---

[1] Coram Rege Roll 482, Rex 1. See also Arch. Cant. Vol. IV.

point of numbers, not far inferior to that of which the interest centred in the march on London.

As far as Norfolk and Cambridgeshire are concerned the suppression of the revolt would appear to have been entirely due to the prompt action of Henry Spenser. It does not however appear that the king cherished any deep gratitude to this martial prelate for the important service then rendered to the state; for on his return from his unsuccessful expedition to Flanders in the autumn of 1383 he was impeached in Parliament by the king's direction and his temporalities seized for the payment of a fine[1].

It would, I think, be impossible to form any accurate idea of the total numbers of the insurgent forces during the revolt, and even with regard to the numbers present on any of the various occasions: the legal documents as a rule confine themselves to such expressions as "magna societas," "comitiva," or the like, without venturing on figures. There are however occasions on which figures are given. At Thetford as we have seen the number was only 17; and at Snettisham in Norfolk a body of 30 men under John Spanye of Lynn[2] was considered large enough to approach the town to search for men of Flanders to kill, while at the attack on the house of Stephen de Langham in Norfolk on 17 June, a body of 200 men were employed. Again in Suffolk on the occasion of the first attack on Mettingham Castle, where one would imagine they would muster as strong as possible, the numbers present are estimated in the indictments at 500.

At the fierce nocturnal assault made on the Abbey of St Benedict de Hulm in Norfolk the attacking party, we are told, were thought to number about 400 men. Again the Mayor of Cambridge, when on trial for the part he took in the riots there, estimates the number of rioters who met before the Guildhall at over one thousand men, a number which, by the way, would have exceeded half the population of the town at this time. In Essex indeed, where according to Walsingham's account, as many as eight hundred horses were taken from the rebels on their final defeat, it is possible

---

[1] Stubbs, Const. Hist. II. 466.   [2] Appendix, p. 135.

that the muster may have been much larger, being perhaps collected in as great force as possible for a final effort. I doubt however if his figures can be relied on as correct.

The bulk of the insurgent forces were no doubt composed, for the most part, of the labouring and servile classes who formed so large a proportion of the population; but, as we have seen, the country gentry, whose guidance in military matters must have been much required, were by no means unrepresented at their musters: so much indeed were their services in demand that on some occasions it seems their presence and active assistance were forcibly compelled by the rioters. Many of the minor clergy[1], it is also to be noted, were eager partizans in the insurrection; several who are described as "capellani" were actively engaged in the scenes of violence that took place, and did not shrink from dyeing their hands in blood.

On the other hand the regular clergy who inhabited the larger religious houses, had evidently made themselves the object of the intense hatred of the common people, and were persistently attacked during the rising.

From the lists of names which occur on the Coram Rege Rolls and elsewhere, it would seem also that a fair proportion of the tradesman and artizan class from the towns had thrown in their lot with the insurgents.

In spite of considerable inconsistency of action, we may certainly deduce from the conduct of the insurgents some of the more prominent ideas which animated them. First, no doubt, was that of resistance to exorbitant taxation, of which the late developments came as the crowning evil of a period of intolerable oppression brought about by the Statutes of Labourers.

The idea also which was expressed by their destruction of the records of the Manorial Courts, namely, that now was the opportunity to break the chain which bound the native to the soil, and at the same time to destroy the weapon which the Manorial lords were ruthlessly using to regain and enforce such service as had been withdrawn, was one which seems to

---

[1] Among these we note a Nicholas Bacon, and John Oxeford "clericus hostiarius scole de Clare." List of indicted persons, Ant. Indictments, 128.

have been ever present to the minds of the insurgents, and to have largely influenced their action. No doubt also to this idea must be traced the great hatred evinced to any who were skilled in the study and practice of the law.

It would seem indeed that the natives and customaries must have been in a desperate condition, or very certain of complete success, before they would have thus willingly destroyed in their struggle for liberty the title-deeds to their own estates, which were contained in the Court Rolls of the Manor. It is also to be noted that an intense and deeply rooted hostility, only to be appeased by savage and immediate slaughter, appears to have been felt by the insurgents throughout the country against the men of Flanders, whose immigration had been encouraged for financial reasons by the late king. Perhaps indeed from Chaucer's allusion to this in the Nonne's Tale we may suppose that the slaughter of Flemings was popularly considered as a very leading feature in the revolt.

We may perhaps not be wrong in thinking that by the frequency of attack upon men who had sat in various parliaments since 1376, of which in the three counties of Norfolk, Suffolk and Cambridgeshire there are not less than 10 instances, some idea of bringing home to burgess and knight of the shire an increased sense of the responsibility attaching to their position may have been intended, especially perhaps in the matter of taxation.

- The question as to how far and in what directions the rising of 1381 effected a permanent change for the better in the condition of the working classes, it is not my purpose now to consider; but it may be interesting to take a glance at some evidence as to the condition of affairs in two Suffolk Manors, during the period more immediately succeeding the revolt.

It is certainly rather surprising to find, in a manor in the midst of a disturbed district, where one would naturally expect that there would have been great difficulty in enforcing services at all, that during the period 1377–1384 there is no indication on the Court Rolls that anything unusual was going on in the way of defect of service; but such is the case.

The following instance however is I think worth quoting to show that after the rising it was considered advisable on this manor, at least, to make great efforts to enforce the legal rights of the owner, which for some time previously had been allowed to lapse.

The case in question occurs on the Court Rolls of the Manor of Barton Parva in Suffolk, which at this time belonged to the Cellarer of the Abbey of St Edmundsbury, and of which the Court Rolls from 1377 to 1384 are extant. A small Manor within this Manor was held by Sir John Shardelow, Knight and Chivaler by the service of 15 precariæ in autumn. In the first few rolls there is the yearly note that the service had not been rendered and that a fine should be levied and no further notice apparently taken. In the years 1383 and 1384 however the matter is much more carefully gone into, and it is then stated that these services had now been withheld for no less than 30 years (which shows that the withdrawal of service had begun soon after the pestilence), and a distraint is made upon Shardelow's goods. Two of his horses are seized and he is ordered to answer to the lord for 28 years of arrears; unfortunately the rolls end here, so that we cannot trace the matter further, but this is enough to show that energetic steps were taken to enforce the rights of the owner.

But while there is evidence that service and custom where they had fallen in abeyance were frequently claimed, and the claims supported by the law, there is also evidence to show that in the country districts a sturdy resistance to rendering predial service of any kind was organised afresh soon after the rising. In illustration of this point I will give a short report of a case which came before the Ipswich Assizes in September 1385, and which is recorded at length on Assize Roll No. 861, preserved in the Record Office.

The case refers to the Manor of Littlehawe in Thurston, near Bury St Edmunds, of which Robert de Ashfield was lord.

A charge is here brought against the "natives by blood," and the "customaries who held as natives," of this Manor to the number of 15, which probably was the total number of them, that they, acting with the counsel and advice of Robert the parson of Thurston Church, Simon his chaplain, John Aubrey and four others, had for the last three years past withdrawn their services due to the lord, claiming to be free from all, with the single exception of a rent of fourpence per acre. One of the larger holders of the 15 was Robert Soutere of Thurston, a native by blood, who held 24 acres and two messuages for which he paid a yearly rent of 4*d.* per acre besides 1*d.* per acre which was paid in accordance with an ancient custom called "le unyeld." Three hens were due from him to the lord at Christmas, and 15 eggs at Easter, he was bound to perform two days' ploughing[1] in the year, and four half-days mowing grass, and in haymaking he was to have the help of the other customaries when needful. He also had to hoe for two half-days, and reap for six days in autumn, and to carry corn one day, if he had a cart and horses. Fines were also due if he or his sons or his daughters should marry, his tenement was subject to a heriot of a "better beast" on his death, and his heir paid a fine on entry. He also had to fulfil the office of Propositus and Messor (or head reaper) when it fell to his turn. The other tenants held similarly in proportion to their various holdings. They were further charged with being in diverse clubs and bound together by oath to resist the lord's claims.

The jury after due investigation found a true bill against the defendants, namely that they had withdrawn their services, refused to allow distraint, and threatened the lord's agents; and further that they were "bound together by words," in clubs (conventiculis), though not by oath, as was stated in the charge, for the purpose above mentioned; also that they had made collections "tallagia" among themselves and others for their common cost amounting in each year to about the sum of six pounds.

We are also told that they had obtained exemplifications from Domesday under the great seal, but that these were of no use in the matter.

---

[1] "Cum caruca sua si jungat tempore seminationis frumenti et avene sine resumsione."

It was decided that their claim to be free could not be upheld and that they had ever been and were "nativi."

The punishments inflicted were fines which amounted in all to nearly £3. And there seems reason to believe that cases of this kind were not uncommon, especially on manors where the customs were irksome or strictly enforced.

In looking back across the five centuries that separate us from the portentous outbreak of 1381, when the great working class of England, roused to fury by the goad of relentless taxation, turned so fiercely to bay, we cannot, even while justly condemning their violence, withhold a large measure of sympathy both for the ideas which prompted, and for the results which followed their action.

And though the attempt was then frustrated and the rising crushed, and that to the great and unquestionable advantage of the nation as a whole, yet, apart from the objects which were more consciously pursued, the effort marks an important epoch.

It emphasized to the country at large, in a way there was no possibility of mistaking, the fact that the working classes had arrived at a position of great power; and though perhaps in disclosing that power they had also disclosed their inability, as yet, to use it to the greatest effect, yet their strength and position had been shown to be such as no rulers could with safety ignore.

APPENDIX I.

TRANSCRIPTS OF ALL THE POLL TAX LISTS WHICH REMAIN IN THE RECORD OFFICE FOR THE COUNTY OF SUFFOLK.

HUNDRED OF THINGO

Analysis of Poll Taxes (1381)

	Inhabitants over 15	Male	Female	Armigeri	Agricole	Artifices	Laboratores	Servientes
Barrow	71	42	29	—	6	16	28	21
Brockley cum Rede	70	39	31	2	10	17	8	33
Chevington	78	41	37	—	1	8	34	35
Flempton	33	17	16	—	8	—	13	12
Fornham All Saints	32	23	9	—	2	10	10	10
Hargrave	39	20	19	—	—	5	34	—
Hawsted[1]	63	32	31	—	2	6	38	17
Hengrave	36	21	15	1	1	—	17	17
Horningsheath Magna	53	33	20	—	—	5	21	27
,, Parva	21	9	12	—	2	—	10	9
Ickworth	47	28	19	2	—	3	21	21
Lackford	49	28	21	—	—	8	20	21
Nowton	28	17	11	—	1	—	15	12
Risby	57	30	27	—	—	—	11	46
Saxham Magna	38	22	16	—	—	5	23	10
,, Parva	57	34	23	4	14	6	—	33
Westley	36	18	18	—	6	4	10	16
Whepsted	62	33	29	—	—	9	31	22
Total	870	487	383	9	53	102	344	362

[180 Lay Subsidy]
[49   Suffolk   ]

HUNDREDUM DE THYNGOWE

VILLA DE BARWE

Hec indentura tripartita facta inter Willelmum Tendrynge chivaler et socios suos assessores et contra irrotulatores ultimi

[1] It is interesting to compare with this the return of inhabitants over 16 made by the Rector to the Bishop of Norwich in April 1706, which was 81 men and 93 women. (Hawsted Par. Reg.)

subsidii domino Regi concessi videlicet de qualibet persona laica tres grotas anno regni regis ejusdem quarto ex una parte et Willelmum Rosschebroke chivaler et socios suos collectores dicti subsidii ex altera parte Willelmum Lyly Johannem Meriel Johannem Smyt Symonem Warner constabularios et subcollectores ejusdem subsidii ville de Barwe ex tercia parte de numero et nominibus subscriptis de statu et gradu eorum.

Agricole	s.	d.	*Laboratores (cont.)*	s.	d.
Stephanus Hegeman - -⎫	iij		Johannes Boys - - -⎫	ij	
Alicia uxor ejus - - -⎭			Agneta uxor ejus - - -⎭		
Johannes Lyly - - - -⎫	iij		Robertus Mud - - - -⎫	ij	
Claricia uxor ejus - - -⎭			Isabella uxor ejus - -⎭		
Johannes Prycke - - -⎫	iij		Walterus Slautere - -		xij
Christiana uxor ejus -⎭			Johannes Hamund - -⎫	ij	
			Margeria uxor ejus - -⎭		
Artifices			Walterus Deke - - -		xij
Johannes Warde, *drapere*⎫	ij		Johannes Meryel - - -⎫	ij	
Matildis uxor ejus - -⎭			Agneta uxor ejus - - -⎭		
Johannes Norman, *messer*⎫	ij		Adam Warner - - - -⎫	ij	
Isabella uxor ejus - -⎭			Katerina uxor ejus - -⎭		
Johannes Soutere, *soutere*⎫	ij		Walterus Dey - - - -⎫	ij	
Emma uxor ejus - - -⎭			Margeria uxor ejus - -⎭		
Johannes Dekne, *talyor*⎫	ij		Caterina Schot - - -		xij
Margareta uxor ejus - -⎭					
Johannes Smyth, *smyt* -⎫	ij		*Servientes*		
Johanna uxor ejus - -⎭					
Ricardus Meryel, *bocher*⎫	ij		Ricardus Norman - -		viij
Agneta uxor ejus - - -⎭			Sibilia Meryel - - - -		iiij
Johannes Spark, *webstere*⎫	ij		Ricardus Ayloch, junior		viij
Johanna uxor ejus - -⎭			Johannes Wyfford - -		iiij
Walterus Turnour, *turnur*⎫	ij		Johannes Gautron - -		viij
Sibilia uxor ejus - - -⎭			Henricus Holm - - -		iiij
			Ricardus Trim... - -⎫	ij	
Laboratores			Alicia uxor ejus - - -⎭		
Agneta Doraunt - - -		xij	Johannes Scherwy... -		xij
Johannes Lane - - -⎫	ij		.... Meryel - -		xij
Alicia uxor ejus - - -⎭			Johannes Kyneyston -		xij
Henricus Lane - - -		xij	Walterus Calle - - -⎫	ij	
Willelmus Lylye - - -⎫	ij		.... uxor ejus - -⎭		
Isabella uxor ejus - -⎭			Katerina Bele - - - -		xij
Johannes Brustal - -⎫	ij		Ricardus Calve - - -		xij
Margeria uxor ejus - -⎭			Johannes Lyly - - -		xij
Petrus Ferr - - - - -⎫	ij		Ricardus Ayloch, senior		xij
Claricia uxor ejus - -⎭			Johannes Ketyl - - -⎫	ij	
Johannes Adam - - -		xij	.... uxor ejus - -⎭		
Johannes Massote - -⎫	ij		Johannes Aylnot - - -		xij
Johanna uxor ejus - -⎭			Johannes Dey - - - -		xij

Summa nominum, lxxi
Summa denariorum, lxxis.

APPENDIX 1.   69

$\left[\frac{180}{49} \& \frac{180}{34} \begin{array}{l} \text{Lay Subsidy} \\ \text{Suffolk} \end{array}\right]$

Hec indentura tripartita facta inter Willelmum de Tendrynge chivaler et socios suos assessores et contra irrotulatores ultimi subsidii domino Regi concessi videlicet de qualibet persona laica tres grotas anno regni regis ejusdem quarto ex una parte et Willelmum de Rosshebrok et socios suos collectores dicti subsidii ex altera parte et Simonem le Smyth Johannem Shortnekke Johannem Hybele Johannem le Bole Johannem Wysman et Johannem Cressener constabularios et subcollectores ville de Brokleygh cum Reede ex tercia parte de numero et nominibus subscriptis et de gradu et statu eorundem videlicet.

VILLA DE BROKELE CUM REDE THYNGHOWE

Armiger	s.	d.	*Artifices (cont.)*	s.	d.
Willelmus de Walsham	vj		Johannes Hibele, *pedder*	ij	
Elizabetha uxor ejus			Caterina uxor ejus		
			Johannes Wysman, *carpenter*	ij	
Agricole			Petronilla uxor ejus		
Johannes de Somerton	v	vj			
Beatrix uxor ejus			*Laboratores*		
Johannes Shortnekke	ij	vj	Johannes Mayhew, junior, *laborer*	xviij	
Beatrix uxor ejus					
Thomas Alston	ij	vj	Alicia uxor ejus		
Caterina uxor ejus			Johannes Sculton, *laborer*	xviij	
Galfridus Alisander	ij	vj	Agneta uxor ejus		
Agneta uxor ejus			Johannes .... ag *laborer*	xvj	
Simon Aubry	ij		Alicia uxor ejus		
Johanna uxor ejus			Galfridus Soneman	ij	iiij
			Semila uxor ejus		
Artifices			*Servientes*		
Simon Smyth, *faber*	ij	iiij	Johannes Baronn, *carucarius* Willelmi de Brokleygh	ij	
Idonia uxor ejus					
Johannes Bole, *brasiator*	xx				
Alicia uxor ejus			Alicia uxor ejus		
Willelmus Walspryng, *sherman*	ij		Stephanus Gardener *serviens* Johannis de Rokwode	ij	
Johanna uxor ejus					
Johannes Mayhew, senior	ij		Johanna uxor ejus		
Isabella uxor ejus			Johannes Styward *serviens persone* de Brokleygh	xviij	
Johannes le Grom, *brasiator*	ij		Margeria uxor ejus		
Margeria uxor ejus			Johannes Wotton *serviens*	ij	
Robertus Sourale, *webbestere*	xij		Cecilia uxor ejus		
Johannes Wrytgh, *carpenter*	ij		Ricardus Shortnekke *bercarius* Willelmi le Hore	xviij	
Isabella uxor ejus			Alicia uxor ejus		

Servientes (cont.)	s.	d.	Servientes (cont.)	s.	d.
Willelmus Sonem serviens		ij	Johannes filius Johannis de Somerton		iiij
Isabella uxor ejus[1] Ricardus Meller serviens W. le Hore Anna uxor ejus		ij	..... bel filia et serviens dicti Johannis Walterus ...... serviens dicti Johannis		iiij iiij
Johanna Fouke serviens Ricardi Fouke		xij	Simon Shepherd serviens dicti Johannis		iiij
Johannes Alisander shepherde, mortuus est		xij	Caterina Freman serviens Thome Alston		iiij
Willelmus Lyng serviens Simonis le Smith		vi	Johannes Mayhew serviens W. Hore		ij
Ricardus ... llin serviens Willelmi de Walsham ..... serviens Willelmi de Brokleygh		viij x	Caterina uxor ejus Johannes Cressener carucarius .... Brokleygh Amicia uxor ejus		xx
Johannes Gardener serviens Johannis de Rokwode		x	Walterus Neng serviens in Villa		xii
Isabella Bole vannator et serviens		viij	Johannes filius et serviens Johannis Wysman		vi
...... Shortnekke serviens Johannis Shortnekke		iiij			

Summa personarum, lxx
Summa denariorum, lxxs.

[180 Lay Subsidy]
[49   Suffolk   ]

HUNDREDUM DE THYNGOWE

VILLA DE CHEWYNGTON

Hec indentura tripartita facta inter Willelmum Tendryng chivaler et socios suos assessores et contra-irrotulatores ultimi subsidii domino Regi concessi videlicet de qualibet persona laica tres grotas anno regni ejusdem quarto ex una parte et Willelmum de Rosschebrok chivaler et socios suos collectores dicti subsidii et altera parte Johannem Cartere Willelmum Pumpyn Willelmum Martyn Robertum Mayhew constabularios et subcollectores ejusdem subsidii ville de Chewyngton ex tercia parte de numero et de nominibus subscriptis et de gradu et statu eorundem.

[1] The subsequent part of this document is in the parcel marked $\frac{180}{34}$, and is endorsed " Hundredum de Thyngo Rotuli collectoris ... Tudenham summa .... istorum xviij rotulorum ... DCCCLXX. ...... xliij . li . x . s."

APPENDIX I. 71

Villa de Chevyngton

Agricola	s.	d.	Laboratores (cont.)	s.	d.
Johannes Peke	ij		Johannes Page	ij	
			Julia uxor ejus		
Artifices			Robertus Lane	ij	
Michaelus Writhe, *carpenter*	ij		Alicia uxor ejus		
			Robertus Hardfot	ij	
Johanna uxor ejus			Margareta uxor ejus		
Johannes Sped, *webstere*	ij		Johannes Cawynham	ij	
Johanna uxor ejus			Johanna uxor ejus		
Willelmus Coupere, *broustere*	ij		Willelmus Chyld	ij	
			Margareta uxor ejus		
Sabbe uxor ejus			Willelmus Fot	xij	
Willelmus Fuller, *fuller*	ij		Alicia Nicole	xij	
Isabella uxor ejus					

Laboratores			*Servientes*		
Johannes Cartere	ij		Agneta Osburn	xij	
Margareta uxor ejus			Ehud Deye	xij	
Willelmus Pumpyn	ij		Robertus Spak	xij	
Sabbe uxor ejus			Alicia Stonham	xij	
Willelmus Martyn	ij		Matildis Meller	xij	
Alicia uxor ejus			Willelmus Pumpyn, junior	xij	
Robertus Mayhew	ij		Johannes Tornor	xij	
Agneta uxor ejus			Johannes Redynhale	xij	
Johannes Russyn	ij		Marion Attemer	ij	
Alicia uxor ejus			Johannes Falis		
Johannes Osbern	ij		Elena Hamind	xij	
Margareta uxor ejus			Rosa Ide	xij	
Willelmus Dicere	ij		Agneta Mery		
Johanna uxor ejus			......elle..	xij	
Johannes Smalwode	ij		Henricus Bernerewe	xij	
Isabella uxor ejus			Johannes Deye		
Henricus Mayster	ij		Rosa uxor ejus		
Margareta uxor ejus			Johannes Nottynge		
Johannes Tyle	ij		Johannes Hoo	ij	
Ebota uxor ejus			Johanna uxor ejus		
Salamon Melk	ij				
Alicia uxor ejus			(remainder of Roll gone[1])		

[180 Lay Subsidy
  43   Suffolk]

Hundredum de Thynghowe

Villa de Flempton

Hec indentura tripartita facta inter Willelmum de Tendryng chivaler et socios suos assessores et contra rotulatores ultimi subsidii domino regi concessi videlicet de qualibet persona laica

---

[1] On the back of the Roll for Brockley is a statement to the effect that the total number of names on the 18 rolls for the Hundred of Thingo amounted to 870. As this Chevington Roll is the only one imperfect of the 18, we can infer that there were 15 more *Servientes* here than are given above.

tres grotas anno regni regis ejusdem quarto ex una parte et Willelmum de Russhebrok chivaler et socios suos collectores dicti subsidii ex parte altera et Edmundum Edryck et Johannem Bele subcunstabularios et Johannem Mayhew Johannem Walhous subcollectores ville de Flempton ex tercia parte de numero et nominibus subscriptis et de gradu et statu eorundem videlicet.

VILLA DE FLEMPTON

Servientes	s.	d.	Augrecole (cont.)	s.	d.
Willelmus West - - -		iiij	Isabella uxor ejus - -		xviij
Johanna uxor ejus - -		iiij	Willelmus Peyton - -	ij	
Johannes West - - -		xvi	Emma uxor ejus - - -	ij	
Ricardus Dun - - - -		xii			
Margareta uxor ejus - -		xii			
Willelmus Gosse - -		xii	Laboratores		
Alicia uxor ejus - - -		xii	Robertus Clere - - -		iiij
Alexander Saylour - -		xii	Johanna uxor ejus - -		iiij
Agneta Wade - - - -	ij		Thomas Sare - - - -		iiij
Johannes Bele - - -		xii	Johannes Barat - - -		iiij
Agneta uxor ejus - -		xii	Edmundus Chapeleyn -		iiij
Robertus Donne - - -		xii	Willelmus Pope - - -		xviii
			Agneta uxor ejus - - -		xviii
Augrecole			Johannes Ber . . . . -		xii
Johannes Welhous - -		xviii	Isabella uxor ejus - -		xii
Alicia uxor ejus - - -		xviii	Margareta Dun - - -		iiij
Johannes Hemysby - -		xviii	Alicia Clement - - -		iiij
Matildis uxor ejus - -		xviij	Margareta Goche - - -		iiij
Edmundus Edryk - -		xviij	Agneta Saylour - - -		iiij

Nomina personarum, xxxiij
Summa denariorum, xxxiijs.

⎡184 Lay Subsidy⎤
⎣ 49   Suffolk ⎦

HUNDREDUM DE TYNGHOWE

VILLA DE FORNHAM OMNIUM SANCTORUM

Hec indentura tripartita facta inter Willelmum Tendryng chivaler et socios suos assessores et contra irrotulatores ultimi subsidii domino Regi concessi videlicet de qualibet persona laica tres grotas anno regni ejusdem quarto ex una parte et Willelmum Rosschebrok chivaler et socios suos collectores dicti subsidii ex parte altera Walterum Payn Thomam Payn Hugonem Mason Willelmum Chapman constabularios et subcollectores ejusdem subsidii de Fornham omnium sanctorum ex tercia parte de numero et nominibus subscriptis et de gradu et statu eorundem videlicet.

APPENDIX I. 73

Agrecola	s.	d.	*Artifices (cont.)*	s.	d.
Robertus Batissforde		iij	Johannes Walcard, *barker*		
Mabbilia uxor ejus			Emme Walcard mater ejus		ij
			Henricus Smyth, *faber*		xij
			Nicholaus Smith, *faber*		xij
Laboratores			Walterus Taylor		xij
Walterus Payn, *browster*		ij	Johannes Wodecok, *taylor*		xij
Alicia uxor ejus					
Johannes Colkyrke, *browster*		ij	Robertus Calf		xij
			Johannes Wrythe		xij
Agneta uxor ejus					
Galfridus Angold		xij	*Servientes*		
Hugo Mason		ij	Alicia Dockynge		iiij
Christiana uxor ejus			Sarra Calf		viij
Willelmus Schapman		ij	Ricardus ate Brygge		xij
Margeria uxor ejus			Johannes ate Fen		xij
Johannes Bettys		xij	Johannes Warde		xij
			Stephanus Storych		xij
			Johannes Angold		xij
Artifices			Adam Roggere		xij
Thomas Payn		ij	Galfridus Horn		xij
Matildis uxor ejus			Ive Warde		xij

Summa nominum, xxxij
Summa denariorum, xxxij*s.*

[180 Lay Subsidy / 49 Suffolk]

Hundredum de Thynghowe

Villa de Hardgrave

Hec indentura tripartita facta inter Willelmum Tendryngc chivaler et socios suos assessores et contrairrotulatores ultimi subsidii domini Regis ei concessi videlicet de qualibet persona laica tres grotas anno regni ejusdem quarto ex una parte et Willelmum Rosshebrok chivaler et socios suos collectores dicti subsidii ex altera parte Robertum Hoketon Adam Anable Johannem Frost Walterum Anable subcollectores dicti subsidii ville de Hargrave ex tercia parte de numero et de nominibus subscriptis de gradu et statu eorundem.

Laboratores	s.	d.	*Laboratores (cont.)*	s.	d.
Robertus Hoketon		ij	Walterus Anable		ij
Emme uxor ejus			Alicia uxor ejus		
Adam Anable		ij	Walterus Riche		ij
Cissilia uxor ejus			Margeria uxor ejus		
Johannes Frost		ij	Johannes Nicole		ij
Alicia uxor ejus			Alicia uxor ejus		
Johannes Thurgor		ij	Rogerus Algi		ij
Alicia uxor ejus			Margeria uxor ejus		

74   SUFFOLK POLL TAX LISTS, 1381.

Laboratores (cont.)	s.	d.	Laboratores (cont.)	s.	d.
Robertus Kyppynge - ⎫	ij		Thomas Smith - - -		xij
Alicia uxor ejus - - ⎭			Alicia uxor ejus - - -		xij
Ricardus Page - - - ⎫	ij		Ricardus Chawseler - -⎫	ij	
Johanna uxor ejus - ⎭			Alicia uxor ejus - - -⎭		
Robertus Anable - - ⎫	ij				
Agneta uxor ejus - - ⎭					
Willelmus de Kent - ⎫	ij		*Artifices*		
Johanna uxor ejus - ⎭					
Johannes Page - - ⎫	ij		Willelmus Carpon, *talyor*⎫		xij
Alicia uxor ejus - - ⎭			Emme uxor ejus - - -⎭		xij
Johannes Kyppynge - ⎫	ij		Willelmus Powgwene,⎫	ij	
Isabella uxor ejus - ⎭			*brewstere* - - - - -⎬		
Ricardus Tankard - ⎫	ij		Caterina uxor ejus - -⎭		
Agneta uxor ejus - - ⎭			Robertus Parys - - -		xij

Summa nominum, xxxix

⎡180 Lay Subsidy⎤
⎣ 49   Suffolk   ⎦

HUNDREDUM DE TYHYNGOWE

VILLA DE HAWSTED[1]

Hec indentura tripartita facta inter Willelmum Tendrynge chivaler et socios suos assessores et contra irrotulatores ultimi subsidii domino Regi concessi videlicet de qualibet persona laica tres grotas anno regni regis ejusdem quarto ex una parte et Willelmum Roschebroke chivaler et socios suos collectores dicti subsidii ex parte altera Johannem Moryel, Willelmum Walkelynge, Johannem Boydyn, Johannem Warde, constabularios et collectores ejusdem subsidii [de] villa de Hawsted ex tercia parte de numero et nominibus subscriptis et de gradu et statu eorundem.

[1] From an extent of the manor of Hawsted, it appears that there were at Hawsted in 1358, thirty 'libere tenentes,' two of whom lived at Bury, and eleven 'nativi.' The former class held only 104½ acres between them, many apparently holding only a messuage, while the latter class held 146¼ acres. On comparing these figures with the poll tax record, we find that the number of householders given there as laboratores and artifices together is twenty-six, and that of the servientes eleven, a coincidence of numbers which seems to point to the use of the word servientes in the poll tax as equivalent to 'nativi,' and that the laboratores and artifices corresponded very much to the 'libere tenentes' of the manors. On comparing the names in the two documents, one is struck at once by the great change which had taken place in them, for of the thirty 'libere tenentes' in 1358 only four, viz.: John Ward, John Boydyn, John Kertlyng, and William Walk-lynge appear in the poll tax, and of the eleven nativi only one, Thomas Frame, remains. Such a change, I think, can only be accounted for on the supposition that this parish was subjected to a very severe visitation of the plague in 1361 or 1369.

APPENDIX I.

Agricola	s.	d.	Laboratores (cont.)	s.	d.
Johannes atte Grene }	ij		Johannes Heyward }	ij	
Genne uxor ejus }			Alicia uxor ejus }		
			Johannes Hebyl }	ij	
			Katerina uxor ejus }		
Laboratores			Johannes Moryel }	ij	
Walterus Bernard }			Alicia uxor ejus }		
Agneta uxor ejus }	ij		Willelmus Walkelynge }	ij	
Petrus Ward }	ij	xij	Margareta uxor ejus }		
Alicia uxor ejus }		xij			
Emma Gekes			Johannes Wryte, *carpen-* }		xij
Alicia Clark			*tarius* }		
Edmundus Stonham }	ij		Willelmus Smyth, *faber* }	ij	
Ebote uxor ejus }			Rosa uxor ejus }		
Johannes Pypere }	ij		Johannes Fouke, *faber* }	ij	
Matildis uxor ejus }			Robertus Hurt, *webstere* }	ij	
Johannes Fullere }	ij	xij	Emma uxor ejus }		
Elena uxor ejus }					
Johannes Godhall			*Servientes*		
Johannes Cokeman }	ij		Johannes Clerk		
Agneta uxor ejus }			Johannes Heyward }		xij
Johannes Boydyn }	ij	xij	Elsete uxor ejus }		
Emma uxor ejus }			Johannes Tyby }	ij	
Johannes Certlenge			Johanna uxor ejus }		
Ricardus Kes }	ij		Willelmus Cokerel }	ij	
Katerina uxor ejus }			Isabella uxor ejus }		
Sandre Ide }	ij		Willelmus Clerk }	ij	
Isabella uxor ejus }			Ebete uxor ejus }		
Johannes Ward }	ij		Thomas Frame }	ij	
Claricia uxor ejus }			Matildis uxor ejus }		
Johannes Deye }	ij	xij	Thomas Mower }	ij	xij
Alicia uxor ejus }			Cristina uxor ejus }		xij
Johannes Benyth			Claricia Hoppere		xij
Johannes Wastel }	ij	xij	Amy Deyc		xij
Leticia uxor ejus }			Simon Mors		xij
Katerina Wele			Katerina Norfolke		xij

[180 Lay Subsidy]
[49   Suffolk]

Hundredum de Thynghowe

Villata de Hemgrave

Hec indentura tripartita facta inter Willelmum de Tendringge chivaler et socios suos assessores et contrarotulatores ultimi subsidii domino Regi concessi videlicet de qualibet persona laica tres grotas anno regni regis ejusdem quarto ex parte una et Willelmum de Rosshebrok chivaler et socios suos collectores dicti subsidii ex parte altera et Willelmum atte Crouch Nicholaum atte Heth subconstabularios et Robertum Fulhond Edmundum Bogeys subcollectores ejusdem ville de Hemgrave ex tercia parte de numero et nominibus subscriptis et de gradu et statu eorundem videlicet.

Armiger	s.	d.	Laboratores	s.	d.
Thomas Hemgrave - -	vij		Petrus Sebourgh - - -	viij	
			Benedictus Wynyeve -	viij	
Servientes			Robertus West - - -	vj	
Robertus le Qwte - -	x		Alicia uxor ejus - - -	vj	
Margeria uxor ejus - -	x		Johannes Langham - -	xviij	
Johannes Barkere - -	x		Caterina uxor ejus - -	xviij	
Margareta uxor ejus - -	x		Jacobus Trenchemere -	xij	
Robertus le Qwyte - -	vi		Alicia le Smyth - - -	xij	
Agneta uxor ejus - - -	vi		Laurence Wysman - -	vj	
Johannes Clement - -	xij		Alicia uxor ejus - - -	vj	
Margareta uxor ejus -	xij		Thomas Bayly - - -	iiij	
Johannes Bogeys - - -	vj		Nicholaus atte Heth -	viij	
Sarra uxor ejus - - -	vj		Alicia uxor ejus - - -	viij	
Robertus Fulhond - -	ix		Willelmus atte Crouch -	xviij	
Beatrix uxor ejus - -	ix		Margeria uxor ejus - -	xviij	
Willelmus Dawe - - -	vi		Edmundus Bogeys - -	viij	
Walterus Brese - - -	vij		Beatrix uxor ejus - -	viij	
Dulcia Bullok - - - -	ix				
Robertus Angold - - -	xij		*Agricola*		
Beatrix uxor ejus - -	xij		Galfridus Clement - -	ij	

Summa nominum, xxxvi
Summa denariorum, xxxvis.

[180 Lay Subsidy]
[49   Suffolk   ]

HUNDREDUM DE THYNGOWE

VILLA DE HORNYNGESERTH MAGNA

Hec indentura tripartita facta inter Willelmum Tendrynge chivaler et socios suos assessores et contra irrotulatores ultimi subsidii domini Regis ei concessi videlicet de qualibet persona laica tres grotas anno regni ejusdem quarto ex una parte et Willelmum Rosschebrok chivaler et socios suos collectores dicti subsidii ex altera parte Johannem Bricete Johannem Dane Galfridum Wepstede Robertum Gobet constabularios et subcollectores ejusdem subsidii [de] villa de Hornyngeserth Magna ex tercia parte de numero et nominibus subscriptis de gradu et statu eorundem.

	s.	d.	Laboratores (cont.)	s.	d.
Robertus Gobet, *draper* ⎱	iij		Johannes Brycete - ⎱	ij	
Alicia uxor ejus - - -⎰			Johanna uxor ejus - -⎰		
Michaelis Gos, *carpenter* ⎱	ij	iiij	Galfridus Wepstede - ⎱	ij	
Alicia uxor ejus - - -⎰			Agneta uxor ejus - - -⎰		
Robertus Prest, *carpenter*	xij		Johannes Bare - - ⎱	ij	iiij
			Isabella uxor ejus -⎰		
Laboratores			Thomas Coupere - - ⎱	ij	
Johannes Dane - - - ⎱	ij		Margeria uxor ejus - -⎰		
Alicia uxor ejus - - -⎰			Symon Jent - - - -	xij	

APPENDIX I. 77

Laboratores (cont.)	s.	d.	*Servientes* (cont.)	s.	d.
Benedictus Knyth -⎫	ij		Johannes Ryngedale - -		viij
Johanna uxor ejus - ⎬			Robertus Asscheman -		xij
Willelmus Brend - -⎫	ij		Thomas Brend - -		xij
Johanna uxor ejus - ⎬			Willelmus Godefrey - -		xij
Johannes Busschop - ⎫	ij	iiij	Ricardus Goos - - -		xij
Cristina mater ejus - ⎬			Johannes Newhawe - -		viij
Alanus Noble - - -⎫	ij	viij	Matildis Lewote - - -		xij
Katerina uxor ejus - ⎬			Margeria Lewote - - -		xij
Nicholaus Gandawe - ⎫	ij		Thomas Rose - - -		xij
Johanna uxor ejus - ⎬			Agneta Rungeton - - -		xij
			Johannes Clerk - - -		xij
			Thomas Blok - - -⎫	ij	
Servientes			Agneta uxor ejus - ⎬		
Johannes Alysawe - -		viij	Willelmus Driwer - ⎫	ij	
Johanna Fyssche - - -		viij	Johanna uxor ejus - ⎬		
Robertus Boyler - - -		viij	Johannes Pypere - -		xij
Adam Godefrey - -⎫	ij		Thomas Clenewalle - -		xij
Katerina uxor ejus - ⎬			Johannes Pye - - -⎫	ij	
Edmundus Kynch - -		xij	Margaria uxor ejus - ⎬		
Johannes Godefrey - -		viij	Robertus Godefrey - -		xij

Summa nominum, liij
Summa denariorum, liiis.

⎡180 Lay Subsidy⎤
⎣ 49   Suffolk ⎦

HORNYNGESHERTH PARVA IN HUNDREDO DE THYNGHOWE

Hec indentura tripartita facta inter Willelmum de Tendryng chivaler et socios suos assessores et contrarotulatores ultimi subsidii domino Regi concessi videlicet de qualibet persona laica tres grotas anno regni regis ejusdem quarto ex una parte et Willelmum de Rosshebroke chivaler et socios suos collectores dicti subsidii ex altera parte.

Augricola	s.	d.	*Laboratores*	s.	d.
Johannes Lacford - -⎫	ij		Rosia le Smyth - - -		xij
Emma uxor ejus - - ⎬	ij		Alicia Hermer - - - -		xij
			Emma Hermer - - -		vj
Servientes			Johannes Goldynge - -		xij
Robertus Hermer - - -		xij	Sabina uxor ejus - -		xij
Rosia uxor ejus - -		xij	Emma Goldynge - - -		xiiij
Thomas Lacford - - -		xij	Thomas Pulrose - - -		iiij
Caterina uxor ejus - -		xij	Alicia uxor ejus - - -		iiij
Johannes Goldynge, junior		xij	Johannes Aubry - - -		xij
Matildis Goldynge - -		xij	Emma Dun - - - -		viij
Rogerus Gardiner - -		xij			
Johannes Rudham - -		xij			
Margeria uxor ejus - -		xij			

Summa personarum, xxi
Summa denariorum, xxis.

$\begin{bmatrix} 180 & \text{Lay Subsidy} \\ \overline{49} & \text{Suffolk} \end{bmatrix}$

Hundredum de Thynghowe

Villa de Icworth

Hec indentura tripartita facta inter Willelmum Tendryng chivaler et socios suos assessores et contrairrotulatores ultimi subsidii domino Regi concessi videlicet de qualibet persona laica tres grotas anno regis ejusdem quarto ex una parte et Willelmum Rosschebrok chivaler et socios suos collectores dicti subsidii ex altera parte Johannem Barker, Nicholaum Barker, Thomam Bonys, Johannem Taylor constabularios et subcollectores ejusdem subsidii de Icworth ex tercia parte de numero et nominibus subscriptis et de gradu et statu eorundem.

Armiger	s.	d.	*Artifices*	s.	d.
Thomas Icworth - - -)		vj	Simon Canon, *browstere*)	ij	
Agneta uxor ejus - - -)			Alicia uxor ejus - - -)		
			Petrus ate Halle - -		xij
			Servientes		
			Thomas Goldeford - -		xij
Laboratores			Agneta *serviens* Thome)		viij
			Ikworth - - - - -)		
Johannes Barker - - -)	ij		Radulfus *serviens ejusdem*		viij
Isabella uxor ejus - -)			Radulfus Choke - - -)		iiij
Nicholaus Barkere - -)	ij		Johannes Schabayle - -)		iiij
Alicia uxor ejus - - -)			*servientes domino*)		
Thomas Bonys - - -)	ij		Johannes Hary - -		viij
Margeria uxor ejus - -)			Matildis Beneyt - -		xij
Johannes Taylor - - -)	ij		Robertus Pye - -		xij
Johanna uxor ejus - -)			Margeria uxor ejus - -		xij
Rogerus Godffrey - - -)	ij		Johannes Tracy - -		vj
Matildis uxor ejus - -)			Willelmus Bareleg - -)		xvj
Walterus Beneyt - - -)	ij		Caterina uxor ejus - -)		
Johanna uxor ejus - -)			Johannes Sayham - -)		xviij
Thomas Page - - - -)	ij		Amissia uxor ejus - -)		
Alicia uxor ejus - - -)			Willelmus Borel - - -)	ij	
Johannes Caunceler - -)	ij		Agneta uxor ejus - - -)		
Alicia uxor ejus - - -)			Thomas filius Johannis)		xij
Johanna ate Park -		xij	Barkere - - - - -)		
Willelmus de Saxham -		xij	Johannes Cartere - -		xij
Stephanus Chetebere -		xij	Alicia Baron - - -		xij
Ricardus Canon - - -)	ij		Thomas Benyngton - -		xij
Agneta uxor ejus - - -)			Petrus atte Halle - - -		xij

Summa nominum, xlvij
Summa denariorum, xlviis.

[180/49 Lay Subsidy Suffolk]

HUNDREDUM DE THUNGOW

VILLA DE LAKFORD

Hec indentura tripartita facta inter Willelmum Tendrynge chivaler et socios suos assessores et contrairrotulatores ultimi subsidii domino Regi concessi videlicet de qualibet persona laica tres grotas anno regni regis ejusdem quarto ex una parte et Willelmum Rosschebrok Chivaler et socios suos collectores dicti subsidii ex altera parte Benedictum ate Cherche Johannem Schepperde Adam Ate Well Johannem Flemton constabularios et subcollectores ejusdem subsidii ville de Lacforde ex tercia parte de numero et nominibus subscriptis de gradu et statu eorundem.

Laboratores	s.	d.	*Artifices (cont.)*	s.	d.
Benedictus ate Sherche } Agneta uxor ejus - - -}		iij	Walterus Webbe, *webbe* } Ibote uxor ejus - - -}	ij	
Johannes Schepperde -} Margeria uxor ejus - -}		iij	Willelmus Thashere, } *thashere* - - - - -} Caterina uxor ejus - -}	ij	
Adam ate Well - - -} Isabella uxor ejus - -}		ij	*Servientes*		
Johannes Flemton - -} Agneta uxor ejus - - -}		ij	Johannes Page - - -} Alicia uxor ejus - - -}	ij	
Robertus Buk - - - -		xij	Johannes Hervy - - -		viij
Willelmus Brese - - -} Alicia uxor ejus - - -}		ij	Radulfus Thommyssone } Amissia uxor ejus - -}		xvj
Johannes Cartere - - -} Agneta uxor ejus - - -}		ij	Johannes Purstone - -} Matildis uxor ejus - -}	ij	
Willelmus the Heyr - -		xij	Willelmus Page - - -} Johanna uxor ejus - -}	ij	
Bartolomaus Brese - -} Isabella uxor ejus - -} Johannes Kennygale - -} Margeria uxor ejus - -}		ij	Humfrey Mowere - - -} Agneta uxor ejus - - -}		xvj
Petrus Dowe - - - -} Alicia uxor ejus - - -}		ij	Nicholaus Schompayn -} Caterina uxor ejus - -}	ij	
			Petrus Rolf - - - -		xij
Artifices			Willelmus Dowe - - -} Margeria uxor ejus - -}	ij	
Radulfus Baldewene, *taylor* - - - - - -} Margeria uxor ejus - -}		ij	Johannes Deye - - -} Agneta uxor ejus - - -}	ij	
Simon Schordewaner, } *schordewaner* - - -} Amissia uxor ejus - -}		ij	Johannes Baldewene -		viij
			Johannes Tyncewyk - -		xij
			Walterus Mayster - -		xij

Summa nominum, xlix
Summa denariorum, xlix*s*.

[180/49 Lay Subsidy Suffolk]

HUNDREDUM DE THYNGHOWE

VILLA DE NOWTON

Hec indentura tripartita facta inter Willelmum de Tendryng chivaler et Socios suos assessores et contrarotulatores ultimi subsidii domino Regi concessi videlicet de qualibet persona laica tres grotas anno regni regis ejusdem quarto ex una parte et Willelmum de Rosshebrok chivaler et socios suos collectores dicti subsidii ex parte altera.

Augricola	s.	d.	*Laboratores*	s.	d.
Simon Serjaunt - - -		ij	Nicholaus Horsecroft -		xviij
			Alicia uxor ejus - -		xviij
Servientes			Willelmus Godwene - -		viij
Rogerus Sterme - - -		xviij	Caterina uxor ejus - -		viij
Margeria uxor ejus - -		xviij	Johannes Norman - -		x
Johannes Welham - -		xviij	Alicia uxor ejus - - -		x
Johanna uxor ejus - -		xviij	Willelmus Godfrey - -		vi
Thomas le Koo - - -		xij	Isabella Serjaunt - - -		viij
Anna uxor ejus - - -		xij	Ricardus le Koo - - -		iiij
Henricus Buttre - - -		xviij	Johannes Welham, junior		iiij
Beatrix uxor ejus - -		xviij	Thomas Horsecroft - -		viij
Alyn Sheperd - - -		xij	Adam Sterme - - - -		x
Matildis uxor ejus - -		xij	Johannes Pascale - - -		xij
Johannes Bullok - - -		xij	Johannes Ariforde - -		iiij
Alicia uxor ejus - - -		xij	Christina (?) Bretthinham		ij

Summa hominum, xxviij
Summa denariorum, xxviijs.

[180/49 Lay Subsidy Suffolk]

HUNDREDUM DE TYNGHOWE

VILLA DE SAXHAM MAGNA

Hec indentura tripartita facta inter Willelmum Tendryng chivaler et socios suos assessores et contra irrotulatores ultimi subsidii domino Regi concessi videlicet de qualibet persona laica tres grotas anno regni ejusdem quarto ex una parte et Willelmum Rosschebrok chivaler et socios suos collectores dicti subsidii ex altera parte Ricardum Andrew Willelmum Doraunt, Johannem Mayster seniorem Willelmum Schot constabularios et subcollectores ejusdem subsidii ville de Saxham Magna ex tercia parte de numero et nominibus subscriptis de gradu et statu corundem.

APPENDIX I.

Laboratores	s.	d.	Laboratores (cont.)	s.	d.
Ricardus Sannty			Ricardus Andrew		
Amissia uxor ejus	ij		Alicia uxor ejus	ij	
Isabella Bradley			*Artifices*		
Ubelye filia ejus	ij		Willelmus Page, *webstere*	xij	
Margeria Caunseler	xij		Robertus Clerk, *taylor*	xij	
Robertus Foul			Robertus Cokedon, *browstere*	ij	
Mabylye uxor ejus	ij				
Johannes Mayster senior	xij		Alicia uxor ejus		
Walterus Horold			Walterus Merel, *taylor*	xij	
Isabella uxor ejus	ij				
Ricardus Hermer			*Servientes*		
Margeria uxor ejus	ij		Ricardus Deye	xij	
Rogerus ate Hawe			Willelmus Hermer	xij	
Rosa uxor ejus	ij		Ricardus Caunseler	xij	
Johannes Mayster junior			Willelmus Adam	xij	
Agneta uxor ejus	ij		Ricardus Chestey		
Alicia Mayster	xij		Agneta uxor ejus	ij	
Willelmus Doraunt			Walterus in the lane	xij	
Margeria uxor ejus	ij		Nicholaus Schepperde	xij	
Willelmus Schot			Isabella Kyppyng	xij	
Johanna uxor ejus	ij		Johannes Andrw	xij	

Summa nominum, xxxviij
Summa denariorum, xxxviijs.

[180 Lay Subsidy]
[49 Suffolk]

Hundredum de Tynghow

Villa de Saxham Parva

Hec indentura tripartita facta inter Willelmum Tendryng chivaler et socios suos assessores et contrarotulatores ultimi subsidii domino Regi concessi videlicet de qualibet persona laica tres grotas anno regni regis ejusdem quarto ex una parte et Willelmum Rosschebrok chivaler et socios suos collectores dicti subsidii ex altera parte Johannem ate Hawe Willelmum Hethe Johannem Lawney Henricum Julle constabularios et subcollectores ejusdem subsidii ville de Saxham parva ex tercia parte de numero et nominibus subscriptis et de gradu et statu eorundem.

Armigeri	s.	d.	Argrecole (cont.)	s.	d.
Johannes de Hethe			Henricus Julle		
Amissia uxor ejus	vj		Margeria uxor ejus	ij	
Rogerus Hethe	iij		Willelmus de Hethe		
Johanna uxor ejus			Margeria uxor ejus	ij	
			Galfridus Warde		
Argrecole			Agneta uxor ejus	ij	
Johannes atte Hawe			Johannes ate Hel		
Meliora uxor ejus	ij		Alicia uxor ejus	ij	
Johannes Lawney			Johannes Norman		
Agneta uxor ejus	ij		Liticia uxor ejus	ij	

Artifices	s.	d.	Servientes (cont.)	s.	d.
Johannes Smyth, *smyth* }	ij		Ricardus Slawtere - -		iiij
Margeria uxor ejus - -}			Johannes Cartere - - -		vj
Henricus Wryth }		xij	Thomas Hethe - - -		x
Willelmus atte *wrythys* }			Johannes Shepperde - -		xij
Hawe }		xij	Margeria Ricard - - -		xij
Willelmus Port, *tachere*		xij	Claryssia Peytevyn - -		xij
Ricardus Berd - - - -		xvj	Johannes Barwe - - -		xij
			Johannes Danyel - - -		xij
Servientes			Gilbertus Howard - -}		
Ricardus Coupere - -		vj	Alicia uxor ejus - -}	ij	
Robertus ate Hawe - -}	ij		Henricus Peytevyn - -}		xij
Agneta uxor ejus - -}			Amissia uxor ejus - -}		xij
Stephanus Fryote - -}			Margeria ate Hel - -		xij
Mabilia uxor ejus - -}	ij		Beatrix filia Margerie Hel		xij
Lenota Norman - - -		xij	Johannes Holdernesse -}		
Edmundus Knyth - -		xij	Johannes filius ejusdem }	ij	
Stephanus Calfawe - -		xij	Johannes Slade - - -}		
Robertus Navys - - -		iiij	Caterina uxor ejus - -}	ij	
Oliva Spenser - - - -		iiij	Johannes Osbern - - -}		
Sarra Schepperde - - -		iiij	...... uxor ejus - -}	ij	
Stephanus Donewych -		vj	...... lfus Osbern - -		xij

Summa Nominum, lvij
Summa denariorum, lvijs.

[180 Lay Subsidy]
[49 Suffolk   ]

HUNDREDUM DE THYNGHOW

VILLATA DE RYSBY

Hec indentura tripartita facta inter Willelmum de Tendringe chivaler et socios suos assessores et contra rotulatores ultimi subsidii domino Regi concessi videlicet de qualibet persona laica tres grotas anno regni regis ejusdem quarto ex una parte et Willelmum de Rosschebrok chivaler et socios suos collectores dicti subsidii ex altera parte et Simonem de Heryngwelle Jacobum Page constabularios et Johannem le Verdonn Simonem le Smyth Johannem Haukyn de Thodynham et Simonem Heryngewelle ex tercia parte de numero et nominibus subscriptis de gradu et statu eorundem.

Servientes	s.	d.	*Servientes* (cont.)	s.	d.
Jacobus Page - - - -		xij	Edmundus Bunnynge -		xij
Mariota uxor ejus - -		xij	Thomas Julle - - - -		xij
Alicia Bullok - - - -		xij	Johannes Verdon - -		xij
Johannes Heyward - -		xij	Alicia uxor ejus - - -		xij
Caterina uxor ejus - -		xij	Johannes Hopton - - -		ix
Isabella Meller - - -		xviij	Alicia uxor ejus - - -		ix
Simon Heryngewelle -		xviij	Johannes Hanlyn - -		xij
Clare uxor ejus - - -		xviij	Beatrix uxor ejus - -		xij
Robertus Christemasse -		xviij	Anna le Meller - - -		xij
Loveday uxor ejus - -		xviij	Johannes Bunynge - -		xij

APPENDIX I. 83

Servientes (cont.)	s.	d.	Servientes (cont.)	s.	d.
Beatrix uxor ejus - -		xij	Agnes uxor ejus - - -		xij
Johannes Meller - - -		vj	Johannes Blek - - -		vj
Isabella atte Grene - -		xij	Margareta uxor ejus - -		vj
Alicia atte Grene - - -		xij	Walterus atte Dale - -		xij
Johannes atte Grene		vj	Mariota uxor ejus - -		xij
Thomas Haukyn - - -		xij	Edmundus Taylor - -		xij
Willelmus Walcard - -		vj			
Alicia uxor ejus - - -		vj	*Laboratores*		
Alicia atte Hache - -		xij			
Agneta atte Hache - -		xij	Walterus Belamy - - -		xij
Johannes Clere - - -		ix	Alicia uxor ejus - - -		xij
Margareta uxor ejus - -		ix	Johannes Sumper - -	ij	
Isabella de Wode - - -		xij	Margareta uxor ejus - -	ij	
Simon le Smyth - -		xij	Ricardus Herist junior -		xij
Juliana uxor ejus - -		x	Johannes Verdon junior		xij
Willelmus Okele - - -		xij	Ricardus Yongwone junior		xij
Rosia uxor ejus - - -		xij	Johannes Webster - -		xij
Nicholaus de Wode - -		xij	Edmundus atte Hache -		xij
Alicia uxor ejus - - -		xij	Henricus Bullok - - -		vj
Johannes Acke - - -		xij	Agneta uxor ejus - - -		vj

Summa personarum, lvij
Summa denariorum, lvijs.

[180 Lay Subsidy]
[49   Suffolk]

VILLA DE WESTLE

Hec indentura tripartita facta inter Willelmum Tendringe chivaler & socios suos contra irrotulatores ultimi subsidii domino Regi concessi videlicet de qualibet persona laica tres grotas anno regni ejusdem quarto ex una parte et Willelmum Ruschbrok chivaler et socios suos collectores dicti subsidii ex altera parte et Thomam Thurmood Thomam Gyle Edmundum Amy constabularios et subcollectores ejusdem subsidii de villa de Westle ex tercia parte de numero et nominibus.

Agricole	s.	d.	*Laboratores (cont.)*	s.	d.
Thomas Thurmood - -			Edmundus Amy - - -		
Margeria uxor ejus - -	ij		Christiana uxor ejus -	ij	
Thomas Gyle - - - -			Seman de Cavenham -		
Isabella uxor ejus - -	ij		Alicia uxor ejus - - -	ij	
Robertus Welyngham -			Johannes Bounend - -		
Margeria uxor ejus - -	ij		Alicia uxor ejus - - -	ij	
			Willelmus Bonde - - -		
Artifices			Matildis uxor ejus - -	ij	
Johannes Lamber, carpenter - - - - -					
Johanna uxor ejus - -	ij		*Servientes*		
Ricardus Dye, *webstere* -			Nicholaus Shepherd - -		
Matildis uxor ejus - -	ij		Isabella uxor ejus - -	ij	
			Thomas Buntyfeld - -		
Laboratores			Johanna uxor ejus - -	ij	
Matildis Murwell - - -		xij	Ch ... Julle - - -		
Mariota Welingham - -		xij	Beatrix uxor ejus - -	ij	

6—2

84 SUFFOLK POLL TAX LISTS, 1381.

Servientes (cont.)	s.	d.	Servientes (cont.)	s.	d.
Walterus Thurmood	ij		Johannes Deth		xij
Mar... uxor ejus			Thomas S... nde	ij	
Henricus Cavenham	ij		Alicia uxor ejus		
Alicia uxor ejus			Ricardus Smyht	ij	
Edmundus Welyngham		xij	Agneta uxor ejus		

Summa nominum, xxxvi
Summa, xxxvis.

[180/52 Lay Subsidy Suffolk]

HUNDREDUM DE THYNGHOWE

VILLA DE WHEPSTED

Hec indentura tripartita facta inter Willelmum Tendryng chivaler et socios suos assessores et contrairrotulatores ultimi subsidii domino Regi concessi videlicet de qualibet persona laica tres grotas anno regni regis ejusdem quarto ex una parte et Willelmum Rosschebrok chivaler et socios suos collectores dicti subsidii ex parte altera et Ricardum Fayrchild Johannem Lamberd Walterum Cage et Robertum Pylgrey constabularios et subcollectores ejusdem subsidii de villa predicta ex tercia parte de numero et nominibus subscriptis et de gradu et statu eorundem videlicet.

Artifices	s.	d.	Laboratores (cont.)	s.	d.
Johannes Fleg, carpenter	ij	vj	Galfridus Neith	ij	vj
Alicia uxor ejus			Johanna uxor ejus		
Johannes Boydyn, carpenter		xij	Johannes Brend	ij	
			Elen uxor ejus		
Willelmus Deye, carpenter	ij	vj	Johannes Pye	ij	vj
Amy uxor ejus			Christiana uxor ejus		
Johannes at hel, taylor	ij	vj	Johannes Cage	ij	vj
Matildis uxor ejus			Rosa uxor ejus		
Willelmus Norman	ij		Petrus de Toune	ii	vj
Matildis uxor ejus			Olive uxor ejus		
			Alicia Cage		xviij
			Radulfus Menewod		xij
Laboratores			Ricardus Fayrchilde	ij	vj
			Marion uxor ejus		
Simon Raph	ij	vj	Johannes Lamberd		xij
Johanna uxor ejus			Willelmus Cage	ij	vj
Walterus Mundeford	ij	vj	Agneta uxor ejus		
Beatrix uxor ejus			Robertus Pylgrey	ij	
Willelmus atte Moor	ij	vj	Alicia uxor ejus		
Alicia uxor ejus					
Rogerus Donyton	ij		*Servientes*		
Alicia uxor ejus					
Christiana Dolyngham	ij	vj	Johannes Bulbrok	ij	
Johannes filius ejus			Alicia uxor ejus		
Ricardus Taylor	ij		Willelmus Smyth		xij
Johanna uxor ejus			Christiana uxor ejus		

APPENDIX I. 85

Servientes (cont.)	s.	d.	Servientes (cont.)	s.	d.
Johannes Whytman - } Margeria uxor ejus - }		xviij	Edmundus Meller - - Johannes Cage, junior -		iiij iiij
Johannes Tofeld - - } Isabella uxor ejus - }		ij	Johannes Parys - - } Isabella uxor ejus - }		ij
Benedictus Menewod - } Johanna uxor ejus - }		viij	Rogerus Brythren - } Agneta uxor ejus - - }		ij
Johannes Gyle - - - } Johanna uxor ejus - }		xviij	Margeria Menewod - - Rogerus Wattys... -		viij iiij
Willelmus Bulbrok - } Beatrix uxor ejus - - }		viij			

[180 Lay Subsidy]
[38   Suffolk   ]

VILLATA DE MILDENHALE IN HUNDREDO DE LACFORD

Hec indentura tripartita facta inter Willelmum de Tendryng chivaler et socios suos assessores et contra irrotulatores ultimi subsidii domino Regi concessi videlicet de qualibet persona laica tres grotes anno regni ejusdem iiij^{to} ex una parte et Willelmum de Russhebrok et socios suos collectores dicti subsidii ex altera parte et Henricum Purs Henricum Chapman Thomam Clerk Robertum' Dyke et Willelmum. Greyne constabularios et sub-collectores ejusdem subsidii ex tercia parte de numero et nominibus subscriptis et de statu et gradu eorundem videlicet.

Agricole	s.	d.	Brasiatores	s.	d.
Willelmus Sopere - } Agneta uxor ejus - - }	ij	vj	Johannes Gilbonu - } Margeria uxor ejus - }	ij	vj
Dionis Ereswell - -	•	xviij	Willelmus Neb - - } Katerina uxor ejus - }	ij	
Johannes Kelfynch - } Isabella uxor cjus - }	ij		Thomas Clerk - - - } Agneta uxor ejus - - }	ij	
HenricusChapman senior } Emma uxor ejus - - }	ij	vj	Johannes Lanwade - } Katerina uxor ejus - }	ij	
Katerina Walcham - -	ij				
HenricusChapman junior } Johanna uxor ejus - }	ij	vj	Robertus Revenhal - } Elena uxor ejus - - }	ij	
Simon Childreston - -		xij	Thomas Wylde - - } Agneta uxor ejus - - }	ij	
Simon Childreston junior } Margeria uxor ejus - }	ij	vj	Johannes Rande - - } Elizabetha uxor ejus - }	ij	
Rogerus Childreston - } Beatrix uxor ejus - - }	ij		Pannarii		
Robertus le Reve - - } Alicia uxor ejus - - }	ij		Nicholaus Partrich - } Dionis uxor cjus - - }	ij	vj
Willelmus Greyne - } Emma uxor ejus - - }	ij		Henricus Purs - - - } Margareta uxor ejus - }	ij	
Johannes Everard - } Agneta uxor ejus - - }	ij	vj	Petrus Berton - - - } Margeria uxor ejus - }		xviij
Robertus Dyk - - - } Isabella uxor ejus - }	ij		Artifices		
Robertus Claver - - } Alicia uxor ejus - - }	ij	vj	Thomas Barker - - } Matildis uxor ejus - }	ij	

Artifices (cont.)	s.	d.	Artifices (cont.)	s.	d.
Robertus Gennote } Matildis uxor ejus }	ij		Willelmus Cavenham } Margeria uxor ejus }	ij	
Johannes Webstere } Margeria uxor ejus }	ij		Willelmus Sygo } Agneta uxor ejus }	ij	
Thomas Eton } Margareta uxor ejus }	ij		Johannes Sygo } Margeria uxor ejus }	ij	
Johannes Barbour	xij		Robertus Sygo } Margeria uxor ejus }	ij	vi
Johannes Gilbonn junior } Johanna uxor ejus }	ij		Johannes Thorndon } Felis uxor ejus }	ij	
Henricus Taillor } Margeria uxor ejus }	xviij		Robertus Goche } Margeria uxor ejus }	ij	
Walterus Bocher } Isabella uxor ejus }	xviij		Johannes Sly } Margeria uxor ejus }		xviij
Willelmus Coupere	xij		Willelmus Sly } Margeria uxor ejus }	ij	
Johannes Skarlet } Margeria uxor ejus }	ij				
Johannes Smyth	xviij		Johannes Symond } Margeria uxor ejus }	ij	
Rogerus Castel } Margeria uxor ejus }	ij	vj	Thomas Northern } Anna uxor ejus }		xii
Thomas Fenhowe } Alicia uxor ejus }	ij		Johannes Fraunceys } Beatrix uxor ejus }	ij	
Radulfus Baxtere	x		Willelmus Cotton } Alicia uxor ejus }	ij	
Johannes Page } Margeria uxor ejus }	ij				
Rogerus Rondham	xij		Thomas Symond } Johanna uxor ejus }	ij	
Adam Cote } Isabella uxor ejus }	ij		Johannes Fremond } Margeria uxor ejus }	ij	
Petrus Messager	ij				
Robertus Soutere } Alicia uxor ejus }	ij		Johannes Turnay } Johanna uxor ejus }	ij	
Willelmus Mustardar } Margeria uxor ejus }	ij		Willelmus Parmater } Alicia uxor ejus }	ij	
Robertus Smyth } Anna uxor ejus }	ij		Ricardus Mulberye } Margareta uxor ejus }	ij	
Johannes Lister } Johanna uxor ejus }	ij		Johannes Cotton } Alicia uxor ejus }	ij	
Johannes Mannyng } Alicia uxor ejus }	ij		Johannes Taillour		vj
Simon Baxtere } Margeria uxor ejus }	ij		Johannes Calcher	ij	vj
Edmundus Elvedon } Alicia uxor ejus }	ij		Johannes Skynner		
			Willelmus Taillor		xij
			Willelmus Webster		xij
Johannes Webestere } Isabella uxor ejus }	ij		Johannes Taillour		xij
Henricus Sadiller } Margeria uxor ejus }	ij		*Servientes*		
Thomas Fullere } Katerina uxor ejus }	ij		Petrus *serviens* W. Neb		vj
			Robertus *serviens* Johannis Smyth }		xij
Robertus Waryn } Beatrix uxor ejus }	ij		Cecilia Souter		xij
			Johannes *serviens* H. Purs }		iiij
Thomas Loksmyth } Johanna uxor ejus }	xij		Johannes *serviens* W. Sopere }		vj
Willelmus Baxtere } Katerina uxor ejus }	ij		Johannes Brownyng		vj
Simon Penne } Agneta uxor ejus }	ij		Margareta Ally		xij
Simon Gregory } Isabella uxor ejus }	ij		Margeria *serviens* Johannis Childreston }		vj
			Henricus Petrisburg		iiij
Johannes Sly } Beatrix uxor ejus }	ij		Amabilia Brethenham		iiij
			Alicia Gundel		iiij

APPENDIX I. 87

Servientes (cont.)	s.	d.	Laboratores (cont.)	s.	d.
Emma Ally		iiij	Rogerus B .... rd		xviij
Robertus Kirkowe		iiij	Johannes Algood	ij	
Johannes Borel		iiij	Leticia uxor ejus		
Alicia serviens K. Walcham		viij	Johannes Bernard		xij
			Johannes Costyn		xij
Petrus Hardy		iiij	Johannes Tollote		xij
Margeria serviens W. Benet		iiij	Margeria uxor ejus		
			Ricardus Halstede		xij
Ricardus Brid		iiij	Margeria Elveden		xij
Constancia Kytebote		iiij	Agneta le Hyne		xij
Etheldreda Elyman		iiij	Willelmus Prat		xij
Thomas Cote		xij	Margeria uxor ejus		
Katerina Soutere		xij	Ricardus Gennote	ij	vj
Johannes serviens H. Purs		vj	Beatrix uxor ejus		
			Johannes Gennote		xij
Robertus serviens J. Kelfynch		vj	Johannes Lardy	ij	vj
			Agneta uxor ejus		
Margeria Succlyng		vj	Johannes Ally		xij
Margeria Hy		xij	Petrus Coneynhton		xij
Johannes filius Adami		xij	Robertus Millere		xij
			Willelmus Martyn		xij
Katerina Elmham		xij	Thomas Miller		vj
Katerina Cake		ij	Ricardus Bambonn		xij
Johannes Pykrel		ij	Johanna uxor ejus		
Em...		ij	Johanna Succlyng		xij
Cecilia ... Bullok		ij	Margeria filia ejus		xij
Johanna ... yte		ij	Margeria Succlyng		xij
Johannes serviens T ...		xij	Adam Chadenhalk	ij	viij
Thomas filius ...		xij	Beatrix uxor ejus		
Rogerus Sygo		xij	Johannes filius ejus		viij
			Robertus filius ejus		viij
Laboratores			Enota le Hyne		xij
Robertus Gilbert	ij		Willelmus le Hyne	ij	
Alicia uxor ejus			Beatrix uxor ejus		
Johannes Hoot		xviij	Johannes Childreston	ij	vj
Johanna uxor ejus			Alicia uxor ejus		
Johannes Cotton	ij		Reginaldus Tyd	ij	
Cecilia uxor ejus			Cecilia uxor ejus		
Johannes Legt		xij	Willelmus Miller		xij
Agneta uxor ejus			Johannes Place	ij	
Ricardus Odam	ij		Katerina uxor ejus		
Margareta uxor ejus			Etheldreda Goldwyn		xij
Robertus Morle	ij		Johannes Golwyn		xij
Sarra uxor ejus			Radulfus Thaccher	ij	
Radulfus Fouldon	ij		Isabella uxor ejus		
Margeria uxor ejus			Emma Elmham		xij
Willelmus Thacher		xij	Willelmus Hallested		xij
Willelmus Kent		xij	Ricardus de Berton		xij
Willelmus Fisher	ij		Willelmus Hamond	ij	
Johanna uxor ejus			Agneta uxor ejus		
Philippus Ged	ij		Adam Playford	ij	
Alicia uxor ejus			Johanna uxor ejus		
Etheldreda Wayte		xij	Robertus Holm	ij	
Cecilia Cotton		xij	Agneta uxor ejus		
Robertus Langemere		xij			
Johannes Rederc		xviij	*Serjiantes de payes*		
Alicia uxor ejus					
Johannes Catelyn		xij	Radulfus de Walcham	x	
Johanna Skynner		xij	Walterus Beneyt	x	
Thor		viij	Matildis uxor ejus		

Laboratores	s.	d.	Laboratores (cont.)	s.	d.
Rogerus .... - - -		xij	Henricus Morle - - -⎫	ij	
Willelmus .... - - -		xij	Isabella uxor ejus - -⎭		
Johannes Fenhow - -		xij	Henricus Harg ... - -		viij
Johannes H .... - -			Thomas Morle - - - -⎫	j	
Gilbertus S .... ake -			Agneta uxor ejus - - -⎭		
...... - - - - -		(?)	Galfridus Langmere - -⎫	ij	
...... - - - - -⎫		xij	Agneta uxor ejus - - -⎭		
...... - - - - -⎭			Willelmus Ratlesden - -⎫	ij	
Willelmus Cake - - -		xij	Margeria uxor ejus - -⎭		
Symon Tymeworth - -⎫	ij		Johannes Penyman - -		xij
Matildis uxor ejus - -⎭			Johannes Wylde - - -⎫	ij	
Ricardus Felyrs - - -⎫	ij		Agneta uxor ejus - - -⎭		
Agneta uxor ejus - - -⎭			Johannes Bernygham -⎫		xviij
Willelmus Wright - -		xij	Johanna uxor ejus - -⎭		
Bertholomaus Tyby - -⎫	ij		Johannes Berton - - -		xviij
Johanna uxor ejus - -⎭			Robertus Symond - -		xviij
Johannes Hallested - -⎫	ij		Alicia Sly - - - -		xij
Anna uxor ejus - - -⎭			Johannes Co ... er - -⎫	ij	
Walterus Cole - - - -		xij	Matildis uxor ejus - -⎭		
Ricardus Cole - - - -		xij	Willelmus Thurston - -⎫	ij	
Alexander Cole - - -⎫	ij		Alicia uxor ejus - - -⎭		
Agneta uxor ejus - - -⎭			Johannes Messager - -⎫	ij	
Johannes Costyn - - -⎫	ij		Johanna uxor ejus - -⎭		
Matildis uxor ejus - -⎭			Robertus Hulet - - -⎫	ij	
Ricardus Penne - - -⎫	ij		Agneta uxor ejus - - -⎭		
Alicia uxor ejus - - -⎭			Willelmus .... - - -	j	
Galfridus Penne - - -⎫	ij		Henricus .... - - -		xij
Katerina uxor ejus - -⎭			Robertus .... - - -		xij
Johannes Bullok - - -		xij	Maria Hyne - - - -		xij
Matildis Aunsel - - -		xij	Johannes Fisher - - -		xij
Julia le Swon - - - -		xij	Johannes Ty ... - - -		iiij
Rogerus Man - - - -⎫		xij	Johannes Watton - - -⎫	ij	
Cecilia uxor ejus - - -⎭			Margeria uxor ejus - -⎭		
Alicia Grigory - - - -		xij	Johannes Parmeter - -		xij
Johannes Gregory - -		xij	Johanna Symond - - -		xij
Hamo Childreston - -⎫		xij	Johannes Beconn - -		xij
Agneta uxor ejus - - -⎭			Robertus Aleyn - - -		xij
Johannes filius S. Childreston - - - - -		viij	Margeria Gardener - -		xij
			Etheldreda Algood - -		xij
Edmundus frater ejus -		viij	Alicia Skynnere - - -		xij
Johanna soror ejus - -		viij	Robertus Reymond - -		xij
Thomas Sly - - - -⎫	ij		Simon Mekke - - - -		xij
Agneta uxor ejus - - -⎭			Thomas serviens W. Mustarder - - - -		xij
Johannes Mildeman - -⎫	ij		Margeria le Smyth - -		xij
Margeria uxor ejus - -⎭			Willelmus Thresshere -		xij
Johannes Dawes - - -⎫	ij		Martinus Wylkok - -		xij
Johanna uxor ejus - -⎭			Johanna serviens W. Sopere		vj
Edmundus Dawes - -⎫	ij		Johanna Halstede - -		xij
Agneta uxor ejus - - -⎭			Johannes Tymworth - -		xij
Willelmus Symon - -⎫	ij		Beatrix Gundel - - -		iiij
Agneta uxor ejus - - -⎭			Alicia filia Ricardi Penne		xij
Johannes Swage - - -		xij	Willelmus Pyteman - -		iiij
Petrus Mayner - - -⎫	ij		Alanus le Man - - -		xij
Walterus Wryght - - -⎫	ij		Thomas Pyteman - - -		vj
Margeria uxor ejus - -⎭			Emma serviens H. Chapman - - - - -		vj
Willelmus Mariot - - -⎫	ij		Thomas Attebregge - -		xij
Alicia uxor ejus - - -⎭			Thomas Mayner - - -		xij
Rogerus Rolf - - - -⎫		xviij	Johannes Bronewyn - -		xij
Cecilia uxor ejus - - -⎭					

Laboratores (cont.)	s.	d.	Laboratores (cont.)	s.	d.
Beatrix serviens .... der		xij	Willelmus .... sel		xij
Willelmus Hubert - -		xij	Thomas Sygo - - -		xij
Johannes Hert - - -		xij	S... Messager - -		xij
Thomas Reche - - -		xij	Thomas Thaccher - -		xij
Robertus filius R. Reve -		xij	Isabella Messager - - -		xij
Robertus Marchand - -		xij	Johannes Cook - - -		xij

Summa, xixli. xviiis.

$\left[\dfrac{180}{45}\text{ Lay Subsidy} \atop \text{Suffolk}\right]$ *Skin damaged*

HUNDRED OF STOWE

STOWEMARKET

Indentura de subsidio ville de Stowemarket domino nostro Ricardo Regi Anglie concesso anno regni sui quarto.

	s.	d.	Artifices (cont.)	s.	d.
De			De		
Radulpho Clement armigero et Katerina uxore -	iij	iiij	..... (Sh)akerys sutore ..... Smyth et Katerina	ij	
Amicia Houtot generosa	ij		uxore - - - - -	ij	vj
			.... Mellere flecher cum		
Artifices			Margareta uxore - -	ij	vj
De			..... Furbesshor - -		xij
Roberto Frend pistore			.... Agneta		
cum Matilde uxore -	iij	iiij	uxore - - - - - -	iij	vj
Ricardo Eston firmario -	iij		..........tice uxore -	iij	
...... S ... ford sutore			.... Johanna		
cum Agneta uxore - -		xviij	uxore - - - - -		xviij
Roberto Wyngge chinchere cum uxore Elena		xviij	...... cum Christiana		xij
Johanne Aubry cissore			uxore - - - - -	ij	
cum Katerina uxore -		xviij	.... uxore -	ij	vj
Stephano Sarle tinctore					xij
cum Agneta uxore - -	iij		.... Margareta		
.... questore.			uxore - - - - -		xviij
cum Johanna uxore -	iij	vj	...... cum Margareta		
.... cum			uxore - - - - -	ij	
Johanna uxore - - -	iij	vj	....	ij	
....		vj	.... Margeria		
.... cum			uxore - - - - -		xviij
Matilde uxore - - -	ij	vj	.... cum Issabella		xij
....		xij	uxore - - - - -	ij	
.... cum					
Christiana uxore - -	ij	vj	.... Smyth -		xij
.... carpenter			.... herf sutore		
cum Johanna uxore -	ij		cum Mariota uxore -		xviij
.... matore			.... bonn celarer -		xij
cum Johanna uxore -	ij	vj	.... ery - - -		xij
.... sutore			... nardiston carpenter		
cum Margeria uxore -	ij		cum Mariota uxore -		xviij
.... cue colermaker			... otele ... cum Elena		
cum Margeria uxore -	ij		uxore - - - - -		xviij

SUFFOLK POLL TAX LISTS, 1381.

Artifices (cont.)	s.	d.
De		
.........*inchere* cum Alicia uxore - - - -	ij	vj
..... s b ... *maker* cum Johanna uxore - - -		xviij
.... cum Matilde uxore - - -		xviij
.... Alicia uxore - - - - -		xviij
.... Margareta uxore - - - - - -	ij	
Johanne Leg *pelliparrio* cum Margareta uxore -	ij	
Willelmo Stanton *cissore* cum Agneta uxore - -	ij	
Johanne Hoo *baskatmaker* cum Margeria uxore et Cecilia matre	iij	
Dionisia Chaundeler -		xij
Edmundo Bethwold *pistore* cum Katerina uxore	ij	
Katerina Neve *brasiatrice* cum Edmundo filio suo	iiij	
Thoma Clerk cum Johanna uxore - - - -	ij	
Alicia Kent *spinstere* -		xij
Nicholao Partre *colermaker* cum Amicia uxore - - - - - -	ij	
Laurentio Spot *carnifice* et Agneta uxore - -	ij	vj
Willelmo Keteryngham *carpenter* - - - - -		xij
Katerina Childirhous -		xij
Thoma Cook - - - -		xij
Johanna Coldhacle *scherewoman* - - - -		xij
Rogero Frost *chinchere*		xij
Johanne Flecher cum Matilde uxore - - -	ij	
Thoma Chese *sutore* cum Basilia uxore - - -	ij	
Willelmo (Wilde?) ..*elar* cum Mabilia uxore -	ij	
Willelmo P...h *habirdassher* cum Johanna uxore - - - - - -	iij	
.... kyn *hoxstere* -		xij
Johanne Frie *pistore* cum Johanna uxore -	ij	
Johanne Dextere cum Matilde uxore - - -		xviij
...... Guntre *spinster* -		xij
Elia Dranton *brasiatore* cum Christiana uxore -	ij	
Johanne Randolf *cissore* cum Mariota uxore -	ij	
Johanne Tostoke *molendinario* cum Isabella uxore - - - - -	ij	vj

Artifices (cont.)	s.	d.
De		
Roberto Boyo et Johanne *tegulatoribus* cum uxoribus Margeria et Katerina - - - - -	iiij	
...... Chalonner - -		xij
Roberto Potte cum Alicia uxore - - - - -	ij	
Johanne Clubbe *tannatore* cum Margeria uxore - - - - -	ij	
Johanne Holterelyn *cooperator* cum Alicia uxore - - - - -		xviij
Reginaldo Senker cum Bassilia uxore - - -		xviij
Johanne Wekys *fuller* cum Matilde uxore -		xviij
Johanne Hoo (*gleente*?) cum Katerina uxore -	iij	ij
...... Robeld		xij
...... Langlyf *p*.. cum Christiana uxore - -	iij	vj
.... kyn - - - -		xij
.... cum Alicia uxore - - - - -	ij	
.... Johanna uxore - - - - -		xviij
Willelmo Barbour cum Johanna uxore - - -	ij	
Johanne Robeld *carpenter* cum Matilde uxore	ij	
Petro Byl *fouller* et Margeria uxore - - -	ij	

Laboratores

	s.	d.
De		
Simone Skulton *laboratore* cum Johanna uxore - - - - -	ij	
Johanne Reed *laboratore*		xij
Johanne Plumbe *laboratore* cum Alicia uxore -		xviij
Rogero Badele *laboratore* cum Alicia uxore - -	ij	
Roberto Carter *laboratore* - - - - - -		xij
Willelmo Leg *laboratore* cum Juliana uxore -		xij

Servientes

	s.	d.
De		
Roberto et Margareta *servientibus* Stephani Sarle		xij
Katerina *serviente* Roberti Sarle - - - -		vj
Roberto *serviente* Johannis Hervy - - - - -		?
Johanne *serviente* Willelmi Dey - - - -		xij

APPENDIX I. 91

Servientes (cont.)	s.	d.	Servientes (cont.)	s.	d.
De			De		
Johanne *serviente* Johannis Schakeris - -		xij	Isabella *serviente* Nicholai Partre - - - -		xij
Johanna *serviente* Gilberti Smyth - - - -		vj	Christiana *serviente* Amicie Houtot - - -		xij
Johanna *serviente* Thome Meller - - - - - -		vj	Margareta *serviente* Katerine Childrous - - -		xij
Willelmo et Thoma *servientibus* Willelmi Crane		xij	Edmundo *serviente* Thome Chese - - -		xij
Johanne et Stephano *servientibus* Willelmi Sparwe - - - - -		xij	Johanne *serviente* Willelmi Wilde - - - -		xij
Roberto *serviente* Roberti Smyth - - - - - -		vj	Alicia *serviente* Johannis Tostoke - - - -		vj
Johanne *serviente* Willelmi Manser - - -		xij	Margeria *serviente* Johannis Hoo - - - -		iiij
Johanne *serviente* Johannis Coo - - - -		vj	Katerina et Johanna *servientibus* Willelmi Langlyf - - - - -		xij
Johanne, Egidio, et Katerina *servientibus* Katerine Neve - - -	ij		Isabella Brastrete - - Amabilia Ferour - - -		vj vj
Johanne, Johanne, Thoma et Margareta *servientibus* Roberti Frend -	iij		Eloseo, et Matilde, *servientibus* Radulphi Clement - - - - - -		xij
Agneta *serviente* Laurentio Spot - - - - -		vj	Willelmo, Bertholomao, et Johanne *servientibus* Ricardi de Eston - -		xij

Summa personarum ccij
Summa denariorum xli. ijs.

Collectores { Willelmus Crane
Johannes de Hoo
Willelmus Langlyf
Robertus Frend } quia onerantur superius.

[180 Lay Subsidy]
[35   Suffolk   ]

FYNBERGH MAGNA

Indentura ejusdem ville de subsidio domino Ricardo Regi nostro concesso anno regni sui quarto.

Agricole	s.	d.	Agricole (cont.)	s.	d.
Johannes Sorell - - -	ij		Johanna uxor ejus - -		iiij
Johanna uxor ejus - -		xij	Rogerus Cordde - - -		xx
Agneta Cakestrete - -		xij	Alicia uxor ejus - - -		xij
Augustinus Jour - - -		xviij	Nicholaus Wode - - -		xviij
Mariota uxor ejus - -		vj	Alicia uxor ejus - - -		vj
Johannes Lenegor - -		xvj	Thomas ate Fen - - -		xvj
Johanna uxor ejus - -		viij	Alicia uxor ejus - - -		viij
Robertus Bedoun - -		xij	Katerina Neue - - - -		xij
Alicia uxor ejus - - -		xij	Petrus Wetherden - -		xij
Johannes Thedham - -		xviij	Johannes Plant - - -		vj
Margareta uxor ejus - -		vj	Roys uxor ejus - - -		xviij
Johannes Scherwynd -		xx			

SUFFOLK POLL TAX LISTS, 1381.

Panermakers	s.	d.	Laboratores	s.	d.
Johannes Rome - - -		xij	Thomas Stalpy - - -		xx
Elizia uxor ejus - - -		xij	Agneta uxor ejus - - -		iiij
Stephanus Truton - -		vj	Johannes Neue - - -		xvj
Dionisia uxor ejus - -		xviij	Margeria uxor ejus - -		viij
Johannes Coker - - -		xij	Johannes Senlowes - -		xij
Margeria uxor ejus - -		xij	Margeria uxor ejus - -		xij
			Johannes Aylemer - -		xvj
Textatores			Margeria uxor ejus - -		viij
Nicholaus Cros - - -		xv	Johannes Blechepayl -		vj
Emma uxor ejus - - -		ix			
Nicholaus Pirie - - -		xij			
Alicia uxor ejus - - -		xij			
Cissores					
Robertus Edward senior		xvj	*Servientes*		
Alicia uxor ejus - - -		viij	Ricardus Lenegor - - -		x
Robertus Edward junior		xiiij	Agneta uxor ejus - - -		x
Philyppa uxor ejus - -		x	Robertus Seygge - - -		viij
			Robertus Gentil - - -		xij
Fabri			Agneta uxor ejus - - -		xij
Henricus Smyth - - -		xij	Johannes Grene - - -		x
Agneta uxor ejus - - -		xij	Robertus Ossebern - -		x
Robertus Hakoun - - -		xij	Nicholaus Edward - -		x

Summa lvij*s* (erased E. P.)

Colectores { Rogerus Cordde
Johannes Rome
Nicholaus Wode
Thomas Ate Fen

Summa personarum lxi
Summa denariorum lxi*s*.

[180 Lay Subsidy / 42 Suffolk]

BUXHALE

Indentura de Subsidio Ville de Buxhale Domino nostro Ricardo Regi Anglie concesso anno regni sui quarto.

Armigeri	s.	d.	Agricole (cont.)	s.	d.
De Adam Cokerel - - -}	vj	viij	De Nicholao Foot - - -}	ij	
Cecilia uxore ejus - -}			Roys uxore ejus - -}		
Johanne Rouly - - -}	vj	viij	Rogero Smyth - - -}	ij	
Margeria uxore ejus -}			Claricia uxore ejus -}		
			Ricardo Husk - - -}	ij	
			Margeria uxore ejus -}		
Agricole			Rogero Copinger - -}	ij	
De			Alicia uxore ejus -}		
Semano Breton - - -}	iij		Edmundo Langemere -}	ij	
Agneta uxore ejus - -}			Johanna uxore ejus -}		
Ricardo Thurmood - -}	ij		Willelmo Spetylman -}	ij	
Alicia uxore ejus - -}			Deonisia uxore ejus -}		
Willelmo Hare - - -}	xxx		Johanne Cobbe - -}	xviij	
Johanna uxore ejus - -}			Matilde uxore ejus -}		

APPENDIX I.

Agricole (cont.)	s.	d.	*Pelliparii*	s.	d.
De			De		
Edmundo Canon - - -⎫			Thoma Fancebroun - -⎫		
Amicia uxore ejus - -⎬	ij		Alicia uxore ejus - -⎭		xviij
Rogero Saltere - - -⎫	ij				
Margareta uxore ejus -⎭			*Laborarii*		
Cecilia Fancebroun - -		xij	De		
Johanne Spryng - - -⎫	ij		Ricardo Skeyman - -⎫	ij	
Amabila uxore ejus - -⎭			Johanna uxore ejus - -⎭		
Egidio Skut - - - -⎫	ij		Roberto Folke - - -⎫		xviij
Margareta uxore ejus -⎭			Johanna uxore ejus - -⎭		
...... Skut - - -⎫	ij		Roberto Kent - - -		xij
...... uxore ejus - -⎭			Johanne Langemere- -⎫		xviij
Roberto Heyham - - -⎫	ij		Alicia uxore ejus - -⎭		
Alicia uxore ejus - - -⎭			Willelmo Coupere - -⎫		xviij
Roberto Joye - - - -⎫		xij	Emma uxore ejus - -⎭		
Alicia uxore ejus - - -⎭			Johanne ate Hel seniore⎫	ij	
Matilde Chaunteler - -		xij	Katerina uxore ejus - -⎭		
			Johanne ate Hel juniore⎫	ij	
			Sarra uxore ejus - -⎭		
Carnifices			Johanne Baroun - - -⎫	ij	
De			Ositha uxore ejus - -⎭		
...... Bocher - - -		xij	Johanne Pye - - -⎫	ij	
...... Cakebred - - -⎫	ij		Alicia uxore ejus - -⎭		
Clemence uxore ejus -⎭			Johanne Clerk - - -⎫		
			Beatrice uxore ejus - -⎭		
			Willelmo Legat - - -		xij
Carpentarii			Johanne Mesham - -⎫	ij	
De			Agneta uxore ejus - -⎭		
Galfrido Smalbon - -⎫	xx		Rogero Levyrmere - -		xij
Alicia uxore ejus - - -⎭			Henrico Charlys - - -⎫	ij	
Simone Fraul - - - -⎫	ij		Petronilla uxore ejus -⎭		
Cecilia uxore ejus - -⎭			Johanne Foot - - -⎫	ij	
Thoma Wryte - - - -⎫		xviij	Alicia uxore ejus - -⎭		
Margareta uxore ejus -⎭			Johanne Spetylman - -		xij
			Ricardo Freton - - -⎫	ij	
			Agneta uxore ejus - -⎭		
			Thoma Payn - - -⎫	ij	
Sissores			Basilia uxore ejus - -⎭		
De			Rogero Jay - - - -⎫	ij	
Willelmo Taylor - - -⎫		xviij	Margeria uxore ejus -⎭		
Alicia uxore ejus - - -⎭			Johanne Tynton - - -⎫	ij	
Henrico Taylor - - -⎫		xij	Alicia uxore ejus - -⎭		
Amia uxore ejus - - -⎭			Johanna Naunton - -		xij
Johanne Spetylman - -⎫		xviij	Johanne Tynton - - -		xij
Roys uxore ejus - - -⎭			Roberto Breton - - -⎫	ij	
			Christiana uxore ejus -⎭		
Textores			*Servientes*		
De			De		
Johanne Neel - - - -⎫		xviij	Roberto Cokerel - - -		x
Katerina uxore ejus - -⎭			Petro Cook - - - -		viij
Johanne Mylys - - -⎫	ij		Reginaldo Pach(at) - -		vj
Roys uxore ejus - - -⎭			Johanne Resshebrok -		viij
Agneta Costard - - -		xij	Margeria Abot - - -		vj
			Roberto Cartere - - -⎫		xviij
			Inet uxore ejus - - -⎭		
Fabri			Thoma Harre - - - -		viij
De			Agneta serviente Thome		xij
Johanne Smyth - - -⎫	xxx		Roberto Schepperde - -⎫		xvj
Mariota uxore ejus - -⎭			Elena uxore ejus - -⎭		

Servientes (cont.)	s.	d.	Servientes (cont.)	s.	d.
De			De		
Johanna Canoun - - -		vj	Roberto Bardolf - - -		xij
Willelmo Payn - - -		viij	Johanne Pachat - - -⎫		xx
Johanne Lemmer - -⎫		xviij	Johanna uxore ejus - -⎭		
Agneta uxore ejus - -⎭					

Collectores ⎰ Johannes Cobbe
⎱ Rogerus Saltere
⎱ Edmundus Canoun
⎱ Galfridus Smalbon

Summa personarum cxxij
Summa denariorum vili. ijs.

[180 Lay Subsidy / 44 Suffolk]   *Skin damaged*

WESTCRETYNG

Hec indentura tripartita est facta inter Willelmum de Tendryng chivaler et socios suos assessores et contrarotulatores ultimi subsidii domini Regis nunc concessi videlicet de qualibet persona laica tres grosses anno regni predicti Regis iiij^{to} ex una parte et Willelmum de Reshebrok chivaler et socios suos collectores ejusdem subsidii ex altera parte et Johannem Caketon et Johannem Pyn subconestabularios et subcollectores ejusdem subsidii villate de Westcretyng ex tercia parte de numero et nominibus subscriptis ac de statu et gradu eorundem.

Agricole	s.	d.	*Laborarii et Servientes* (cont.)	s.	d.
Johannes Mounpelers -⎫	iiij		...... Boor... - -⎫	ij	
Johanna uxor ejus - -⎭			Agneta uxor ejus - -⎭		
...... de Cretyng - -⎫	iij		Thomas Moor - - -		xij
...... uxor ejus - -⎭			Johannes Moor - - -		xij
(4 names gone)	ij		...... Shepherde - - -		xij
	ij		Katerina Shepherde *spinnere* - - - - -		vj
Johannes Stede - - -⎫	ij				
Agneta uxor ejus - -⎭			Margareta Strotel *spinnere* - - - - -		vj
Edwardus Reynold - -⎫	ij				
Isabella uxor ejus - -⎭			Christiana Stede *spinnere*		vj
...... Dunch - - -⎫	ij		...... Be... - - -		vj
...... uxor ejus - -⎭			Rosea Hosbond - - -		xij
Johannes Pyn - - -⎫	iij		Johannes Shitte junior -		xij
Agneta uxor ejus - - -⎭			Willelmus Baday - - -⎫		xviij
(3 names gone)		xij	Alicia uxor ejus - - -⎭		
Laborarii et Servientes			Katerina Clerk *spinnere* -		vj
Johannes Tyler - - -⎫	ij		Elizabetha filia Margarete Cretyng *spinnere* -		vj
...... uxor ejus - - -⎭			Willelmus Katerinesson -		xij
...... Shitte - - -⎫	ij		Margareta Stede *spynnere*		vj
...... uxor ejus - - -⎭					

Summa personarum xl
Summa denariorum xls.

APPENDIX I.

[180 Lay Subsidy / 53 Suffolk]

ELDENEUTON

Armigeri	s.	d.	Artifices et Laborarii	s.	d.
Willelmus W..rd			Edwardus ..... textor -		viij
Isabella uxor ejus	iiij		Robertus Stoke fuller -		viij
Johannes de Brecete			...... Arnold - - - -		xij
Alicia de Brecete	ij	vj	Johannes Blake fuller -		xij
			Thomas Apelthweith - -		xij
[Agricole?]			Johannes Gurnay sutor - ⎫		xx
Ricardus de Brecete - -		xij	Margeria uxor ejus - - ⎭		
Margeria de Brecete - -		xij	Ricardus Geffrey sutor -		viij
Johannes Cokerel			Johannes Gyste - - -		xij
Johanna uxor ejus	ij		Johannes Reve peliparius ⎫	ij	
Johannes Marl...			Agneta uxor ejus - - ⎭		
Matilda uxor ejus	ij	vj	Petrus Cuttyng fleicer - ⎫	ij	
Johannes Coupere			Ismania uxor ejus - - ⎭		
Margeria uxor ejus	ij		Thomas Brown piscator - ⎫	ij	
Galfridus Coupere			Alicia uxor ejus - - - ⎭		
Jonhott uxor ejus	ij		Johannes Dunken faber -		viij
Rogerus Apilthweit			Margareta Cuttyng - -		viij
Johanna uxor ejus	ij	vj	Galfridus Smyth faber -		xij
Robertus Adgor			Radulfus Capons - - -		x
Margeria uxor ejus	ij	vj	Johannes Taillor - - -		xij
Henricus Bouel			Martinus fiz Martyni -		viij
Cristina uxor ejus		xx			
W.... Caperoun					
...... uxor ejus		xx			
...... Caperoun			Servientes		
Margeria uxor ejus	ij	iiij	Johannes Plat - - - -		viij
Ricardus Hotot			Thomas Masselyn - -		viij
Isabella uxor ejus		xx	Johannes Payn - - -		iiij
Henricus Coupere			Margareta Cope - - -		iiij
Isabella uxor ejus	ij		Edwardus Mellere - - ⎫	ij	
Ri.........			Alicia uxor ejus - - - ⎭		
Margareta uxor ejus - ⎫	ij		Thomas Appeltwheit fi- ⎫		xij
...... Massyn - - ⎭			lius Henrici Apeltiweit ⎭		
Alicia uxor ejus - -	ij	vj	Massot Frencheman - -		viij
Johannes Arnold - - ⎫	ij		Johannes Larke - - - ⎫	ij	
Margeria uxor ejus - ⎭			Cristina uxor ejus - - ⎭		

Summa personarum lxv
Summa denariorum lxvs.

[180 Lay Subsidy / 46 Suffolk]

WETHERDEN

Hec est indentura tripartita facta inter Willelmum Tendryng chivaler et socios suos assessores et contrairrotulatores ultimi subsidii domino Regi concessi videlicet de qualibet persona laica tres grotes anno regni ejusdem quarto ex una parte et Willclmum

96   SUFFOLK POLL TAX LISTS, 1381.

Rosshebrok chivaler et socios suos collectores dicti subsidii ex altera parte et Johannem Westbroun et Willelmum Banyngham constabularios et Johannem Bonde Johannem Bole Robertum Cokerel et Walterum Bereiweie subcollectores ville de Wetherden ex tercia parte videlicet de numero et nominibus subscriptis et de gradu et statu.

	s.	d.		s.	d.
Rogerus Schales *armiger* ⎱ Denisia uxor ejus - - ⎰	v		Alicia Lerling *webber* -		xij
Johanna Motonn *agricola* - - - - -		iij	Johannes Densi *carucator* ⎱ Alicia uxor ejus - - - ⎰		xviij
Johannes Motonn - - ⎱ Alicia uxor ejus - - - ⎰		iiij	Johannes Densi *pastor* -	iiij	
			Robertus Weneis *agricola* ⎱ Caterina uxor ejus - - ⎰		ij
Johannes Moton senior -		xij	Robertus Hoo *agricola* -⎱ Hesabel uxor ejus - - ⎰		ij
Johanna Fermer *webber* ⎱ Johanna filia sua - - - ⎰		ij	Johannes Hoo *coopertor*		xij
Johannes Browster *cissor* ⎱ Gundre uxor ejus - - - ⎰		ij	Galfridus Netherstrete -		xij
Robertus Hessete *triturator* - - - - -		ij	Edmundus Hok *agricola* ⎱ Alicia uxor ejus - - - ⎰	ij	iiij
Margeria uxor ejus - - ⎰			Robertus Ros *agricola* -⎱ Alicia uxor ejus - - - ⎰	ij	ij
Tomas Neele *laborator* -		xij	Johannes Ros *carucator*		iiij
Johanna Bauleie - - -		xij	Hissabel Ros - - - -		viij
Ade Schepperde *pastor* -⎱ Johanna uxor ejus - - ⎰		ij	Masselie Toke - - - -		xij
			Caterina Boldiro - - -		viij
Robertus Lerling *faber* -⎱ Alicia uxor ejus - - - ⎰		ij	Hissabel Counte - - -		iiij
			Alicia Fraw . . . . - -		iiij
Alicia Bauleie *webber* -⎱ Angueta felia sua - - - ⎰		ij	Johannes Walsham - -		xij
			Robertus Multon - - -		xviij
Willelmus Bauleie *sacrista* - - - - -		xij	Margareta Brewster - -		xviij
			Johannes Grene *laborator* ⎱ Willelmus filius ejus - ⎰		ij
Johannes Lane *agricola* -⎱ Alicia uxor ejus - - - ⎰	ij	vj	Willelmus Wergowns *meller* - - - - -		iiij
Walterus Bereiweie *agricola* - - - - - ⎱ Alicia uxor ejus - - - ⎰	ij	iiij	Robertus Cokerel *agricola* ⎱ Alicia uxor ejus - - - ⎰		ij
Johannes Thelich *laborator* - - - - -		xij	Johannis Bonde *chinchere*		xviij
			Johanna Bonde *browster*		xviij
Rogerus Wodecok - -		xij	Johannes Cobold *pastor*		iiij
Petrus Sudbery *triturator*		xij	Robertus Beri *pedder* -⎱ Johanna uxor ejus - - ⎰		ij
Hur Wangeforthe *triturator* - - - - - ⎱ Alicia uxor ejus - - - ⎰		ij	Willelmus Banyngham *agricola* - - - - ⎱ Caterina uxor ejus - - ⎰		ij
Johannes Wodecok - -⎱ Hisabella Wodecok - - ⎰		ij	Willelmus Bonde - - -		iiij
Raf Manser - - - -		vj	Walterus Tipping *carucator* - - - - -		x
Johannes Sudberi - -		xij	Johannes Thresher - -		iiij
Johannes Westbron *agricola* - - - - - ⎱ Alicia Westbroun - - - ⎰		iij	Johanna Palmere - - -		iiij
			Margeria Fectere - - -		iiij
Johannes Westbroun *agricola* - - - - -⎱ Helisabeth uxor ejus - ⎰		ij	Ade Densi - - - - -		iiij
			Margerie Wode - - -		iiij
			Margeria Talihowr - -		iiij
Johannes Bole - - - -⎱ Necolaa uxor ejus - - ⎰		ij	Margareta (Ormer?) - -		iiij
			Johannes Hassele - - -		iiij

Summa personarum iiij v
Summa denariorum iiij*li.* vs.

APPENDIX I.

[180 Lay Subsidy / 46 Suffolk]

GYPPYNG NEUTON

Agricole	s.	d.	Laboratores	s.	d.
Willelmus de Neuton		iiij	Galfridus Cook	ij	
Johanna uxor ejus			Matildis uxor ejus		
Robertus atte Grene		ij	Johannes Cake	ij	
Alicia uxor ejus			Johanna uxor ejus		
Willelmus Cook		ij	Laurencius (. . . . ion?)		xviij
Juliana uxor ejus			Agneta uxor ejus		
Johannes de Sprouton		ij	Mariota Ky...		xij
Cecilia uxor ejus			Ricardus Kyng	ij	
Johannes Brungor junior		xij	Margereta uxor ejus		
Johannes Brungor senior	ij	vj	Agneta Barker		xij
			Cristina atte Hyl		xij
Agneta uxor ejus			Willelmus Dunken		xviij
Johannes atte Hyl		ij	Alicia uxor ejus		
Margeria uxor ejus			Semanus Ryche	ij	
Johannes Cook	ij	vj	Matilldis uxor ejus		
Matildis uxor ejus			Mabilla Gobelet		vj
			Matilldis Cook		xij
			Johannes Manning		vj
			Ricardus Barker		xviij
			Amicia uxor ejus		
Artifices			*Constabularii. Agricole*		
Henricus Lacy *carnifex*		xij			
Johanna uxor ejus			Galfridus Cook *carnifex*	ij	vj
Johannes Kyng *carpentarius*		ij	Alicia uxor ejus		
			Johannes Osbern	ij	vj
Matildis uxor ejus			Katerina uxor ejus		

Summa personarum xliij
Summa denariorum xliijs.

[180 Lay Subsidy / 46 Suffolk]

DAGWROTH

Agricole	s.	d.	Artifices	s.	d.
Adam Markys	ij		Willelmus Gannuld *textor*	ij	
Alicia uxor ejus					
Robertus ate Brigge	ij	vj	Matildis uxor ejus		
Mariota uxor ejus			Robertus Hardhefd *cissor*		xij
Hawota Brigg		vj			
Johannes Schene	iij				
Beatrix uxor ejus					
Alicia Schene filia ejus		vj			
Margeria atte Brigge		xviij	*Servientes*		
(two names erased)					
			Elena *serviens* Margerie atte Brigg		xij
Robertus Waketon	ij	vj			
Deonicia uxor ejus			Henricus Newman *serviens manerii*		xviij
Nicholaus de Hampton	ij				
Margareta uxor ejus			Johanna uxor ejus		

P.

98   SUFFOLK POLL TAX LISTS, 1381.

Servientes (cont.)	s.	d.	Constabularii. Agricole	s.	d.
Galfridus Neuman servi- ens manerii	ij		Johannes atte Lee -⎫ Alicia uxor ejus -⎬	ij	
Matildis uxor ejus - -⎪ Johannes Fermer - - -		xij	Johannes Wryth - -⎫ Katerina uxor ejus -⎬	ij	
Johannes Hamound - -		xij			
Nicholaus Shepherde		xij			

Summa nominum xxviij
Summa denariorum xxviijs.

$\left[\dfrac{180}{53} \text{ Lay Subsidy} \atop \text{Suffolk}\right]$

Shellond Harleston and Onehouse

Subsidium domini Regis Ricardi secundi anno quarto deliberatum per Johannem Hamond Johannem de Freton et per Rogerum de Corper constabularios ville de Shellond Harleston et Onhows et Johannem Vaus eisdem constabulariis associatum Ricardo de Pakynham et collectori et receptori subsidii predicti.

	s.	d.	Harlistone Hameletum	s.	d.
Johannes de Hegsete		xx	Johannes de Freton -⎫	ij	viij
Johannes Hamond - -⎫ Alicia uxor ejus - -⎬	ij	iiij	Matilldis uxor ejus -⎬		
Johannes atte Fen -⎫ Cecilia uxor ejus - -⎬	ij		Rogerus Shaldrye -⎫ Margeria uxor ejus -⎬	ij	iiij
Thomas Tynton - -⎫ Margeria uxor ejus -⎬	ij	vj	Rogerus Cokeman -⎫ Margareta uxor ejus -⎬	ij	iiij
Johannes Vaus - -⎫ Rosea uxor ejus - -⎬	ij		Johannes Alderyd - -		viij
Johannes Mundegome -⎫ Margeria uxor ejus -⎬	ij		Johannes Lilye - -⎫ Agatha uxor ejus - -⎬		xx
Johannes atte Hell -⎫ Agneta uxor ejus - -⎬		xvj	Robertus Syre - - -⎫ Johanna uxor ejus -⎬		xx
Johannes Scot - - -		vj	Robertus Mere - - -⎫ Margereta uxor ejus -⎬		xx
Margeria Broun - -		viij	Johannes Sl.... - -⎫ Agneta uxor ejus - -⎬	ij	iiij
Willelmus Tynton - -		xij	...... Trust - - -⎫		xx
Mariota Hamond - -		xij	Margeria uxor ejus -⎬		
Robertus Cokeman -⎫ Margeria uxor ejus -⎬	ij		Onhows Hameletum		
Johannes de Halle -⎫ Margeria uxor ejus -⎬	ij		Rogerus Corper - -⎫ Alicia uxor ejus - -⎬	ij	iiij
Amicia de Halle - -		xij	Johannes Hevy - -⎫ Margareta uxor ejus -⎬	ij	iiij
Johannes atte cros -⎫ Johanna uxor ejus -⎬	ij	iiij	Lucia H...nt - -		viij
Willelmus Letyl - -⎫ Margareta uxor ejus -⎬	ij	iiij	Henricus - - - -⎫ Matildis - - - - -⎬	ij	iiij
Rogerus Benet - - -		viij	Agneta Al... - - -		viij
Johannes Cobbe -⎫ Amicia uxor ejus - -⎬	ij		Robertus Hell... -⎫ Cristiana uxor ejus -⎬		ij
Matildis Trrist - -		x	Johannes - - - -⎫		ij
Margeria B...oun - -		x	Alicia uxor ejus - -⎬		

APPENDIX I. 99

Onhows Hameletum (cont.)	s.	d.	Onhows Hameletum (cont.)	s.	d.
Johanna			....		xij
Johannes		xij	...... Letyl		xij
....		xij	...... Letyl		xij
....		xx	....		xvj
....		xij	....		xij
....		xij	...... Bryd		viij

Summa nominum lxxij
Summa denariorum lxxijs.

[180 Lay Subsidy / 36 Suffolk]   *Skin damaged.*

[COMBES?]

...... Ricardo concessum de denariis pro capite duodecem anno regni sui quarto in Michaelis termino ...... subsidii Willelmus de R ...... miles Ricardus de Pakynham et eorum socii.

Cultores	s.	d.	Cultores (cont.)	s.	d.
De			De		
Roberto Cokerel - - -			Johanne Frend - - -⎫		
Rosa uxore sua - - -			Agneta uxore sua - -⎬	ij	
...... Glanvyle - - -			Johanne filio suo - -⎭		
...... sua - - - -	iiij		..... Man - - - -⎫	ij	vj
...... Gardener - - -		xij	Johanna uxore sua - -⎬		
			..... Bron - - - -⎭		
(3 names gone)			Matilde uxore sua - -⎫		
			Simone Gunne - - -⎬	ij	
Johanne Talbot - - -⎫			.....uxore sua - -⎭		
Mariota uxore sua - -⎬	ij		Johanne Blaxhale - -⎫	ij	
...... Gobbe - - -⎭		xij	Katerina uxore sua - -⎭		
...... Backe - - -⎫					
Agneta uxore sua - -⎬	iiij		*Artificiarii*		
...... filia sua - -⎭			De		
Edmundo Boure - - -			Thoma Rigge - - -⎫		
Margeria uxore sua - -⎫	iiij		Isabella uxore sua - -⎬	iiij	
...... filia sua - -⎬			Willelmo filio suo - -⎭		
...... Alayn - - -⎭			Johanne *famulo* - -		xij
... et uxore sua - -⎫	ij		Roberto Dalkys - - -		xvj
......Cartere - - -⎬			Johanne Smyth - -⎫	ij	
......uxore sua - -⎭	ij		Margareta uxore sua -⎭		
Willelmo Frend - -⎫	ij		Johanne *famulo* - -		
Johanna uxore sua - -⎭			Adam Dalkys - - -		
Alicia Mot - - - -		xij	Willelmo Martyn - -		xij
Johanne Wynge - - -⎫	ij		Johanne Chene - - -	ij	
Agneta uxore sua - -⎭			Johanna uxore sua - -		
Johanne Bellous - - -			Roberto Sorel - - -	v	
Sara uxore sua - -⎫	iiij		Isabella uxore sua - -		
....na filia sua - -⎭			Michaele filio suo - -		
Galfrido Hoot (Hooc?) -⎫	ij		Thoma Gaysle - - -		xij
Rosa uxore sua - -⎭			Rogero Soutere - - -	ij	
Thoma Turnor - -⎫	ij		Amicia uxore sua - -		
.... uxore sua - -⎭					

7—2

Artificiarii (cont.)	s.	d.	Artificiarii (cont.)	s.	d.
De			De		
Thoma Snellyng - - -		xviij	Johanne Qwyte - - - ⎫		
Margareta uxore sua -			Cristiana uxore sua - - ⎬	ij	
Roberto Schyth - - -		xviij	Roberto Alayn - - - ⎫		
Isabella uxore sua - -			Alicia uxore sua - - - ⎬	ij	
Petro Stantone - - -	ij		Willelmo Wrythe - - ⎫		
Matildo uxore sua - -			Alicia uxore sua - - - ⎬	ij	
Roberto Schyth - - -		xviij	.... Lowys - - - ⎫		
Margareta uxore sua -			.... uxore sua - - - ⎬	ij	
Adamo Gundre - - -		viij	Bartolomao ..... - -		viij
Emma uxore sua - -					
Johanne Hashard - -					
Juliana uxore sua - -			*Laborarii*		
Henrico Raneld - - -		xviij	De		
Margereta uxore sua -			A... Puddy - - - ⎫		
Edmundo Raneld - -	iij		.... uxore sua - - - ⎬		
Katerina uxore sua - -			Hugone Dale - - - ⎫		
Steffano Cristemasse -	ij		Johauna uxore sua - ⎬		
Alicia uxore sua - - -			Johanne Browe... - ⎫		
Roberto W .... - - -		xij	A... uxore sua - - - ⎬		
Willelmo .... - - -	ij		Johanne Bole - - - ⎫		
Matilde uxore sua - -			Alicia uxore sua - - ⎬	ij	
Willelmo Kegyl - - -		xviij	Johanne Manysbody - ⎫	ij	
Isabella uxore sua - -			Mabilia uxore sua - - ⎬	ij	
Adalyia Crane - - -		xij	Johanne Sterde - - - ⎫		
Johanne Tryker - - - ⎫			Alicia uxore sua - - ⎬	ij	
Margareta uxore sua - ⎬	ij		Johanne Wynge - - ⎫		
Johanne Glesne - - -		xij	Margareta uxore sua - ⎬	ij	
Roberto Wente - - - ⎫			Hugone Benyth - - -		xij
Matilde uxore sua - - ⎬	ij		Roberto Peyntor - - ⎫		xviij
Willelmus Coldhakyl - ⎫			Agneta uxore sua - - ⎬		
Margareta uxore sua - ⎬	ij		Thoma ... ow ... - ⎫		
Alano Coldhakyl - - - ⎫			Matilde ..... - ⎬		
Johanna uxore sua - - ⎬	ij		Roberto (? G)re - - ⎫		
Johanne Bole - - - - ⎫			Isabella uxore sua - - ⎬	ij	vj
Juliana uxore sua - - ⎬	ij	vj	Steffano Bole - - - ⎫		
Johanne Trot - - - - ⎫			Johanna uxore sua - ⎬	ij	
Margareta uxore sua - ⎬	ij				
Roberto Barker - - - ⎫		xviij			
Agneta uxore sua - - ⎬			*Famuli*		
Ricardo Burs - - - - ⎫		xij	De		
Johanna uxore sua - - ⎬			Nicholao Jackysonne -		xij
Reginaldo Qwytyng - - ⎫	ij		Johanne Beste - - -		xij
Rosa uxore sua - - - ⎬			Katerina Dalkys - - -		xij
Johanne Rome - - - ⎫		xvj	Elena Stanton - - -		xij
Alicia uxore sua - - - ⎬			Thoma Blaxhale - - -		xij
Johanne Mellere - - - ⎫	iij		Radulffo Adgor - - -		xij
Cristiana uxore sua - ⎬			Hugone Spot - - - ⎫		xviij
Johanne Tryker - - - ⎫	ij		Matilde uxore sua - - ⎬		
Nicholao uxore sua - - ⎬			Johanne ..... - - - ⎫		
Johanne Adgor - - - ⎫	iij		Alicia uxore sua - - ⎬		
Isabella uxore sua - - ⎬			.... Deye - - -		vj
Radulfo Jery - - - - ⎫	ij		.... Codynham - - ⎫	ij	
Beatrice uxore sua - - ⎬			Sara uxore sua - - - ⎬		
Johanne Prentys - - -		xij	Johanne Cler - - -		
Willelmo Gyrling - -		xij	....		
Johanne Malkyn - - ⎫		ij	.... Mot - - - -		xij
Margareta uxore sua - ⎬			Johanne Cokerel - - ⎫		
Johanne Doye - - - ⎫	ij		Isabella uxore sua - - ⎬	iij	
Cristiana uxore sua - ⎬			.... filia sua - - - ⎫		

APPENDIX I. 101

Famuli (cont.)	s.	d.	Famuli (cont.)	s.	d.
De			De		
...... Bateman - - -		xij	...... Adgor - - - -		xij
...... Webber - - -		xij	...... Tyler - - - -		xij
...... Waryn - - -)		xviij	...... Qwytewyng - -		xij
Margareta uxore sua -)			...... Fermer - - -		xij
Elena Adgor - - - -		xij	...... Helle - - - -		xij
...... Gosselene - -		xij	...... Fermer - - -		xij
Johanna Gardener - -			...... Helle - - - -		xij

Summa omnium nominum c iiij ix.

Colectores
{ Willelmus Estone xijd. }
{ Johannes Gardener xijd. } subconstabularii
{ Willelmus Gosselene xijd. }
{ Ricardus Adgor xijd. } coadjutores

[180 Lay Subsidy] *Name and part of skin gone.*
[53 Suffolk   ]

[THORNEY[1]]

	s.	d.	Servientes (cont.)	s.	d.
Stephanus Swalwe *webber*)	ij		Johannes Wlvard *serviens*)		xij
Margeria uxor ejus - -)			eodem - - - - - - }		
Willelmus Ker *webber* -)	ij		Matildis uxor ejus *serviens*)		
Agneta uxor ejus - -)			eodem - - - - - }		
Thomas Webber - - -		xij	Johannes ...... *serviens*		
Johannes de Padenhale -		xij	eodem - - - - -		vj
Agneta Lacy - - - -		xij	.... *serviens* eodem		vj
Willelmus Kyng *carpenter*)	ij		.... *serviens* eodem		vj
Mariota uxor ejus - -)			An ... le Ros *serviens*		
Agatha Goldyng - - -		xviij	eodem - - - - -		vj
Thomas Mey - - -)	ij	vj	Rogerus Schepherd *ser-*)	ij	
Margareta uxor ejus- -)			*viens* eodem - - - -)		
Ricardus Schitte - - -)	ij	vj	Johanna uxor ejus - -)		
Isabella uxor ejus - -)			Johannes Melewey *ser-*)	ij	
Johannes Bregge - - -)	ij		*viens* Thome Goney -)		
Katerina uxor ejus - -)			Margareta uxor ejus - -)		
Willelmus Glannvill - -		xij	Johannes Neuman *ser-*)	ij	
Thomas Cardoun - - -)	ij		*viens* eodem - - - -)		
Alicia uxor ejus - -)			Alicia uxor ejus - -)		
Ricardus Gerard - -)	ij		Matildis Blower *serviens*		
Matilldis uxor ejus - -)			eodem - - - - -		vj
Willelmus Proude - -		xij	Alicia atte Grene - - -		vj
Johannes Carter - -)	ij		Petrus Keneld *serviens*		
Matilldis uxor ejus - -)			Galfrido atte Grene -		vj
			Johannes Whederyld -		vj
Servientes			Margeria Whederyld - -		vj
Thomas Stonton *serviens*			Johanna Kyng - - - -		vj
Robt Hotost - - - -		vj	Galfridus Mauger *servi-*		
Ricardus Gerard *serviens*			*ens* Johanni Sewale -		vj
eodem - - - - -		vj	Johannes atte Wode - -		xij

[1] The name of Thorney appears to be the right one after comparing this Poll Tax list with a Court Roll of Thorney of 20 Ric. II. Cf. Court Rolls, General Series, Port. 204, No. 21. P. R. O.

Servientes (cont.)	s.	d.	Servientes (cont.)	s.	d.
Johanna Fenkele - - -		xij	Johannes Berche - - -⎫	ij	
Johannes Fenkele - -		xij	Custancia uxor ejus - -⎭		
Nicholaus Kent - - -		vj	Robertus Ode - - - -		xij
Willelmus Kent - - -		vj	Ricardus Bol - - - -		xij
Cecilia Hotot serviens			Johannes Pe... - - -		xij
Ricardo Hotot - - -		vj	Walterus Aleyn - - -		xij
Mabillia Cake - - -		xij	Ricardus Sawer - - -		xij
Johannes Hamond - -			Johannes serviens		
Ricardus Cook - - - -		vj	ma[rcial?] atte Ford -		xij
Margeria Colman - - -		vj	Thomas Berwe - - -		xij
Johannes Padenhale - -		xij	Johannes Cook serviens		
Alicia Shitte - - - -		vj	Roberti Hotot - - -		xij
Agneta serviens Rogero			Walterus Crinyte - - -		xij
Hoo - - - - - -		vj	....		xij
Johannes C.... - - -		xij	Nicholaus Cake - - -		xij
Johannes Gunnild - -		vj	Johanna Cake serviens		
Sabella Goldyng - - -		vj	Petri atte Kent - - -		xij
Godefridus serviens Jo-⎫	ij		Johannes ... - - -		xij
hanni Moriel - - -⎬			Johanna Cur ... - - -		xij
Alicia uxor ejus - - -⎭			Johannes Badynhale - -		xij
Robertus Mauger - - -		xij	Matilldis Ode - - - -		xij
Alicia Hamond serviens			Johanna Osbern - - -		xij
Johanni Dawys - - -		vj	Walterus Carter - - -		xij
Matilldis Cole - - - -		vj	Johannes Leman - - -		xij

Summa personarum clxxix
Summa denariorum viijli. xixs.

⎡180 Lay Subsidy⎤
⎣ 48   Suffolk   ⎦

HUNDREDUM DE BLAKEBORN

VILLA DE FAKYNHAM MAGNA

Hec indentura tripartita facta inter Willelmum Tendryng chivaler et socios suos assessores et contra irrotulatores ultimi subsidii domino Regi concessi videlicet de qualibet persona laica tres grotas anno regni ejusdem quarto ex una parte et Willelmum Rosschebrok chivaler et socios suos collectores dicti subsidii ex altera parte et Willelmum Grenegres Galfridum Gerard Johannem Clement Galfridum Calf constabularios et subcollectores ejusdem subsidii de villa predicta ex tercia parte de numero et nominibus subscriptis et de gradu et statu eorundem videlicet.

Agricole	s.	d.	Artifices	s.	d.
Willelmum Grenegres -⎫	iiij		Thomas atte Grene car-⎫	ij	
Isabella uxor ejus - -⎭			pentarius - - - - -⎬		
Galfridus Gerard - - -⎫	ij		Matildis uxor ejus - -⎭		
Alicia uxor ejus - - -⎭					
Johannes Clement - -⎫	ij	vj	Laboratores		
Katerina uxor ejus - -⎭					
Galfridus Calf - - - -⎫	ij		Benedictus Rowe - - -		xij
Agneta uxor ejus - - -⎭			Johannes Rowe - - -		xij

APPENDIX I. 103

Laboratores (cont.)	s.	d.	Servientes	s.	d.
Ricardus Rowe - - -		vj	Johannes Grenefeld - -⎫		xviij
Willelmus Gerard - -⎫	ij		Juliana uxor ejus - -⎭		
Agneta uxor ejus - -⎭			Emma Smyth - - -		xij
Emma Smyth - - - -		xij	Johannes Cres - - -		xij
Edmundus Breton - -⎫		xviij	Robertus Calf - - -		xij
Lucia uxor ejus - -⎭			Agneta Cartere - - -		vj
Nicholaus Gerard - -	ij		Thomas Cakebred - -⎫	ij	
Alicia Gerard - - -		xij	...... uxor ejus - -⎭		
			Joh........... - -		vj

Summa xxix*s*.

⎡ 180 Lay Subsidy ⎤
⎣ 41   Suffolk ⎦

EUSTON IN HUNDREDO DE BLAKBORNE

Hec indentura tripartita facta inter Willelmum Tendryng chivaler et socios suos assessores et contra irrotulatores ultimi subsidii domino Regi concessi videlicet de qualibet persona laica tres grotes anno regni ejusdem quarto ex una parte et Willelmum Russhebrook et socios suos collectores ejusdem subsidii ex altera parte et Petrum Baa Thomam Jade Petrum Pakkeman et Willelmum atte Chirche constabularios et subcollectores ejusdem subsidii in villa predicta ex tercia parte de numero et nominibus et de statu et gradu eorundem videlicet.

Agricole	s.	d.	Bercarii	s.	d.
Willelmus atte Chirche -⎫	ij	vj	Henricus Bouecold - -⎫	ij	
Alicia uxor ejus - -⎭			Cristina uxor ejus - -⎭		
Henricus Blauncpayn -⎫	v	iiij	Petrus Knyth - - -		xviij
Margareta uxor ejus - -⎭			Robertus Wauton - - -	ij	
Thomas Jade - - - -⎫	ij		Johannes Cole - - -		xij
Agneta uxor ejus - -⎭			*Servientes*		
Petrus le Baa - - - -⎫		xviij	Margareta Aleyn - - -		iiij
Katerina uxor ejus - -⎭			Walterus *serviens* Henrici Blauncpayn - -		vj
Artifices			Alicia Baa - - -		xij
Walterus Leneve - - -		xij	Agneta *serviens* Johannis Jade - - - - -		vj
Johannes Runtyng - -	ij		Johannes Jade junior -		vj
Edmundus Rogger - -⎫	ij	vj	Walterus Jade - - - -⎫		xx
Katerina uxor ejus - -⎭			Margeria uxor ejus - -⎭		
Johannes Lucas - - -		xviij	Johannes Deye - - -		xviij
Johannes Droughte - -⎫		xx	Johannes Jade senior -		xij
Katerina uxor ejus - -⎭			Johanna Wauton - - -		iiij
Walterus Barat - -⎫	ij		*Laboratores*		
Alicia uxor ejus - -⎭			Walterus Boydon - -⎫	ij	
Petrus Pakkeman - -		xij	Alicia uxor ejus - -⎭		
Meter[1]			Johanna Lucas - - -		vj
Johannes Jade - - -⎫	iij				
Agneta uxor ejus - -⎭					

[1] Possibly 'mecer'; a slip for 'mercer.'

Laboratores (cont.)	s.	d.	*Laboratores* (cont.)	s.	d.
Johanna Barat		xij	Alicia Pakkman		viij
Petrus Lenedey		viij	Galfridus Poyt		xij
Alicia Leneve		viij	Petrus atte chirch		vj
Nicholaus Hascard }		ij	Alicia *serviens* H. Blauuc-		
Margeria uxor ejus }			payn		vj
Matilldis Horn		xij	Margeria Knyt		vj
Margeria Leneday		iiij	Matilldis atte Chirch		iiij
Willelmus Note }		xviij			
Margeria uxor ejus }					

Summa personarum liij
Summa denariorum liij*s*.

[180 Lay Subsidy
 47 Suffolk]

GNATTESSAL

.... Willelmum de Tendryng chivaler......assessores et contra irrotulatores ultimi......concessi videlicet de qualibet persona laica tres grotes anno regni ejusdem quarto ex una parte Willelmum de Russhebrok et socios suos ...... ex altera parte et Ricardum Baldry et Nicholaum Baldry constabularios Johannem Baxtere Willelmum Coppyng Johannem Betteson Johannem Ilbert subcollectores ville de Gnattessal ex tercia parte de numero et nominibus subscriptis et de statu et gradu eorundem videlicet.

Agricole	s.	d.		s.	d.
Thomas de Stanton }	v		Willelmus Rook }	ij	
Margeria uxor ejus }			Amya uxor ejus }		
Ricardus Baldry }	v		Johannes Mannyng		xij
Christiana uxor eius }			Johannes Shepherd }	iij	
Nicholaus Baldry	iij		Matildis uxor ejus }		
			Willelmus Turgy }	ij	
			Alicia uxor ejus }		
Laborarii			Robertus Gernoun }	xx	
			Denise uxor ejus }		
Johannes Clytermere }	ij		Ricardus Hunte }	ij	
Mess.... uxor ejus }			Agneta uxor ejus }		
Johannes Betteson }	iij	vj	Margareta Slaug....		
Beatrix uxor ejus }			Agneta God.....		
			.....ad ...... }		
Johannes Baxter *pistor* }	ij		Isabella uxor ejus }		
Margareta uxor ejus }			Margareta Coppyng		
Willelmus Coppyng *webe-* }	ij		Willelmus Rash }		
ster }			Agneta uxor ejus }		
Alicia uxor ejus }			.... }	ij	
[1] Ricardus Taillor	i	iiij	Alicia uxor ejus }		
Matildis uxor ejus			Cecilia		iiij
Willelmus Mabbesson }	xviij		Alicia Turgy		xij
Roes uxor ejus }			Johannes ...hilbon }	ij	
Petrus Rolle		xij	Alicia uxor ejus }		

[1] The rest of the trade names are illegible.

APPENDIX I. 105

Servientes	s.	d.	Servientes (cont.)	s.	d.
.... filius Ricardi			Alicia Godard - - -		vj
Baldry - - - - -		xij	Reginaldus Elfred - -		viij
			Alicia Hunte - - - -		iiij
[Skin damaged]			Johannes Smyth - - -⎫		xij
			Margareta uxor ejus - -⎭		
Johannes *serviens* Nicho-			Christiana Soutere - -		vj
lai Baldry - - -		vj	Agneta Bettesen - - -		iiij
...... Shephard - - -		iiij	Willelmus Wyse - - -		vj
Johannes Judy - - -		iiij	Agneta Wyse - - - -		vj
Johanna le Man - - -		iiij	Johanne Shapestre - -		vj

Summa hominum lxij
Summa denariorum lxijs.

⎡180 Lay Subsidy⎤
⎣ 47   Suffolk   ⎦

HYNDERKLE

Hec est indentura tripartita facta inter Willelmum de Tendryng chivaler et socios suos assessores et contrairrotulatores ultimi subsidii domino Regi concessi videlicet de qualibet persona laica tres grotas anno regni ejusdem quarto ex una parte et Willelmum Rosshebrok chivaler et socios suos collectores dicti subsidii ex altera parte et Henricum Folkmere et Johannem Basely constabularios Robertum le Clerk Willelmum Setard Thomam Schepherde Hugonem Benne subcollectores ejusdem subsidii ville de Hynderkle ex tercia parte videlicet de numero et nominibus subscriptis et de gradu et statu eorundem videlicet.

	s.	d.		s.	d.
Adam Botonn *agricola* -⎫	ij		Robertus Clerk *agricola*-⎫	v	
Matildis uxor ejus - -⎭			Katerina uxor ejus - - ⎭		
Willelmus Toly *sutor* -⎫			Willelmus *serviens* dicti		
Petronilla uxor ejus - -⎭	ij		Roberti - - - -		
Alicia filia ejus - - -⎭			Willelmus Edward *famu-*		
Robertus Burgeys *tritu-*	ij		*lus carucator* - - -⎫		xij
rator - - - - -⎭			Amya uxor ejus - - -⎭		
Amya uxor ejus - - ⎫			Alicia Crane - - - ⎫	iiij	
Johannes Burgeys -⎬	ij		Johannes filius suus -⎭		
Gundreda uxor ejus - -⎭			Hugo Doke *sutor* - - ⎫		
HenricusBoyboy*brasiator*⎫			Margeria uxor ejus - -⎬	iij	iiij
Agneta uxor ejus - - ⎬	ij		Margeria filia eorundem ⎭		
Margeria filia eorundem⎭			Amya Schepherde *spyn-*		
Henricus Harling - - -		ij	*nere* - - - - - -		xij
Adam Deynissone *webe-* ⎫			Willelmus Bole *triturator*⎫	ij	
ster - - - - - - ⎬	ij		Katerina uxor ejus - - ⎭		
Isabella uxor ejus - -⎭			Alicia Hare *spynnere* -		
Adam Donne *webester* -⎫	ij		Johannes Basely *taillor* -⎫	iiij	
Margeria uxor ejus - -⎭			Alicia uxor ejus - - -⎭		
Ricardus Goos *agricola*-⎫			Johannes Heyr *junior* ⎫		
Johanna uxor ejus - -⎬	iij		*cooperator* - - -⎬	ij	
Isabella filia eorundem -⎭			Margeria uxor ejus - -⎭		

SUFFOLK POLL TAX LISTS, 1381.

	s.	d.		s.	d.
Margeria Cokewald *spynner* - - - - - -		x	Ricardus Redere *redere* -⎫ Agneta uxor ejus - - -⎭	ij	
Simon Wyhot *famulus* ⎫ carucator - - - - ⎭	ij		Johannes Fuller *fuller* -⎫ Christiana uxor ejus - -⎭	ij	
Matildis uxor ejus - - ⎭			Willelmus Setard *bocher* ⎫		
Radulfus Folkmere *taillor* ⎫ Margeria uxor ejus - -⎭	iiij		Alicia uxor ejus - - - Thomas *serviens* dicti W. ⎭	v	
Isabella Arnold - -			Tyllot Daye *spynnere* -	xij	
Henricus Buntyng *agricola* - - - - - - ⎫ Isabella uxor ejus - -⎬ ...... fil.. eorundem ⎭	iij	iiij	Robertus Daye *daye* - - Margeria uxor ejus - -⎭ Walterus Hillessone - -	xij iiij	
Margeria Reynald - - -		xx	....	iiij	
Henricus Folkmere *taillor* ⎫ Mariota uxor ejus - -⎬ Johannes filius suus - -⎭	iiij		Amya Cristemesse *spynnere* - - - - - - Margeria *serviens* Roberti	iiij	
Hugo Benne *agricola* -⎫ Alicia uxor ejus - - -⎬ Johannes Personnesman *laborarius* - - - ⎭	iiij ij		Clerk - - - - - Alicia *spynner* - - Benedictus Rasol *laborator* - - - - - ⎭	iiij iiij viij	
Amya uxor ejus - - ⎫			Agneta uxor ejus - - -⎭		
Thomas Schepherde *cooperator* - - - - ⎬	iij	vj	Willelmus Claver - - - Margeria Coke .... - -	iiij iiij	
Katerina uxor ejus - -⎭			Margeria *serviens* Willelmi Setard - - - -	iiij	
Henricus Botonn *agricola* ..... Botonn filius *agricola* - - - - - -			Johannes Schepherde *bercarius* - - - - - ⎭	viij	
Johanna Botonn uxor ejus - - - - -			Alicia uxor ejus - - -⎫ Walterus Crane - - -⎬	viij	
Julianna Benne *spynnere*		x	Agneta uxor ejus - - -⎭		

Summa personarum iiij$\overset{xx}{\ }$ vj
Summa iiij*li.* vj*s.*

⎡180 Lay Subsidy⎤
⎣ 47   Suffolk   ⎦

IXWORTH THORP

Hec indentura est tripartita facta inter Willelmum Tendryng chivaler et socios suos assessores et contrairrotulatores ultimi subsidii domino Regi concessi videlicet de qualibet persona laica tres grotes anno regni ejusdem quarto ex una parte et Willelmum Rosshebrok chivaler et socios suos collectores dicti subsidii ex altera parte et Galfridum Neve Willelmum ...... constabularios Johannem Hog et Thomam Gandawys subcollectores ville de Ixworth Thorp ex tercia parte de numero et nominibus subscriptis et de gradu et statu eorundem.

	s.	d.		s.	d.
.... Pakenham *armiger* ⎫ .... uxor ejus - - - ⎭	ij		Nicholaus Wynyeve - -⎫ Edonea uxor ejus - -⎭		xvj
Edmundus de Pakenham *agricola* - - - - ⎬ Alicia uxor ejus - - ⎭	ij		Thomas Gandawys *mersonarius* - - - - ⎬ Agneta uxor ejus - - ⎭	ij	

APPENDIX I.

	s.	d.		s.	d.
Galfridus .... ay *pastor* ⎫	iij	ij	Henricus Saltebek *architect* ⎫		ij
Cecilia uxor ejus - - - ⎭			*tect* - - - - - - - ⎭		
Galfridus ..... *agricola* ⎫	ij		Rosa uxor ejus - - -⎫		
Agneta uxor ejus - - - ⎭			Radulfus Otysdole *pastor* ⎬	ij	
....		xij	Edenea uxor ejus - - -⎭		
Isabella Mason *spynner* -		vj	Margareta Bette *spynner*		xij
Cecilia Langeton - - -		xij	Willelmus Pucool *caru-* ⎫		
Katerina Spencer *spynner*		xij	*carius* - - - - - - ⎬	ij	
Johannes Hog *servus* -⎫	ij		Isabella uxor ejus - -⎭		
...... uxor ejus - - -⎭			Agneta Fede *sutor* - -		viij
Willelmus Hog *agricola* ⎫	iij	viij	Johannes Fishere *laborarius* - - - - - ⎫		
.... ⎭			*arius* - - - - - ⎬		xvj
...... Smyth *agricola* -		xij	Margareta uxor ejus - -⎭		
Petrus Wynyeve *textor* -		viij	Thomas Toffay *pastor* -⎫	iiij	
Isabella .... *spynner* -		vj	Isabella uxor ejus - -⎭		
Johannes Coupere - -⎫		xij	Johannes (D?)ale *fuller* -		viij
Alicia uxor ejus - - -⎭			Katerina ... og *serviens* -		vj
Ricardus Ford *pastor* -⎫	ij		....		
Alicia uxor ejus - - -⎭					
Adam Maykyn *triturator*⎫	ij		....		xvj
Katerina uxor ejus - -⎭					

Summa personarum xlvj
Summa pecuniarum xlvjs.

⎡239   Lay Subsidy ⎤
⎣174   Divers Counties⎦

LANGHAM

Hec est indentura tripartita facta inter Willelmum de Tendryng chivaler et socios suos assessores et contrairrotulatores ultimi subsidii domino Regi concessi de qualibet persona laica tres grotes anno regni ejusdem quarto ex una parte et Willelmum de Rosschbrok chivaler et socios suos collectores dicti subsidii ex altera parte Willelmum Eldesen Albritum Schypman constabularios Johannem Wode Willelmum Balye Edmundum Sparwe et Johannem Rust subcollectores dicti subsidii ex tercia parte ville de Langham videlicet de numero et nominibus subscriptis et de gradu et statu eorundem videlicet.

	s.	d.		s.	d.
Willelmus de Langham chivaler - - - -	v		Thomas Alcombury *agricola* - - - - - -		xij
Johannes filius ejus - -		xij	Isabella Jakelyn *spynner* - - - - - -		xij
Willelmus filius ejus - -		xij			
Margareta *serviens* ejus -		xij	Margareta Andrew *serviens* - - - - -		iiij
Robertus *serviens* ejus -		xij			
Thomas Warde *famulus* ejus - - - - -		viij	Thomas ..... Willelmi⎫ de Langham - - -⎭		xvj
Robertus *famulus* ejus -		viij	Agneta uxor ejus - -⎭		
Robertus Jakelyn *serviens* ejus - - - - -		iiij	Johanna Raych *serviens*		viij
			Johannes Wymbyl *junior*		iiij

	s.	d.		s.	d.
Thomas atte Hagwe *agricola* - - - - -			..... Rumbald *famulus*-		viij
			Adam le Rede *laborator*	ij	
Margeria uxor ejus - -	iij		Alicia uxor ejus - -		
Nicholaus filius ejus- -			Amya Lenote - - - -		iij
Amicia filia ejus - - -			Emma filia ejus - -		
Henricus Bras - - - -	ij		Amicia Prentys - - -	ij	
Isabella uxor ejus - -			Agneta *serviens* ejus - -		
Johanna Forth *spynner*		xij	Willelmus Dygge *cornloder* - - - - - -	ij	
Johannes Wroo *bercarius*	ij				
Agneta uxor ejus *webstere*			Margeria uxor ejus - -		
Margeria filia ejus *webstere* - - - - -		vj	Sarra Ingold - - - -		xvj
			Johannes Wode *agricola*		
Thomas *serviens* J. Wroo		viij	Basilia uxor ejus - - -	iij	
Beatrice *serviens* dicti Johannis - - - - -		viij	Johannes *serviens* eorundem - - - - -		
Alicia Cook *spynner* - -		xij	Ricardus Helle *webster*		xvij
Robertus Snowyth *triturator* - - - - -	ij		Margareta uxor ejus - -		
			Willelmus Balye - - -		
Matildis uxor ejus - -			Agneta uxor ejus - - -		
Henricus Snowyth *cissor*	ij		Isabella mater dicti Willelmi - - - - -	v	
Johanna uxor ejus - -					
Johannes Raych *carpentarius* - - - - -	ij	iij	Adam *serviens* dicti Willelmi - - - - -		
Johanna uxor ejus - -			Willelmus Eldesen *cornloder* - - - - - -	iij	iiij
Rosa Wymbil - - - -					
Bartholomaus filius ejus *agricola* - - - -	iiij		Johanna uxor ejus - -		
			Margareta filia ejus - -		
Margareta filia dicte Rose .... *serviens* dicte Rose - - - - -			Edmundus Sparwe *cissor*		
			Rosia uxor ejus - - -	iij	iij
			Margeria filia eorum - -		xij
Johannes Schepherde -	ij		Cecilia Meller *spynner* -		
Isabella uxor ejus - -			Johannes Keneman - -	ij	
Thomas atte Cherch *serviens* - - - - -	ij		Emma uxor ejus - - -		
			Sabina *serviens* eorundem		
Alicia uxor ejus - - -			Thomas Geg - - - -		xiij
Mabilia Lambyn - - -		xij	Katerina uxor ejus - -		
Albritus Schypman *agricola* - - - - - -	iij	iiij	Thomas Burgeys *carpentarius* - - - - -	ij	x
Olyva uxor ejus - - -			Katerina uxor ejus - -		
Agneta Skynner - - -		xvj	Alicia Helle - - - - -		xij
Johannes Rust *agricola* -			Thomas Meller *meller* -		xx
Matildis uxor ejus - -	iij		Johanna uxor ejus - -		
Willelmus filius eorundem - - - - - -			Johannes Scot *carpentarius* - - - - -	ij	
..... Warde *triturator* -			Katerina uxor ejus - -		
..... uxor ejus - - -	ij	vj			
..... fil.. ejus - - -					

Summa personarum iiij x̄
Summa denariorum iiij*li*. x*s*.

[180 Lay Subsidy]
[39   Suffolk   ]

STOWELANGETOT

Hec est indentura tripartita facta inter Willelmum de Tendryng chivaler et socios suos assessores et contrairrotulatores ultimi subsidii domino Regi concessi videlicet de qualibet persona laica tres grotes anno regis ejusdem quarto ex una parte et Willelmum Rossbrok chivaler et socios suos collectores dicti subsidii ex altera parte et Willelmum Marchal et Johannem Crows constabularios et Johannem Rogyn Johannem Tyller Johannem Bere Eliam Wythlok subcollectores ejusdem subsidii ville de Stowelangtot ex tercia parte de numero et nominibus subscriptorum et de gradu et statu eorundem videlicet.

	s.	d.		s.	d.
Robertus de Aisschfeld armiger	xv		Johannes Homite laborarius	ij	
Margareta uxor ejus			Christiana uxor ejus		
Johanna Wykes	ij		Ricardus Thatcher cooperator		xvj
Katerina serviens dicte Johanne		viij	Matildis uxor ejus		
...... serviens Roberti Aisschfeld		vj	Christiana Stambourne		x
Johannes Kenne serviens dicti Roberti		vj	Robertus Clement triturator		xx
Ade serviens dicti Roberti		vj	Alicia uxor ejus		
Johannes Cook serviens dicti Roberti		vj	Johannes Smith faber	ij	
Simon Baxster serviens dicti Roberti		vj	Alicia uxor ejus		
Henricus Bakouu serviens dicti Roberti		vj	Johannes serviens dicti Johannis		viij
Matildis serviens dicti Roberti		iiij	Geffrius Wo....		xij
Katerina serviens dicti Roberti		iiij	Agneta uxor ejus		
Willelmus Bryd serviens dicti Roberti		iiij	Johannes Tyller		
Johannes Carter serviens dicti Roberti		iiij	Amya uxor ejus brasiatrix	ij	
Robertus Man serviens dicti Roberti		iiij	Johannes Kentford schreveyner	ij	
.... serviens dicti Roberti		iiij	Katerina uxor ejus		
Johannes Sel bercarius dicti Roberti		iiij	Willelmus Meller molendinarius		viij
Johannes Boteler brasiator dicti Roberti		iiij	Johannes Bere bercarius	iij	
Elias Boteler serviens dicti Roberti		iiij	Margereta uxor ejus		
Johannes Waler serviens dicti Roberti		iiij	Johannes Rogyn agricola	iij	
			Alicia uxor ejus brasiatrix		
			Thomas Edward triturator		xij
			Margeria uxor ejus		
			Margeria Gernon serviens		
			Johannis Pope capellani		viij
			Elias Wytlok laborarius	ij	
			Margeria uxor ejus		
			Johanna Jay spynner		

	s.	d.		s.	d.
Willelmus Holboy tenta- tor carucarum		xij	Matildis Marchal - - -		viij
Agneta uxor ejus - - -			Thomas serviens W. Marchal - - - - -		xij
Johannes Schepherde bercarius - - - - -		ij	Johannes Pattemere triturator - - - -		ij
Amicia uxor ejus - - -			Agneta uxor ejus - - -		
Willelmus Brewster laborarius - - - -		xij	Robertus serviens Rectoris Isoude uxor ejus - - -		ij
Margeria uxor ejus - -			Johannes Masonn serviens dicti Rectoris -		iiij
Christiana Nugge - - -		xij			
Robertus Aubry agricola Johanna uxor ejus - -		iiij	Johannes Holboy serviens dicti Rectoris -		iiij
Alicia Threin - - - -		xij	Johannes Clement serviens dicti Rectoris -		iiij
Willelmus serviens Roberti Aubry - - - -		iiij	Ricardus Wyth serviens Roberti Aisschfeld - -		vj
Johannes Crowes agricola Agneta uxor ejus - -		ij	Rogerus Seman serviens dicti Roberti - - -		iiij
Willelmus filius eorundem		vj			
Agneta Wade - - - -		xvj			
Willelmus Marchal corsour - - - - - -		vj			
Margeria uxor ejus - -					

Summa lxxvs.

[180 Lay Subsidy]
[40   Suffolk]

WYRDEWELL

Hec est indentura tripartita facta inter Willelmum Tendryng chivaler et socios suos assessores et contrairrotulatores ultimi subsidii domino Regi concessi videlicet de qualibet persona laica tres grotes anno regni ejusdem iiij^{to} ex una parte et Willelmum Rosshebrook chivaler et socios collectores dicti subsidii ex altera parte et Galfridum Osbun seniorem Willelmum Sampsonn constabularios Galfridum Osbun juniorem Johannem Porter juniorem subcollectores ejusdem subsidii ville de Wyrdewelle ex tercia parte de numero et nominibus subscriptis et de gradu et statu eorundem videlicet.

	s.	d.		s.	d.
Johannes Porter junior agricola - - - -	ij	iiij	Galfridus Osbun junior agricola - - - - -	ij	iiij
Johanna uxor ejus - -			Alicia uxor ejus - - -		
Johannes Wetherde bercarius - - - - -	ij	iiij	Galfridus Osbun senior laborarius - - - - -	ij	iiij
Agneta uxor ejus - - -			Claricia uxor ejus - -		
Willelmus Sampsonn bercarius - - - - -	ij	iiij	Willelmus Frenssh thacher - - - - - -		xij
Isabella uxor ejus - -			Lucia uxor ejus - - -		

APPENDIX I. 111

	s.	d.		s.	d.
Johannes Porter *senior* bercarius	ij	iiij	Alexander Wulward bercarius	ij	iiij
Agneta uxor ejus			Alicia uxor ejus		
Galfridus Bosard *laborarius*		xij	Sabyn Bosard		xij
Alicia uxor ejus					

Summa personarum xix
Summa denariorum xix*s*.

[180 Lay Subsidy / 34 Suffolk]   *Damaged, faded and incomplete.*

HADLEGHE IN HUNDREDO DE CORSFORDE

	s.	d.		s.	d.
Thomas Falledew *artifex*		xij	Alicia de Bentone *parve* tenure		
Alicia uxor ejus					
Edmundus Faus *agricola*	ij		Cristina filia ejus		
Margareta uxor ejus		j	Johannes Bayn *fuller*	ij	
Johannes Vaus *famulus* ejus		xij	Alicia uxor ejus		
			Cristina *famula* ejus		vj
Rogerus Payn *operarius*		xij	Johannes Clerk *fuller*	ij	
Ricardus Reynold *textor*	ij		Emma uxor ejus		
Agneta uxor ejus			Robertus Costyn *messor*		
Johannes Gowene *carpentarius*		xviij	Lora uxor ejus		
			Margareta *famula* ejus		iiij
Alicia uxor ejus			Johannes Mellere *molendinarius*		viij
Johannes Coyfe *parve* tenure		xij			
			Emma uxor ejus		
Adam Geulond *operarius*		xij	Thomas Wryghte *carpentarius*	ij	
Agneta uxor ejus			Margareta uxor ejus		
Radulfus Mabylonn *agricola*		xij	Alicia filia ejus		iiij
			Alicia Baldewene *famula*		xij
Agneta uxor ejus			Ricardus Coleman *artifex*	ij	
Thomas de Benton *operarius*		xij	Anna uxor ejus		
			Willelmus Bayn *mercator*	x	
Alicia uxor ejus			Margeria uxor ejus		
Johanna *famula* ejus		xij	Johannes Goye *famulus*		xij
Johannes Thedam *textor*	ij		Alicia uxor ejus		
Agneta uxor ejus			Johannes Barat		xij
Stephanus Boteler *mercator*			Alicia uxor ejus		
			Johannes Sayer *bercher*		viij
Isabella uxor ejus			Alicia *famula*		viij
Johannes Parys *famulus*			Johannes Teppyng *famulus*	ij	
Margareta uxor ejus					
Adam Rebat *textor*			Margareta uxor ejus		
Agneta uxor ejus			Willelmus Bette *operarius*		xij
Johannes Rebat *junior textor*			Agneta uxor ejus		
			Agneta filia ejus *famula*		vj
Isabella Cage *famula*		vj	Johannes Waryn *operarius*		xij
Margareta filia ejus		vj			
Rogerus Mentyl *sissor*		xij	Caterina uxor ejus		
Margareta uxor ejus			Johannes Gastonne	ij	
Johanna Hewes *famulus*			Margareta uxor ejus		

	s.	d.		s.	d.
Ricardus Preston *fuller* ⎫ Alicia uxor ejus ⎭	ij		Robertus Bele *carpentarius* ⎫ Agneta uxor ejus ⎭		xij
Willelmus Wryghte *carpentarius* ⎫ Isabella uxor ejus ⎭	ij		Willelmus Wodyer *pannarius* ⎫ Matildis uxor ejus ⎭	x	
Nicholaus Boneyr *fuller* ⎫ Cristina uxor ejus ⎭	ij		Alicia *famula* ejus		vj
Ricardus Pyper *artifex* ⎫ Alicia uxor ejus ⎭		viij	Johannes Rebat *tinctor* ⎫ Margareta uxor ejus ⎭		xij
Thomas Sampson			Johannes .... *pannarius* ⎫ Matildis uxor ejus ⎭	iij	
Alexander Muggard					
.... *mercator*			Johannes *famula* ejus		vj
Isabella uxor ejus			Bartolameus Slontere		
Sara *famula* ejus			Alicia uxor ejus		
[Here the document becomes illegible and is partially gone]			[Several names here are illegible]		
			Ricardus Nel *tinctor* ..... uxor ejus Alicia *famula* ejus		
Johannes Drake *sissor*					
Elena Neeys *famula*		viij	[Several names are illegible here]		
Willelmus Reyner *operarius* ⎫ Alicia uxor ejus ⎭		viij	Ricardus Semer *pannarius* ⎫ Johannes Pelle *fuller*	ij	
Robertus Sparwe *pannarius* ⎫ Ada uxor ejus ⎭			Alicia Skynner		
Caterina uxor *famula* ejus			[Many names illegible here]		
Aug. Crembyl *claud* (?)	iij				
Alicia *famula* ejus	xij		Johanna Chynchere		
Willelmus Hemmyg *chinchere* ⎫ Cristina uxor ejus ⎭	xij		Ricardus Saltere Lucia uxor ejus		
Alicia Meller *famula*	vj		Willelmus Taylor Alicia uxor ejus		
Ricardus Hayl *fuller* ⎫ Alicia uxor ejus ⎭	xviij		Rogerus Preston *cissor* Agneta uxor ejus		
Ricardus Cock *pannarius* ⎫ Agneta uxor ejus ⎭	ij				
Alicia *famula* ejus	iiij		[Several names illegible here]		
Johannes St .. *operarius* ⎫ Johanna uxor ejus ⎭	ij				
Margareta *famula* ejus	iiij		Johanna Alston		
Johannes Pedebef *pannarius* ⎫ Margareta uxor ejus ⎭	ij		Johannes Busch *parve tenure* Lucia uxor ejus		
Alicia filia ejus	vj		Thomas Greyne *pannarius* ⎫ Cristina uxor ejus ⎭		xviij
Johannes filius ejus	vj				
Margareta Broun *brasiatrix*	xij		Willelmus Brounyng *pannarius* ⎫ Cristina uxor ejus ⎭	iiij	
Alicia *famula* ejus	iiij		Thomas Skalman *pannarius* ⎫ A ..... uxor ejus ⎭	ij	
Edmundus Wolleman *agricola* ⎫ ...... uxor ejus ⎭	ij				
...... Cartere	xij		Willelmus Brownyng junior *pannarius* ⎫ Alicia uxor ejus ⎭	ij	
Agneta uxor ejus					
Galfridus Taylor *sissor* ⎫ Johanna uxor ejus ⎭	xij				

APPENDIX I.

	s.	d.		s.	d.
Robertus *famulus* ejus			Nicholaus Dexter *caru-*		
Alicia atte Hel vidua		ij	*carius*		xij
Alicia Pese vidua		xij	Roger frater ejus		xij
Robertus Sprot *sutor*		ij	Johannes Justise *famulus*		xij
Juliana uxor ejus			Cristina uxor ejus		
Johanna *famula* ejus		vj	Johannes Cok *operarius*		ij
Willelmus Heydone		ij	Johanna uxor ejus		
Elena uxor ejus			Johannes Hamond *agri-*		
Alicia *famula* ejus		vj	*cola*		ij
Willelmus Dobbys *pan-*			Cristina uxor ejus		
narius		ij	Johannes Chelisworth		
Rosa uxor ejus			*tinctor*		iij
Johannes Cukhok *car-*			Isabella uxor ejus		
pentarius		ij	Johannes B .. hel *scissor*		ij
Cristina uxor ejus			Cristina uxor ejus		
Stepanus Porter *fuller*		xij	Johannes Barker *textor*		xij
Matildis uxor ejus			Johannes Cytlyng		xij
Petrus Couper			Johanna uxor ejus		
Johannes Mitte *textor*		ij	Thomas Fut *pannarius*		ij
Dennis uxor ejus			Matildis uxor ejus		
Nicholaus Chaundeler		xij	Johannes Medwe *agri-*		
....			*cola*		ij
Agneta Gyssok		viij	Margeria uxor ejus		
Johannes Bonecold *pan-*			Willelmus Ros *agricola*		ij
narius		ij	Johanna uxor ejus		
Johanna uxor ejus			Johannes Ros *pannarius*		
Johannes Achelard *fuller*		xij	Johanna uxor ejus		
Margareta uxor ejus			Johannes *famulus* ejus		xij
Johannes Baxter		viij	Cristena uxor ejus		
Johanna uxor ejus			Elena *famula* ejus		
Thomas Smyth *faber*		ij	Onnfre Denarstone *agri-*		
Johanna uxor ejus			*cola*		xij
Johanna .... *famula*			Johannes Marscal *launter*		
Johannes Chapman *mer-*		viij	Isabella uxor ejus		
cator			Nicholaus Goyer *oper-*		
Johanna uxor ejus			*arius*		xij
Johannes Spr..		viij	Alicia uxor ejus		
Alicia *famula* ejus		vj	Johannes Bowel *agricola*		ij
Johannes Spr..		xij	Agneta uxor ejus		
			Rogerus filius ejus		xij
[Many names are gone here]			Johannes Beneyt		ij
			Ernaburga uxor ejus		
			Aufrid Mauncer *agricola*		x
Johannes Damysfelde		ij	Johannes Mancer filius		
De.... uxor ejus			ejus *agricola*		iij
Ricardus Smyth *agricola*		xij	Margareta uxor ejus		
Alicia uxor ejus			Galfridus Meller		
Johannes Chapman *agri-*			Johanna uxor ejus		
cola		x	Ricardus filius ejus		xij
Margareta uxor ejus			Margareta uxor ejus		
Johannes Salter			Johannes Lyonn		
Caterina uxor ejus			Alicia uxor ejus		
Ricardus Wade			Matildis Schayl *famula*		
Alicia uxor ejus			Johannes Godefrey..		
Johannes filius ejus		ij	Johanna uxor ejus		
Willelmus Wade *famulus*		viij	Willelmus Cappe *textor*		
Johannes Whelwryghte		ij	Alicia uxor ejus		
Alicia uxor ejus			Johannes Herst *carpen-*		
Johannes Alayn *tinctor*		ij	*tarius*		
Lu ... uxor ejus			Alicia uxor ejus		

P.

	s.	d.		s.	d.
Nicholaus Meller - - -			Johannes Colermaker -		
Johannes Prentys *sutor* -			Alicia uxor ejus - - -		
Agneta uxor ejus - - -			Helena Den - - - -		iiij
Cristina Dapys *famula* -			Johannes Schapman		
Alicia Falledew *famula* -			carucator - - - - -		
Johannes Sextayn - -			Alicia uxor ejus - - -		
Cristina uxor ejus - -					

Summa totalis viicv
Summa .... xxxv*li*. v*s*.

[180 Lay Subsidy / 47 Suffolk]

Hartismere Hundred

Tweyt

Hec est indentura tripartita facta inter Willelmum Tendryng chivaler et socios suos assessores et contra irrotulatores ultimi subsidii domino Regi concessi videlicet de qualibet persona laica tres grotes anno regni ejusdem quarto ex una parte et Willelmum Ruschebrok chivaler et socios suos collectores dicti subsidii ex parte altera et Johannem Melforth Jacobum Melle Matheum Sparwe Johannem Elmswelle ...... Alexandrem Neue constabularios et subcollectores ejusdem subsidii de Tweyt ex tercia parte de numero et nominibus subscriptis et de gradu et statu eorundem videlicet:

Agricole	s.	d.	*Sutores*	s.	d.
Matheus Sparwe *agricola*	iiij		Johannes Melforthe *sutor*	ij	iiij
Alicia Sparwe - - - -			Johanna uxor ejus - -		
Johannes Fuller *agricola*	ij		Nicolaus Petel *sutor* - -		iij
Margareta uxor ejus - -			Margeria uxor ejus - -		
Jacobus Melle - - - -		iij	Galfridus Coray *sutor* -	ij	vj
Alicia uxor ejus - - -			Anna uxor ejus - - -		
Alexander Neue *agricola*	ij				
Artifices			[*Laboratores?*]		
Willelmus Garlek *brasiator* - - - - - -	iij		Ricardus Bischop - - -		xvj
Johanna uxor ejus - -			Warrena uxor ejus - -		
Johannes Garlek filius ejus - - - - - -	iiij		Nicolas .... - -	iij	xviij
Johannes Elmswell *carpentarius* - - - - -	ij		Margeria uxor ejus - -		
Anna uxor ejus *brasiatrix* - - - - -			Willelmus Atte Cros		
			Elyna uxor ejus - - -		
			Johannes Chaumber - -		xviij
			Margeria uxor ejus - -		
			Willelmus Tweyt *webber*		xviij
Johanna ...... *brasiatrix* - - - - -		xij	Katerina ...... - -		xij
			Johannes Hil.... - -		

APPENDIX I.

Servientes	s.	d.	Servientes (cont.)	s.	d.
Matildis . . . . . - -			Matildis Dromer - - -		ij
Agneta Deye - - - -			Willelmus Sparwe - -		
Margeria Deye . . . - -			. . . .		
Rogerus Skoyt - - -		vj	. . . .		
Johanna uxor ejus - -			Johannes Holgate - -		
Katerina Neue - - -			Rogerus Fuller - - -		
Walterus E . . . . . rcher			Johannes Folk - - -		
Margeria uxor ejus - -			Rosa uxor ejus - - -		
Agneta filia ejus - - -			Margeria Munk - - -		

Summa nominum personarum xlviij
Summa denariorum ij*li*. viij*s*.

[On dorse of skin]
Summa personarum istorum xxij rotulorum

mmm iiij v   Inde subsidio cliiij*li*. v.*s*.

⎡180 Lay Subsidy⎤   *Part of a skin.*
⎣ 34   Suffolk ⎦

MUTFORD HUNDRED

	s.	d.		s.	d.
Juliana . . . . . . - -		xij	Petrus Webster - - -⎫	ij	iiij
. . . . - -		xij	Agatha uxor ejus - - ⎭		
Willelmus Wyard - -		xij	Ricardus Clericus - - -		xij
Henricus Burghard - -		xij			

Summa omnium personarum de villate de Kessinglond cccv.
Summa denariorum xv. *li*. v.*s*.

Constabularii ⎧ Henricus Donnison ⎫
              ⎨ Johannes Malle   ⎬ Jurati
              ⎩ Alanus Archere   ⎭
              ⎧ Ricardus de Childerhous ⎫   onorantur
Collectores ⎨ Edmundus le Smyth   ⎬   infra
              ⎩ Thomas de Medwe   ⎭ Jurati
                Willelmus de . . . .

⎡180 Lay Subsidy⎤   *A damaged fragment of a skin.*
⎣ 34   Suffolk ⎦

BLYTHING HUNDRED

BUXLOWE

	s.	d.		s.	d.
Johannes Bra-⎫			Willelmus Bo-⎫		
ham - - - ⎬ cultores			kele - - - ⎬ cultores		
Johanna uxor⎪			Mariota uxor⎪		
ejus - - - ⎭			ejus - - - ⎭		
Adam de Tang-⎫		.	Rogerus Put-⎫		
ham - - - ⎬ cultores			tok - - - ⎬ cultores		iij
Margeria uxor⎪			. . . . . yna uxor⎪		
ejus - - - ⎭			ejus - - - ⎭		

8—2

116 SUFFOLK POLL TAX LISTS, 1381.

	s.	d.		s.	d.
Willelmus Dal- ⎫ lyng · · · ⎬ cultores Margaret uxor ⎪ ejus · · · ⎭		iij	Ricardus Derhawe serviens · · · · · Margareta uxor ejus · · Mariota Derhawe · · ·		
Robertus Crofford · · Agneta uxor ejus · · · Johannes ..... cissor · Mariota uxor ejus · · Johannes Da- ⎫ sach · · · ⎬ carpentarius Mabella uxor ⎪ ejus · · · ⎭			Robertus Derhawe · · Johannes Schere · · · ..... uxor ejus · · · Ricardus Fleded · · · Ricardus Pykbon · · · Margareta Crofford · · Margareta Aldech · · Willelmus Aldech · ·		

Summa nominum personarum....
Summa denariorum xxviis.
Willelmus Dallyng constabularius et oneratur superius.

⎡ 240 Lay Subsidy ⎤
⎣ 308 Divers Counties ⎦

BLYTHING HUNDRED

BENACRE

	s.	d.		s.	d.
Willelmus Bol- ⎫ ynge · · · · ⎬ cultor Mabilia uxor ⎪ ejus · · · ⎭			Willelmus Cut ⎫ Agneta uxor ⎬ carucator ejus · · · ⎭		xiij
Johannes Al- ⎫ man · · · ⎬ piscator Agneta uxor ⎪ ejus · · · ⎭			Johannes Rey- ⎫ sonn · · · · ⎬ cultor Margeria uxor ⎪ ejus · · · ⎭	ij	vj
Elenor serviens ejus · ·			Edmundus filius ejus ·		vj
Johanna Alman serviens ejus · · · · ·			Robertus Reysonn piscator · · · · · Margareta uxor ejus · ·		xx
Thomas Mara- ⎫ ille · · · · ⎬ piscator Margeria uxor ⎪ ejus · · · ⎭	ij		Henricus atte ⎫ Newhous · · ⎬ piscator Matildis uxor ⎪ ejus · · · ⎭	ij	iiij
Willelmus Al- ⎫ man · · · ⎬ piscator Agneta uxor ⎪ ejus · · · ⎭	iij	iv	Johannes filius ejus · ·		viij
			Robertus Qua- ⎫ rel · · · · ⎬ piscator Isabella uxor ⎪ ejus · · · ⎭	ij	vj
Johannes filius ejus · ·		xij			
Alexander filius ejus · ·		xij	Johannes Cul- ⎫ ford · · · ⎬ piscator	ij	vj
Michael serviens ejus ·		viij	Alicia uxor ejus ⎭		
Johannes Bond piscator · ⎫ Johanna uxor ejus · · ⎬	ij	vj	Johannes filius ejus · ·		vj
Matildis Burkyn mater ejus · · · · · ·		xij	Willelmus atte see piscator · · · · ·		
Alicia Mincin cultor · ·		xij	Juliana uxor ejus · ·		
Robertus Mincin cultor · ⎫ Alicia uxor ejus · · · ⎬	iij		Johannes atte ⎫ see · · · · ⎬ piscator Margeria uxor ⎪ ejus · · · ⎭	ij	
Alicia filia ejus · · ·		x			
Robertus serviens ejus ·		viij			
Ricardus serviens Roberti Bonde · · · · · ·		viij	[Rest of this illegible]		

APPENDIX I. 117

BULCAMP

	s.	d.		s.	d.
Johannes de Middleton, Isabella uxor ejus } *fermarius*	v	iiij	Johannes Jebbys, Agneta uxor ejus, Johannes Brok, Johanna uxor ejus } *cultor*	ij	
Johannes Mountys *serviens*		iiij	Johannes West, Clemencia uxor, ejus } *cultor*	ij	vj
Johannes Randekyn *serviens*		iiij			
Reginaldus de Cisterne *serviens*		iiij	Walterus ..... *serviens*		vj
Adam Brok *serviens* ejus		iiij	Willelmus		
Alicia Brok *serviens* ejus		iiij	kys, Margareta uxor ejus } *cultor*	ij	
Johannes Atered *cultor*					
Margareta uxor ejus	v	iiij	....		
Willelmus Oliground *serviens*		iiij	Willelmus Bassat, Alicia uxor ejus } *cultor*	ij	
Johannes Byschop *serviens*		iiij	Stephanus Turry	ij	
Ricardus *serviens* ejus		iiij	Margareta uxor ejus		
Johannes Soun *serviens*		iiij	..... Haldene *spynner*		xij
Agnes *serviens* ejus			..... Prillay *spynner*		xij

BREGGE

	s.	d.		s.	d.
Nicholas Fool *firmarius*		ij	Agneta uxor ejus		
Matildis uxor ejus			Willelmus Deye		
Johannes *serviens* ejus			Agneta uxor ejus		
Robertus Brok *cultor*			Katerina *serviens* ejus		

Summa personarum ccxxi
„ denariorum xi . li. xiid.

Johannes Jebbys } onerantur super.
Nicholas Fool

⎡180 Lay Subsidy⎤ *The name of this township is quite illegible.*
⎣ 37 Suffolk ⎦

Indentura facta inter Willelmum Tendryng chivaler et socios suos assessores et contra irrotulatores et Willelmum Rosshebrooke ...... suos collectores subsidii domino Regi nostro concessi in ultimo parliamento apud northampton anno regni sui quarto ex una parte et Ricardum Webstere Johannem Loche constabularios Johannem Souter Thomam Lymghook subassessores ville de .... quallbet capite iij grotes ut patet per nomina subscripta :

Agricole	s.	d.	Artifices? (cont.)	s.	d.
Rogerus Frary	iij		Thomas....... - - -		
Juliana uxor ejus			....		
Adam Schalo... -	iij		Robertus Coupere webber)	xviij	
Matildis uxor ejus			Alicia uxor ejus - - -		
Thomas Bettes		xxx	Johannes Broun ber-		
Agneta uxor ejus			carius - - - - -		
Thomas Simond	iij		Nicholaus Byllyng co-		
..... uxor ejus			opertor - - - -		
..... Goodwyn		ij	Katerina uxor ejus - -		
....			Johannes Goodwyn tur-		
....			ner - - - - - -		xvj
Willelmus Larlyng	iij		*Laboratores*		
Agneta uxor ejus			Alexander Gylles - - -		xviij
Johannes........	iij		Alicia uxor ejus - - -		
Margareta uxor ejus			Thomas Drenkestone -		xij
Ricardus Webestere	iij		Agneta uxor ejus - - -		
Margareta uxor ejus			Willelmus Barker - -		xviij
Willelmus	iij		Alicia uxor ejus - -		
Cecilia uxor ejus -			Matildis Snowwhyte -		xij
Ricardus Fraunceys	iij		Agneta filia ejus - - -		
Matildis uxor ejus			Alicia Wylde - - -		xij
Walterus Reed	ij		Joh..... ejusdem - -		
Katerina uxor ejus			Joh............	ij	
Johannes Loche	iiij		Agneta uxor ejus - - -		
Beatrix uxor ejus			Thomas Nichole - - -	ij	
Willelmus Draper		xxx	Margeria uxor ejus - -		
Katerina uxor ejus			Thomas Parker - - -	ij	
Willelmus Tyller	ij		Katerina uxor ejus - -		
Colleta uxor ejus			Robertus Morel - - -		xij
Willelmus Bencold	ij		Margareta Godard - -		xij
Agneta uxor ejus			Willelmus atte Hel - -	ij	
Thomas Lymghok	iij		Alicia uxor ejus - - -		
Agneta uxor ejus			Johannes Fraunceys -		xx
Johannes Spencer	ij		Isabella uxor ejus - -		
Agneta uxor ejus			Henricus Belee - - -	ij	
Ricardus Gunnyld	ij		Katerina uxor ejus - -		
Matildis uxor ejus			Matildis Belee - - -		xij
			Margareta de Ford - -		xij
Carpentarii			Alicia uxor ejus - - -		xij
..... Massyon	ij	viij	Walterus Hargham - -		
Sibilla uxor ejus -			Agneta Koune - - -		
Thomas Fissher		xij	Agneta Shepherde - -		xij
Johannes Bettes			Margareta Krane - - -		xij
Letitia uxor ejus	ij	ij	Margeria Byllyng - - -		xij
Willelmus Aylmere					
A..... uxor ejus	ij	ij	*Faber*		
			Thomas Resshebrook -	ij	
Cissores			Margareta uxor ejus -		
Johannes Anelye -					
Janet uxor ejus		xviij	*Soutere*		
Ricardus Barker			Robertus Joyze - - -	ij	
Margeria uxor ejus	ij		Clare uxor ejus - - -		
Rogerus Clement					
Matildis uxor ejus	ij		*Servientes*		
			Johannes Frary - - -		xij
[*Artifices?*]			Agneta uxor ejus - - -		
Thomas Kra(ne) -			Agneta Chaloner - - -		vj
Agneta uxor ejus -			Johanna Chaloner - -		vj

APPENDIX I. 119

Servientes (cont.)	s.	d.	Servientes (cont.)	s.	d.
Matildis Bettes			Johannes Perot		
Johannes Symond			Rosa uxor ejus		
Willelmus Symond			Nicholaus Ree		
Alicia.......			Robertus Dayoa		
Agneta Goodwyn			Rosa uxor ejus		ij
Isabell Poreth			Johannes Osborn		
Nicholaus Akk			Alicia uxor ejus		
Johannes Reve			Alicia Perdon		
Matelldis Shepherde			Beatrix Lymghook		
Issabella Resshebrook			Willelmus Spicor		
Willelmus Fraunceys			Mariota Tyller		
Lucia Fraunceys			.... Estryle		
Johannes Love			....		
Agneta Wymdyssh			Sarra Gylley		

Summa nominum ejusdem...
Summa denariorum in toto vili. ixs.

(*A fragment of some place in Plomesgate Hundred.*)

⌈180 Lay Subsidy⌉
⌊ 34   Suffolk ⌋

	s.	d.		s.	d.
Agneta Martyn		xij	Johannes Grenne junior		
Dassella Martyn		xij	Johanna Dotemay		
Johannes Lof		xx	Margeria Martyn		
Sarra uxor ejus		xij	Oliva Martyn		
Johannes Lof junior		xij	Alicia Iken		
Willelmus Fenman		xij	Galfridus Lenyng		
Cristina uxor ejus		xij	Margeria Arnald		
Robertus Cosyn		xij	Ricardus Svyn		
Johannes Sveyn		xiiij	Agneta Burgh		vj
Cristina uxor ejus			Robertus Knot		iiij
Johannes Sueyn junior			Margeria *famula* Thome		iiij
Henricus Va			Ossegut		
Agneta uxor ejus			Margeria Wygg		x
Willelmus Arnald			Agneta Small		
Johannes Reve		xvj	Johannes Smyth		
Saiena Buntyng		viij	Thomas Wescard		
Thomas Donne		xvj	Robertus Nyse		
Alicia Meye		iiij	Thomas Dokes		xij
Mabella del Heth		iiij	Agneta uxor ejus		xij
Willelmus Weyne		vj	Robertus Rede		xij
Mateldis Fynch		iiij	Alicia uxor ejus		xij
Margeria Thyth		vj	Johannes Pynchebek		xij
Alicia Wastell			Matildis Souter		xij
Johannes Arnald			Johannes Baron		xij
Matildis Lose			Alicia Baron		xij
Avelina Neuman			Thomas Schmyth		xij
Margeria Rede			Matildis Frere		xij
Galfridus H....e			Henricus Hers		xij
Johannes Wytyng			.... uxor ejus		xij

Summa personarum ccx
Summa denariorum xli. xs.

POPULATION OF ENGLAND IN 1377 AND 1381.

THE following tables show the Population of England, as given by the returns for the Lay Poll Taxes of 1377 and 1381. The figures are taken from contemporary documents drawn up on the completion of the collections of the taxes, and preserved in the Lord Treasurer's Office.

Two copies of the return for 1377, and one of that for 1381, are to be found in the Public Record Office, referred to as Lord Treasurer's Remembrancer, Enrolled Accounts (Subsidies) No. 13.

It will be observed that the counties of Cheshire, Durham and Monmouth were not included in the returns. The 1377 Poll Tax was levied on all persons over 14 years of age, and that of 1381 on all persons over 15 years.

An abstract of the results of the Poll Tax of 1377 was printed by Mr Topham in Vol. VII. of the *Archæologia*, but no reference was there given, whereby the document from which his returns were taken can be identified. I do not think however that they were taken directly from these enrolled accounts, as in some particulars they differ from them, though the general result is much the same. It may also be mentioned that there is a slip in printing the total in Mr Topham's list, for the figures he gives come to 19203 less than the total which appears at the foot of his table.

The returns on the enrolled accounts are given in the following form, and I give the return for Norfolk in full for the 1381 Tax as an example.

Norff.

Compotus Johannis Harsyk chivaler Thome de Berney chivaler Willelmi Hastyng Johannis Hales Johannis Reed Roberti Hakebeche Willelmi Cursun de Billyngford et Willelmi Burell de Hevyngham collectorum subsidii predicti in comitatu Norffolchie exceptis civitate Norwici et villa de Lenne per breve Regis patens de magno sigillo datum vij. die Decembris dicto anno quarto super hunc compotum restitutum per supervisum et contrarotulacionem Stephani Hales chivaler Edmundi de Reynham chivaler Ricardi Illeye chivaler Georgii Sefoul Johannis de

Fyncham Henrici de Pakenham et Willelmi Ketel de Iteryngham supervisorum et contrarotulatorum subsidii predicti videlicet de eodem subsidio ut infra.

Iidem reddunt compotum de mmm ccc xxxv. *li.* xix. *s.* receptis de predicto subsidio contingentem lxvj m dccxix. personas laicas homines et feminas in predicto comitatu Norffolchie exceptis predictis civitate Norwici et villa de Lenne per supervisum et contrarotulationem predictum quarum quidem personarum nomina status gradus et summe particulares singillatim annotantur in Indenturis ipsorum collectorum et predictorum supervisorum et contrarotulatorum de particulis in Thesauro liberatis videlicet de qualibet persona iij. grossas sicut continentur in indenturis predictis.

Summa recepta mmm ccc xxxv. *li.* xix. *s.* In Thesauro mmm cc iiij xiij. *li.* ij. *s.* iiij. *d.* in ix talliis. Et eisdem collectoribus et contrarotulatoribus pro misis et expensis suis xvij. *li.* iiij. *s.* vj. *d.* Et Willelmo Wenlok[1] clerico misso versus partes Norffolchie predictis negotiis Regem tangentibus super custibus suis eundo in negotiis predictis x. *li.* per breve Regis de privato sigillo prefatis collectoribus directum et unam partem Indenture inter prefatum Johannem Reed collectorem et prefatum Willelmum Wenlock de receptis. De quibus quidem x. *li.* prefatus Willelmus debet respondere Et respondit in rotulo iiij^to in "Adhuc Item Norff." Et Debent xv. *li.* xij. *s.* ij. *d.* Iidem reddunt compotum de eodem debito in Thesauro liberatum et quieti sunt.

THE POPULATION OF ENGLAND AS GIVEN BY THE POLL TAX RETURNS IN 1377 AND 1381.

	1377	1381
Bedfordshire	20339	14895
Berkshire	22723	15696
Buckinghamshire	24672	17997
Cambridgeshire	27350	24324
Cambridge	1902	1739
Cornwall	34274	12056
Cumberland	11841	4748
Penrith	no separate return	75
Carlisle	678	no separate return
Derbyshire	23243	15637
Derby	1046	no separate return

[1] W. Wenlok clerk was one of the inspectors sent to Norfolk under the second commission. L. T. R. Orig. 4 Ric. I. m. 12.

	1377	1381
Devonshire	45635	20656
Exeter	1560	1420
Plymouth	not given[1]	no separate return
Dartmouth	506	" "
Dorsetshire	34241	19507
Essex	47962	30748
Colchester	2955	1609
Gloucestershire	36760	27857
Gloucester	2239	1446
Bristol	6345	5662
Hampshire	33241	22018
Southampton	1152	1051
Isle of Wight	4733	3625
Winchester	not given[1]	no separate return
Herefordshire	15318	12659
Hereford	1903	no separate return
Ludlow	1172	" "
Hertfordshire	19975	13296
Huntingdonshire	14169	11299
Kent	56557	43838
Canterbury	2574	2123
Rochester	570	no separate return
Lancashire	23880	8371
Leicestershire	31730	21914
Leicester	2101	1708
Lincolnshire		
Lincoln	3412	2196
Close of Lincoln	157	no separate return
Boston	2871	" "
Grimsby	no separate return	562
Kesteven	21566	15734
Holland	18592	13795
Stamford	1218	no separate return
Lindsey	47303	30235
Middlesex	11243	9937
London	23314	20397
Norfolk	88797	66719
Norwich	3952	3833
Lynn	3127	1824
Yarmouth	1941	no separate return
Northamptonshire	40225	27997
Northampton	1477	1518
Northumberland	14162	not given
Newcastle	2647	1819
Nottinghamshire	26260	17442
Nottingham	1447	1266
Newark	1178	no separate return
Oxfordshire	24982	20588
Oxford	2357	2005
Rutland	5994	5593
Shropshire	23574	13041
Shrewsbury	2082	1618
Somerset	54604	30384
Bath	570	297
Wells	901	487
Staffordshire	21465	15993
Lichfield	1024	no separate return

[1] Excluded from the return for the county. Topham's list gives population of Plymouth as 4837, and Winchester as 1440.

APPENDIX I.

	1377	1381
Suffolk	58610	44635
Ipswich	1507	963
Bury St Edmunds	2445	1334
Surrey	18039	12684
Southwark	no separate return	1059
Sussex	35326	26616
Chichester	869	787
Warwickshire	25447	20481
Coventry	4817	3947
Westmoreland	7389	3859
Wiltshire	42599	30627
Salisbury	3226	2708
Worcestershire	14542	12043
Worcester	1557	932
Yorkshire		
York	7248	4015
Hull	1557	1124
Scarborough	no separate return	1480
Beverley	2663	no separate return
North Riding	33185	15690
East Riding	38238	25184
West Riding	48149	23029
Total	1355201	896451

THE CLERICAL POPULATION OF ENGLAND AND WALES AS GIVEN BY POLL TAX RETURNS IN 1381[1].

	Regular and Secular Clergy[2]	Deacons, Acolytes and Inferior Clergy over the age of 16 years[2]
Deaneries of Irchenfield and Ross	102	16
Deanery of Bocking	26	1
,, South Malling	24	3
Archdeaconry of Chester	303	5
,, ,, Cornwall	369	81
Deaneries of Weobley, Leominster, Frome and Weston	186	22
Archdeaconry of Hereford	113	15
Deaneries of Shoreham and Croydon	96	
Archdeaconry of Winton	870	80

[1] L. T. R. Enrolled Accounts Subsidies, No. 4 in P. R. O.
[2] L. T. R. originalia, 4 Ric. II. m. 49. To the Archbishop of Canterbury.
Dated December 20, 4 Ric. II.:

'Quod omnes et singuli prelati etiam regulares cujuscunque gradus status ordinis sexus vel condicionis fuerint ac clerici quomodocunque promoti etiam si exempti privilegeati qualitercunque fuerint omnesque presbiteri non promoti tam regulares quam seculares ac etiam moniales infra vestram provinciam constituti omnesque et singuli advocati procuratores examinatores registratores et notarii publici singuli videlicet viginti grossos omnesque et singuli diaconi subdiaconi accoliti et alii inferiores etatis sex decem annorum et ultra in gradu et habitu clericali quomodolicet existentes qui mendicantes notorie non fuerint tres grossos nobis terminis supradictis persolvent.'

	Regular and Secular Clergy	Deacons, Acolytes and Inferior Clergy over the age of 16 years
Archdeaconry of Surrey	317	20
,, ,, Gloucester	355	30
,, ,, Worcester	568	32
,, ,, Salop	164	13
,, ,, Coventry	455	36
Deaneries of Stonehouse, Cirencester, Fairford, Dursley, Hawkesbury, Button, Bristol	372	26
Archdeaconries of Hunts and Beds	980	157
Diocese of Ely	625	134
Archdeaconries of Norfolk and Norwich	1745	168
,, ,, Suffolk and Sudbury	1230	68
,, ,, Chichester	256	22
Cathedral of Chichester	63	14
Deaneries of Ludlow and Burford	74	8
Archdeaconry of Lewes	356	7
City and Diocese of Canterbury	770	17
Archdeaconries of York, Richmond, East Riding, Cleveland	2295	94
Archdeaconry of Totton	326	93
St Albans	127	21
Archdeaconry of Barnstaple	196	12
City of Rochester	275	
Archdeaconries of Bucks and Oxon	1047	77
,, ,, Dorset and Sarum	1051	174
,, ,, Lincoln and Stow	2463	43
,, ,, Bath and Wells	642	72
,, ,, Berks and Wilts	731	108
,, ,, Nottingham	448	21
,, ,, Taunton	298	26
,, ,, Colchester	423	21
,, ,, Northampton and Leicester	1802	25
Deaneries of Clun, Pontesbury and Wenlock	122	
Archdeaconry of Derby	379	13
Deanery of St Mary Bow	102	6
,, Stottesden	22	
Archdeaconry of Essex	394	10
,, ,, London	631	34
City and Diocese of Durham	304	31
County of Northumberland	268	
Archdeaconry of Middlesex	384	49
Cathedral of London	108	14
Archdeaconry of Exeter	259	24
,, ,, Stafford	367	9
	25883	1952

WALES.

Diocese and City of St Asaph	149	5
Archdeaconry of St David	189	8
,, ,, Merioneth and Deanery of Arwestly	70	3
,, ,, Carmarthen	100	7
,, ,, Brecon	124	1
,, ,, Cardigan	105	
,, ,, Anglesea	38	1
	775	25

APPENDIX I.

The clerical return for 1381 is rather smaller than that of 1377; the latter gave a total clerical population in England and Wales of 30,350, but no mention is made of Northumberland or of the Diocese of Durham. There is no return for the Diocese of Carlisle for the 1381 tax; neither do the returns for the Welsh Dioceses for that year appear to be complete, Llandaff being omitted altogether.

APPENDIX II.

TRANSCRIPTS. EXTRACTS FROM VARIOUS DOCUMENTS.

(ANTIENT INDICTMENTS 128. SUFFOLK.)

Placita corone apud Mildenhale coram Willelmo de Ufford comite Suffolcie Rogero Skales Thoma de Morieux Willelmo de Elmham Johanne de Bourgh et Willelmo de Wyngefeld die Jovis proximo post festum nativitatis sancti Johannis Baptiste anno regni Regis Ricardi secundi post conquestum quinto [27 June 1381].

[SUFFOLK] Johannes Poter de Somerton fullere coram prefatis Justiciariis impetitus est per Johannem de Pole nuper camerarium domini Johannis de Cavendyssh nuper capitalis Justiciarii domini Regis de eo quod ipse die veneris proximo post festum Corporis Christi anno regni Regis nunc quarto [14 June 1381] fuit apud Lakyngheth et ibidem cum magna potestate et modo guerrini surexit contra dominum Regem et corone dignitatem et ibidem die et anno supradictis predictus Johannes Poter proditiose et felonice presens abettavit et procuravit alios proditores et inimicos domini Regis predictum Johannem de Cavendyssh ad interficiendum et super hoc predictus Johannes Poter captus et modo coram prefatis Justiciariis per vicecomitem ductus allocutus est qualiter de feloniis et proditionibus predictis se velit acquietare dicit quod ipse in nullo est inde culpabilis et de hoc de bono et malo ponit se super patriam Ideo fiat inde Jurata Juratores veniunt qui de consensu ipsius Johannis Poter adhoc electi et jurati dicunt super sacramentum suum quod predictus Johannes Poter de Somerton fullere est culpabilis de feloniis et proditionibus sibi impositis. Ideo consideratum est quod predictus Johannes Poter decapitetur [decollatus] et quod capud suum figatur super collistridium etc. Inquiratur de terris et catallis.

Placita corone apud Villam de Sancto Edmundo coram prefatis Justiciariis die sabbati in festo Apostolorum Petri et Pauli anno regni Regis Ricardi secundi post conquestum quinto [29 July 1381].

[SUFFOLK] Georgius de Donnesby de Com. Lincoln impetitus est per Johannem Osbern Aldermannum ville predicte et per plures homines fidedignos ejusdem ville de eo quod ipse isto eodem die venit apud sanctum Edmundum et ibidem consulit diversis hominibus ejusdem ville surgere contra dominum Regem et fideles ligeos dicti domini Regis precipiendo et eis firmiter injungendo quod ipsi surgerent sub pena forisfactorum vite et membrorum et ulterius dixit quod ipse est nuntius magne societatis et missus est ad villam Sancti Edmundi predicti ad faciendum comunitatem ejusdem ville surgere et super hoc captus et coram prefatis Justiciariis per vicecomitem ductus et instanter allocutus est qualiter de feloniis et proditionibus predictis se velit acquietare quiquidem Georgius coram prefatis Justiciariis omnes felonias et proditiones sibi impositas sponte et non vi cognovit et bene et aperte sustinuit Ideo consideratum est quod predictus Georgius de Donnesby decapitetur [decollatus] et quod capud suum figatur super collistridium etc. per quod inquiratur de terris et catallis.

(ANTIENT INDICTMENTS 128. SUFFOLK.)

HUNDREDUM LOSE.

[SUFFOLK] Juratores presentant quod Thomas Sampson Johannes de Batisford persona ecclesie de Bokelesham et Ricardus Talmache de Benteleye congregatores sustentores et interligatores hominum in hundredo de Sannford Gippewici Carleford Wylford et Lose tempore levationis modo guerrini contra dignitatem corone domini Regis venerunt in villa de Melton cum multitudine aliorum ignotorum die dominica proxima post festum corporis Christi anno regni domini Regis Ricardi secundi post conquestum quarto [16 June 1381] felonice et fraudulenter fregerunt et delaceraverunt clausum et domos

Willelmi Fraunceys apud Melton et ibidem aurum argentum pecias de argento cokelearia cifos de maser zonas annulos pannos lineos et laneos utensilia domi viz. vessel de peutre bacyns lavours lanam brasium frumentum bestias diversorum generum et alia bona et catalla ad valentiam c marcarum apud Melton felonice depredaverunt et asportaverunt.

Item dicunt quod Willelmus Bernard de Coppedok predicta die dominica anno supradicto tempore levationis modo guerrini et contra dignitatem corone domini Regis felonice venit cum multitudine aliorum ignotorum in villa de Eyk et ibidem clausum et domos Johannis Staverton de Eyk apud Eyk fregit et delaceravit et ibidem diversas pixides dicti Johannis similiter fregit et cartas scriptas cum aliis munimentis dicti Johannis felonice asportavit ad dampnum dicti Johannis Staverton c. solidorum [etc.].

HUNDRED OF LOSE.   JURATORES PRO REGE.

Thomas Crane.	*Juratus.*	Robertus Schort.	*Juratus.*
Johannes Old.	,,	Rogerus Indyben.	,,
Willelmus Webbere.	,,	Johannes Vynte.	
Ricardus Campaignoun.	,,	Thomas Gilbert.	
Gilbertus Barfot.	,,	Ricardus le Zyngge.	
Willelmus Cok.	,,	Johannes Colisson.	
Johannes de Eston.		Johannes Huntyngfeld.	
Walterus Wytnesham.		Nicholaus Lacy.	
Thomas Payn.	*Juratus.*	Johannes Priour.	
Johannes Wysman.	,,	Thomas Sothewynd.	
Edmundus Graunt.	,,	Henricus le Desing.	
Johannes Beverle.	,,		

(ANTIENT INDICTMENTS 128. SUFFOLK.)

SUFFOLK.   HUNDRED OF STOWE.

Juratores presentant quod Johannes Barbour de Huntyndon decollatus Johannes atte Cros de Shellond Galfridus Taillor de Drenkeston congregatores sustentores et manutentores tempore levationis de villa ad villam in hundredo de Stowe modo guerino et contra dignitatem corone domini Regis venerunt felonice et fraudulenter in villa de Eldeneuton videlicet die sabbati proxima post festum corporis Christi anno regni regis Ricardi secundi post conquestum quarto et ibidem clausum et domos Willelmi Berard apud Eldeneuton felonice et proditiose fregerunt et intraverunt cum multis aliis ignotis et ibidem vaccas bidentes lanam bladum brasium ac alia bona et catalla ad valenciam x. li depredaverunt et asportaverunt.

Item dicunt quod Johannes Wrau capellanus Galfridus Parfay vicarius ecclesie omnium sanctorum de Sudbury et Adam Bray Barkere de Sudbury fuerunt capitales congregatores sustentores et manutentores felonice et proditiose tempore levationis et contra dignitatem domini Regis in hundredo de Stowe etc. sic a villa de Sudbury usque villam de Thetford et alibi in diversis locis in Com. Suff.

[NAMES OF JURY MEN.]

Capitales Constabularii { Radulphus Clement. *Juratus.* [armiger. Stowmarket]
Rogerus Apelthweyt. *Juratus.* [agricola. Old Newton]

Rogerus Scales. [armiger. Wetherden]
Adam Frend. *Juratus.*
Johannes Sorrell. [agricola. Grt. Finborough]
Johannes Motoun. [agricola. Wetherden]
Robertus Frend. [pistor. Stowmarket]
Willelmus Langlyf. *Juratus.* [artifex. Stowmarket]
Johannes Gardener. *Juratus.* [cultor. Combes]
Willelmus Banyngham. *Juratus.* [agricola. Wetherden]
Willelmus de Eston. *Juratus.* [Combes]
Gilbertus Iryng. *Juratus.*
Willelmus Glaunvill. *Juratus.* [Thorney]
Johannes Westbronn. *Juratus.* [agricola. Wetherden]
Johannes Hamond. *Juratus.* [Dagworth ?]
Willelmus Crane. *Juratus.* [artifex. Stowmarket]
Johannes Goldyng. *Juratus.*
Willelmus Fenkele.
Galfridus Cook. [carnifex. Gipping Newton]
Johannes Kyng. *Juratus.* [carpenter. Gipping Newton]

Jurati super legianciam et recognitiones quod tenentur domino regi in LX. li. quas vicecomes levabit de terris et catallis etc....si etc.

N.B. the descriptions in brackets are added from the Poll Tax returns.

(ANTIENT INDICTMENTS 128. SUFFOLK.)

HOXNE. Juratores presentant quod Willelmus Assh soutere de Hoxne fuit capitalis congregator sustentor et manutentor tempore levationis falso et proditiose et contra dignitatem corone domini Regis in Hundredis de Hoxne Blythyng et Waynford fecit diversos homines sibi et sociis suis falso et proditiose jurare predicto tempore levationis.

Item dicunt quod Jacobus de Bedyngfeld et Willelmus Alred de Soham monachorum capitales congregatores tempore levationis modo guerrino felonice intraverunt et fregerunt clausum et domos Edmundi lakynghithe apud Geselyngham cum multis aliis ignotis videlicet die dominica proxima post festum sancti Barnabe apostoli anno regni Regis Ricardi post conquestum quarto [16 June 1381] et ibidem decem vaccas cum uno tauro ollas eneas et patellas pannos lineos et laneas ac alia bona et catalla ad valenciam x. li. felonice depredaverunt et asportaverunt de prefato Edmundo de Lakynghithe apud Geselyngham.

Item dicunt quod Johannes filius Galfridi Barat de Cratfield unus congregator tempore levationis modo guerrino et contra dignitatem corone domini Regis felonice venit in villam de Fresyngfeld ad domum Ricardi Suklyng et ibidem felonice intravit videlicet die martis proxima post[1] festum nativitatis Johannis Baptiste anno quarto supradicto [18 June 1381] et ibidem minavit prefatum Ricardum Suklyng de vita et membris quousque predictus Ricardus fecit finem cum prefato Johanne filio Galfridi Barat de iij. li. vj. s. viij. d. quosquidem iij. li. vj. s. viij. d. predictus Ricardus sibi liberavit pro timore mortis et dictus Johannes filius Galfridi Barat felonice asportavit.

Item dicunt quod predictus Jacobus de Bedyngfeld capitalis congregator tempore levationis modo guerrino in villa de Denyngton cum multis aliis ignotis viz. die sabbati proxima post festum sancti Barnabe apostoli anno supradicto [15 June 1381] [venit] ad domum Willelmi Rous capitalis constabularii Hundredi de Hoxne et ibidem precepit prefato Willelmo Rous sub pena decollationis capitis sui ad liberandum sibi et sociis suis decem sagittarios dicti hundredi predictus Willelmus sibi liberavit decem sagittarios de predicto hundredo pro timore mortis

---

[1] Probably we ought to have 'ante' here instead of 'post,' in which case *anno quarto* would be right, otherwise it should be *quinto*.

capiendi per diem quilibet eorum sex denarios per preceptum dicti Jacobi.

HOXNE. JURATORES PRO REGE.

Benedictus de Redyng. *Juratus.* \
Willelmus Rous. } *Capitales Constabularii.*

Adam Goode. *Juratus.*   Ricardus Smyth de Mendham.
Elias de Wirlyngworthe. *Juratus.*   *Juratus.*
    Thomas Calwere.
Thomas Bronger. *Juratus.*   Willelmus Anneys.
Johannes Boteler. *Juratus.*   Ricardus Cullyng.
Robertus Barker. *Juratus.*   Willelmus Sulman.
Willelmus Hynks. *Juratus.*   Johannes Page.
Thomas Wolrich. *Juratus.*   Johannes Smyth de Stradbrok.
Willelmus le Doo. *Juratus.*   *Juratus.*
Willelmus Hobert.   Simon Folcreed.
Ricardus Cook.   Willelmus Child. *Juratus.*

(ANTIENT INDICTMENTS 128. NORFOLK.)

WEST FLEG.

Inquisitio capta apud Hornyng die Martis proxima post festum translationis sancti Thome Martyris anno regni Regis Ricardi secundi post conquestum quinto [9 July 1381] coram Willelmo de Ufford comite Suffolcie et sociis suis Justiciariis domini Regis etc. per Johannem de Pykeryng Johannem Michel Thomam Isbel Willelmum Gunyld Godfredum de Pykeryng Johannem Dawes Johannem Cole Johannem Harald Johannem de Ryssengles Johannem de Holleslee Thomam Jerveys et Robertum Bataille qui dicunt super sacramentum suum quod Ricardus Philymond de Buxton Johannes Gentelombe Johannes Bettes de North Walsham fuerunt capitales ductores populi contra pacem domini Regis injuste levati apud Billokby et Castre in Fleg viz. die Martis proxima post festum sancti Botulphi anno regni Regis Ricardi secundi post conquestum quarto [18 June 1381] et sic de villa in villam in prejudicium corone domini Regis et perturbationem pacis contra proclamationem et defensionem dicti domini Regis.

Item dicunt quod Johannes atte Chaumbre de Heigham Poltere die lune in festo sancti Botulphi anno quarto supradicto

[17 June 1381] apud Norvicum felonice interfecit Reginaldum de Eccles.

Item dicunt quod Robertus Strongehobbe quondam serviens Johannis filii Alexandri Fastolf fuit capitalis ductor populi contra pacem et in prejudicium corone domini Regis injuste levati et idem Robertus simul cum aliis quam pluribus malefactoribus ignotis vi et armis et modo guerrino venit apud Castre in Fleg die martis proxima post festum Sancti Botulphi anno quarto supradicto [18 June 1381] et ibidem domos Johannis filii Alexandri Fastolf felonice fregit et prostravit nec non bona et catalla dicti Johannis ad valentiam viginti librarum ibidem inventa felonice furatus fuit et asportavit.

Item dicunt quod Henricus Roys de Dilham Adam Pulter
decollatus
alias vocatus Adam Martyn simul cum aliis malefactoribus ignotis die lune in festo sancti Botulphi anno quarto supradicto [17 June 1381] apud Mushold juxta hospitale sancte Marie Magdalene felonice interfecerunt et decollaverunt Robertum de Salle Militem Affirmantes......se habere et habuisse regale preceptum in premissis Datum de loco et anno supradictis.

(ANTIENT INDICTMENTS 128. NORFOLK.)

MITFORD HUNDRED.

Juratores presentant quod Rogerus Bacon Miles Thomas filius domini Thome de Gyssyngge militis Johannes Chacchevache qui se facit vocari Johannes de Monnteney de Bokenham et Galfridus Listere de Felmynham erant capitales illorum qui contra coronam et dignitatem domini Regis se elevaverunt in Comitatu Norff. coligentes sibi diversas conventiculas in depredacionem multorum......et occisionem diversorum hominum quorum nomina ignorantur contra coronam domini Regis etc.

Et quod die lune proxima ante festum Nativitatis sancti Johannis Bapt. anno regni regis Ricardi secundi a conquestu quarto [17 June 1381] Johannes filius Philippi de Carleton venit apud Mateshale vi et armis et contra pacem domini regis simul cum aliis multis ignotis et fecit Ricardum vicarium ecclesie predicte finem facere ad dimidiam marcam et plus ad procurationem Johannis Ladde.

Et quod idem Johannes filius Philippi die predicto venit vi et armis et contra pacem ad domum Thome de Bumstede in

Mateshale cum aliis ignotis et illum quesierunt et minaverunt de vita et membris ita quod domum suam reliquit per v dies et amplius.

Et quod Andreas Ballivus de Brigham Rogerus Bole et Thomas de Blofeld cum aliis ignotis venerunt vi et armis et contra pacem etc., et domum ipsius Thome de Bumstede apud Mateshale intraverunt et illum quesierunt et minaverunt de vita et membris Ita quod domum suam reliquit etc. quousque alii pro eo finem fecerunt de xl. d.

Et quod Thomas de Newelle de Craneworth depredavit de bonis et catallis Johannis de Herlyngg ad valenciam dimidie marce.

Et quod idem Thomas de Newelle depredavit bona et catalla domini Thome Clog ad valenciam dimidie marce.

Et quod idem Thomas de Newelle depredavit bona et catalla Adam Galyon ad valenciam dimidie marce.

Villata de Estderham. Mitford.

Juratores presentant quod Johannes de Carleton venit apud Mateshale die lune proxima ante festum Nativitatis S. Johannis Bapt. anno regni Regis nunc quinto [17 June 1381] cum aliis ignotis et in Ricardum vicarium ecclesie de Mateshale insultum fecere de vita et membro et ceperunt de predicto Ricardo vj. s. viij. d.

Item dicunt quod Thomas de Montency Edmundus de Southous et Ricardus de Southous venerunt apud Hoo die mercurii proxima ante festum Nativitatis Johannis Bapt. anno supradicto per requestum Galfridi Dedmor et Willelmum Drake minaverunt per quod pro timore predictus Willelmus weynavit unum messuagium et octodecem acras terre ad opus Galfridi Dedmor.

Item dicunt quod quidam Martinus Mannyngh manens in Sudburi misit litteras die et anno supra dictis apud Estderham per Robertum Agge de Yaxham et Johannem Brung seniorem de Estderham ad Johannem de Longcham Willelmum Ibry et Rodoland Lucas de eadem ex parte Johannis Wraw ut redderent quoddam librum tenementum predicto Martino quequidem litere sunt in villa ista quiquidem Robertus et Johannes cognoverunt quod fuerunt ubi Thomas atte Ook occisus fuit.

Item dicunt quod Willelmus Smyth manens in Estderham et

Willelmus Padinak iverunt per patriam et obviaverunt cum magna societate et jurati fuerunt per societatem qui quidem Willelmus Smyth venit ad constabularios de Derham mandando eis ut deliberarent prisones gaole ut juratus fuit sed nihil ad hoc fecit et sic per consilium constabulariorum sessavit et postea per ballivos domini arestatus fuit causa predicta et est in custodia ballivi hundredi.

Item dicunt quod Hugo Bucher de Caston Johannes Milicent firmarius de Wokilwode Johannes Creyk de Wymondham Willelmus Draper de Lyng fuerunt cum societate in diversis locis asportando catalla diversorum hominum et emerunt catalla per concordiam.

Item dicunt quod Andreas ballivus domini Episcopi Eliensis apud Brigham fuit communis malefactor in diversis locis in societate predicta asportando catalla diversorum hominum videlicet apud Herlyngh et apud Keniston de bonis Thome Clog capellani et aliorum diversorum hominum.

[NAMES OF JURY MEN.]

Henricus Blowere.	*Juratus.*	Galfridus Colle.	*Juratus.*
Laurencius Gybon.	„	Philipum Taylor.	
Robertus Noon.	„	Galfridus Qwenel.	*Juratus.*
Ricardus Pers.		Rogerus Batalyc.	
Johannes de Massyngham.		Ricardus filius Johannis.	
Edmundus Pers.	*Juratus.*	Johannes Demanye.	
Thomas Dyx.	„	Galfridus Norys.	
Johannes Noon.	„	Nicholaus Atte hooc.	
Robertus Flory.	„	Stephanus Ingrode.	
Johannes de Teversham.	„	Willelmus Smyth Lokmakere.	
Edmundus Aquile.	„	Ricardus Maynere.	*Juratus.*
Johannes Palmere.	„	Robertus Stampyn.	

xij *Jurati.*

(ANTIENT INDICTMENTS 128. NORFOLK.)

SMETH.

Inquisitio capta apud Estrudham die lune proxima ante festum sancte Margarete Virginis anno regni Regis Ricardi secundi post conquestum quinto [15 July 1381] per sacramentum Simonis Roberdeson Thome Burgeys Henrici Baylye de Brauncestre Johannis de Walpool Roberti Rust de Sharnebourne Ricardi Aleynesson Johannis Smyth de Holm Henrici Smyth de Brettham Nicolai de Chosele Galfridi Reyner Johannis de Stone Willelmi de Dockyng qui dicunt super sacramentum suum quod Robertus Fletcher *decollatus* manens in Hunstanton cum aliis ignotis venit usque Hecham cum arcubus sagittis et aliis armaturis et incitavit homines de Hecham ad surgendum in hoc rumore contra pacem domini Regis maledicendo venerabilem patrem nostrum dominum Henricum Episcopum Norvicensem eo quod equitavit in patria ad castigandum malefactores in malum exemplum comunitatis totius patrie viz. die lune proxima preterita [8 July 1381].

Et quod Johannes Spanye de Lenn Episcopi cordewaner die lune proxima post octavam sancte Trinitatis ultimam preteritam [17 June 1381] tempore hujus rumoris principalis ductor et manutentor malefactorum surgentium in patria venit usque Snetesham vi et armis cum xxx. hominibus ignotis et incitavit homines dicte ville ad surgendum contra pacem domini Regis ad querendum homines patrie de Flaundres ad eos occidendos et decapitandos et minavit Radulfum Panton ad eum occidendum per quod idem Radulfus desperans de vita et membris suis invenit plegium ad solvendum cuidam servienti dicti Johannis x. s. contra leges et pacem domini Regis.

Et quod Rogerus Loksmyth manens in Snetisham die martis proxima post octavam sancte Trinitatis ultimam preteritam [18 June 1381] principalis malefactor et manutentor malefactorum tempore hujus rumoris insultum fecit Simoni Wylymot apud Snetesham vi et armis et eum vulneravit cum j. dagger in humero suo petendo ab eodem Simone xv. quarteria iiij. busellos brasii et eum minando quod nisi vellet ei dare dictum brasium quod adduceret quandam congregationem malefactorum patrie ad hospitium dicti Simonis ad spoliandum dictum Simonem de bonis et catallis suis per quod dictus Simon desperans de vita sua liberavit ei dictum brasium. Et quod die Martis proxima ante festum Nativitatis sancti Johannis Baptiste ultimum preteritum [18 June 1381] viz. tempore hujus rumoris quidam Thomas Kenman manens in Holm juxta mare incitavit procuravit et congregavit diversos homines patrie ad navigandum cum eo in quadam batella in mari ad arestandum Edmundum Gurnay et Johannem de Holkam in mari navigantes et illos ibidem arestavere et fugavere usque Holmbulke per quod iidem Edmundus et Johannes desperantes de vita et de membris suis fugavere noctanter in salvatione vite eorum[1].

Item dicunt quod Johannes filius Willelmi Rychond de Walton apud Depdale die sabbati proxima post festum Corporis Christi anno regni Regis nunc quarto [15 June 1381] fecit quandam generalem proclamationem contra coronam domini Regis viz. quod si quis potuisset cepisse Edmundum Gurnay et Johannem de Holkam pro stipendio suo haberet xx. s. ac Willelmum Dauntre servientem dicti Edmundi de xx. s. in pecunia numerata felonice dispoliavit dicens quod predicti Edmundus et Johannes fuerunt proditores ac populi domini Regis communes depopulatores etc.

[Assize Roll 103. m. 4. Cambridgeshire.]

Hundredum de Arnyngford & Stowe.

Item xij Jurati ibidem dicunt quod Willelmus Vicory de Lynton & Johannis Webbe de Pampeswurth [sunt] felones associati cum Johanne Hanchach capitali ductore et Johanne Peper. Et quod ipsi die Sabbati proxima post festum Corporis Christi anno domini Regis nunc quarto [15 June 1381] fuerunt preceptores ad prosternendos domos Thome Haselden et venditores bonorum et catallorum dicti Thome ibidem et publice proclamari fecerunt tales oppresiones arsuras et proditiones silicet septies in die vel pluries in prejudicium domini Regis. Et sciendum est quod predictus Willelmus Vicory alias se reddidit prisone occasione felonie super eum existentis. Et remanet sub custodia vicecomitis. Et quod dictus Johannes Webbe die et anno predictis apud manerium Thome Haselden in Stepelmorden simul cum aliis felonibus ibidem minatus fuit diversos fideles homines de vita et membris pro eo quod noluerunt auxiliare ad prosternendos domos et edificia dicti Thome et ad alias felonias faciendas ibidem et hoc ex mera voluntate sua. Et quod idem Johannes Webbe ibidem vendidit unam tassam pisarum predicti Thome pro lx.s.

[1] The Jury of Galhowe and Brothercross state that Kenman with others "apud Holm prosequebatur Edmundum Gurney et Johannem Holkam ... et abinde usque in mari per xx leucas cum quadam batella in maximum affraiamentum predictorum Edmundi et Johannis ... et sic predictos Edmundum et Johannem fugavit usque portum de Brunham."

unde cepit in partem solutionis xij.*d.* de Thoma North in presencia Johannis Martyn de Lityngton Thome Birton et aliorum fidedignorum qui venerunt coram prefatis assignatis et jurati sunt et diligenter examinati super premissis qui ea sic esse plene testantur. Et predictus Johannes Webbe alias captus [est] per Johannem Dengayn militem et Willelmum de Notton pro suspectione mali ut testantur. Et super hoc predictus Johannes venit et de premissis allocutus est qui ea non dedicit. Ideo per discretionem dictorum assignatorum decollatus est. Et preceptum est vicecomiti quod diligenter inquirat de terris et tenementis bonis et catallis predicti Johannis ut ea in manu regis seisire faciat et domino regi inde respondere distincte et aperte etc.

[IBID. 103. m. 4.]

Item dicunt quod Galfridus Cobbe cum aliis subditis suis ignotis felonice et tanquam proditores intraverunt maneria Thome Haselden apud Geldenmordon et Stepelmordon silicet die sabbati proxima post festum corporis Christi anno domini regis nunc quarto et ibidem proclamaverunt publice fingentes se habere commissionem domini regis ad plura malefacta facienda ubi nullum habuerunt. Et vendiderunt ibidem clv quarteria brasii vj quarteria vij bussellos pisarum v quarteria ij bussellos dragii predicti Thome.

[ASSIZE ROLL 103. m. 3.]

HUNDREDUM DE WITLESFORD.

Item Jurati dicunt quod Johannes Hanchach [de Shudycamps[1]] fuit capitalis ductor malefactorum. Et quod ipse cum societate sua et potestate congregata de hominibus ignotis die Sabbati proxima post festum corporis Christi anno domini Regis nunc quarto [15 June 1381] prostravit domos Prioris Hospitalis sancti Johannis in Dokeswurth et diversa bona et catalla ibidem inventa ad valentiam xx.*li*. Ricardi Maisterman firmarii ibidem cepit et asportavit felonice in prejudicium Regis. Et per diversas inquisitiones diversorum hundredorum captas compertum est quod idem Johannes Hanchach fuit toto tempore perturbacionis equitans cum potestate vi armata sibi congregata de pluribus comitatibus. Et quod ipse fuit preceptor et ductor ad maneria Thome Haselden

[1] Thus described in another place on this Roll.

Willelmi Bateman Hospitalis de Shengeye Edmundi Walsyngham Thome Torell Rogeri Harlaston et Johannis Blauncpayn in Cantebriggia et ad alia furta prosternationes domorum et arsuras infra dictum comitatum in prejudicium Regis et magnam perturbationem populi. [*The skin here is damaged and torn but enough of the document remains to show that Hanchach was beheaded "per discretionem Hugonis le Zouch."*]

EXTRACTS FROM COTTONIAN MSS. IN BRITISH MUSEUM.

Claudius A. XII. fol. 128 b.

In die igitur sancti Dionisii, qui tunc dies fuit dominicus, in domo capitulari et tempore capitulari coram Priore, unus de complicibus provisoris, extrahens de sinu suo quasdam copias bullarum, incepit eas perlegere. Prior vero predictus attendens ad solempnitatem diei et ad prolixitatem copiarum, quarum diligens inspectio divinum servicium retardasset, rogavit eum cum magna instancia ut sibi predictas copias traderet post divinum servicium ab ipso diligenter perlegendas. Quo denegante cum aliis complicibus, surgens predictus Prior ad celebrandum divinum officium quamtocieus properabat. Surrexerunt et complices provisoris, ut dicebatur, accincti longis cultellis, id est baselards, cum maximo strepitu et tumultu, quorum unus manus suas sacrilegas cum violentia posuit in Priorem, non solum ei conviciando sed graviter comminando; et alii etiam vultum valde protervum suis fratribus ostendebant, in tantum quod Prior et qui steterunt pro parte electi de mortis periculo timuerunt. Post capitulum vero predicti fautores, nec petita licencia nec obtenta, exierunt suum claustrum transeuntes ad ecclesias parochiales ubi fuerat maxima multitudo populi congregata, quibus dixerunt voce publica licet falsa, quod predictus Prior, et qui fuerunt cum eo, voluerunt eos in domo capitulari crudeliter occidisse. Plures etiam injurias esse eis illatas per Priorem et alios confratres mendaciter retulerunt. Sic que populus, per falsam suggestionem eorum quasi ad misericordiam inclinatus, promisit eis prebere in omnibus suis agendis auxilium et favorem. Ipsos ergo ab ecclesiis parochialibus in monasterium sequebatur populus cum magno strepitu et tumultu, ubi ad magnum altare post evangelium, perturbatis ultra modum ministris, copias bullarum publice perlegerunt.

CLAUDIUS A. XII. fol. 131 b.

Eodem anno, id est tercio a principio vacacionis, ante festum sancti Johannis baptiste bene per decem dies, sumpta occasione de quadam taxa onerosa regno, videlicet duodecem denarii de capite ab anno etatis quintodecimo et supra, surrexit comitiva maledicta villanorum ruralium et rusticorum de orientali plaga anglie, id est de Cancia Essexia Suffolchia Norfolchia et de comitatibus Cantabriggie et herfordie, qui regis consilium jurisperitos generosos et potentes in regno extinguere cogitabant. Extraxerunt enim de turri london, rege ibi presente, archiepiscopum Cantuarie tunc temporis cancellarium Anglie, magistrum hospitalis sancti Johannis militem thesaurarium Anglie et eos decapitaverunt super unum moncium prope turrim. Alios eciam quam plures et precipue de Flandrensibus crudeliter necaverunt, mansum valde solempne vocatum Saveye, quod fuit ducis lancastrie, et hospitale sancti Johannis immanissime cremaverunt, et sicut ipsi londonie qui pro majori parte fuerunt de Cancia, ita alii quasi eodem tempore in predictis comitatibus surrexerunt et mala consimilia perfecerunt. Eodem tempore in comitatu Suffolchie surrexit comitiva omni bellua crudelior, que, instigata per homines de Bury, Priorem conventum et monasterium sancti Edmundi destruere proponebant. De hoc nephando proposito audiens Prior fugit de nocte ad villam de Mildenhale, ubi in domo cujusdam fidelis servientis monasterii per diem naturalem latuit in occulto. Sed undique insurgentibus hominibus maleficis cognovit se non posse diucius ibi latere. Consurgens igitur de nocte temptavit per naviculam ad eliense monasterium transfretasse, sed cum ad naviculam pervenisset, invenit ibi plures malefactores congregatos qui eum naviculam ascendere nullatenus permittebant, sed in cum frementes, tanquam homines furiosi, vix manus suas ab ictu gladii retraxerunt. (fol. 132) Tandem tamen in maxima difficultate fuit dimissus ab eis. Statim enim post, consilio infortunato disposuit se ire versus comitatum Cantabrigie, uno tantum comite ductore vel si dicam verius proditore, sed antequam potuit pertransire terminos ville de Mildenhale, bis vel ter captus fuit et detentus ab hominibus ville illius a quibus, diversis lacessitus injuriis, mortis periculum vix evasit. Tandemque cum suo ductore devenit ad quandam silvam in comitatu Cantabrigie, distantem a novo mercato quasi per tria miliaria, in qua silva latuit nimium timorosus. Ductor vero suus, vel si verius dicam proditor, simulans se velle querere necessaria ad sustentationem sue vite, rediit ad villam de Mildenhale ubi invenit quam plures de villa de Bury querentes Priorem ut mortis supplicio plecteretur. Quibus ipse proditor detexit omnia secreta Prioris et locum in quo eum poterant reperire. Quibusdam ergo illorum circumdantibus silvam per girum, alii intrabant voce furibunda clamantes "ubi latitat proditor, ubi latitat proditor." Quem apprehensum et quam plurimis injuriis lacessitum perduxerunt ad novum mercatum, ubi per noctem sequentem obprobriis et conviciis illudebant, quandoque enim coram ipso genuflectebant dicentes "ave raby," quandoque ei ciphum sine poculo propinabant, quandoque alapis eum cedentes dixerunt "prophetiza quis est qui percussit te." Sic que per totum noctis spacium fremebant et stridebant dentibus super eum, sicut in nocte cene judea gens perfida fecerat super Christum. Mane autem facto, predicti homines de Bury adduxerunt Priorem ad villam de Mildenhale, ubi ad eos confluebant maxima populi multitudo, qui omnes pro majori parte ei consimiliter illudebant clamantes et dicentes "occidatur proditor, proditor occidatur." Extrahens ergo eum de villa per spacium unius stadii, fecerunt eum descendere de equo super quem resedit et inito consilio seorsum a turba quorundam hominum de villa sancti Edmundi decretum finale populus expectabat, qui eum adjudicantes morti eum decapitandum cum populo clamitabant. Quesitus ergo spiculator, qui, facta per prius confessione a Priori cuidam sacerdoti de Mildenhale diutina et morosa, eum decapitavit gladii uno ictu. Cujus corpus truncatum inhumatum jacuit in eodem loco ab hora sexta diei sabbati usque ad crepusculum ferie quinte proxime tunc sequente. (fol. 132 b) Non enim ausus fuit conventus sepelire ejus corpus propter metum hominum de Bury, qui tam ipsum quam eos tunc summo odio habuerunt. Et quod mirum est dictu, toto illo tempore predictum corpus nec tactum fuit a canibus aut avibus, nec fetebat calore tunc nimium estuante, ubi alia corpora tunc occisa non poterant per unius diei spacium a fetere canibus et avibus preservari.

Facta capitis detruncacione statim illud in summitate lancee asportantes usque villam sancti Edmundi quam tocius properabant, et precurrente rumori volatili totus populus ville tam hominum quam mulierum ad tam horrendum spectaculum cum festinacione maxima concurrebant latrantes inter se invicem et dicentes "Ecce caput proditoris, ecce caput proditoris," "Felix sit iste dies in quo nostrum desiderium vidimus adimpletum" ululantes taliter et tumultum horribilem facientes, precedentibus buccinis, caput super collistrigium adduxerunt. In quo collistrigio appensum fuit super lanceolam caput principalis Justiciarii Anglie, qui in nocte precedente decapitatus fuit apud villam de Lakyngheth, qui fuit predicto Priori et ecclesie sancti Edmundi amicus fidelissimus, et propter hoc ut conviciebatur veresimili conjectura, mortis supplicium passus fuit. Capitibus igitur illudentes caput Prioris applicuerunt ad caput Justiciarii nunc ad auriculam quasi consilium postulando, nunc ad os ejus quasi amicicias ostendendo, volentes pro hoc eis improperare de amiciciis et consiliis que inter se invicem vita comite habuerant. Postquam vero propria illusione fuerant lacessiti, caput Prioris super collistrigium dimiserunt, que capita cum aliis de quibus dicetur, super collistrigium remanserunt quousque comes Suffolchie, bene post octo dies postea, missus fuit a rege cum quingentis lanceis ad compescendum malificos et rebelles. Suspenso enim capite Prioris in collistrigio, tota illa maledicta comitiva venit in monasterium nominans quosdam confratres, quorum unum pre ceteris petierunt, videlicet Walterum Totyngdon, quem cum invenire non poterant, petierunt alium, videlicet custodem baronie, qui licet eorum manus potuit affugisse, noluit tamen, asserens se non posse pociori causa occumbere quam pro jure sue ecclesie, quam semper pro viribus defensabat, ideo velle pro ea mortis supplicium expectare si funesta manus exigeret hoc ab eo. (fol. 133) Quidam igitur de villa, eum nimium odientes, simulantes se esse mundos a sanguine ejus, procurabant malificos de patria ut eum caperent tenerent et occiderent. Qui cum advenirent in claustro suo ubi fuerat constitutus clamabant "ubi est ille proditor," quibus ipse respondit "Non sum ego proditor, si tamen vultis me habere eccme presens asto"; clamantes igitur "invenimus proditorem" extraxerunt eum de claustro et perduxerunt ad medium fori, et ducentes eum per viam traxerunt eum hinc inde et non solum eum alapis ceciderunt sed ei plura mortis vulnera intulerunt, ita quod fuit quasi exanimis antequam ad locum predictum devenit; in quo spiculator sepcies cum percussit priusquam amputare potuit ejus caput, quod cum aliis capitibus super collistrigium posuerunt. Quo facto, venit tota illa maledicta comitiva usque monasterium pro aliis duobus fratribus ut eos consimiliter jugularent, et cognito ab illis fratribus quod pro illis venirent, preparaverunt se ad mortem, et valefacientes fratribus suis et tradentes suas zonas et cultellos infirmario, secundum morem morientium, porrexerunt ad sanctum Edmundum ab eo licentiam capientes et deo et sibi suas animas commendantes. Quo facto, per tres horas et amplius coram magno altari sue mortis executores tremuli expectabant. Sed mirabile contigit, dum fuerunt in via ad predictum flagitium perpetrandum rumor volavit quod alius frater monasterii, quem summo odio habuerunt et quesierant perprius, apud Rougham secrecius latitabat. Quo audito, unanimiter conclamant "queramus proditorem, queramus proditorem." Et cum essent extra portam orientalem in itinere usque Rougham, respicientes a tergo viderunt unum stantem in campanili superius, et estimantes illum esse quem querebant, ad monasterium redierunt, et intrantes ecclesiam transierunt per medium presbiterii usque campanile. Quo tempore et post quam diu fuerunt in ecclesia, steterunt predicti duo fratres coram magno altari mortis supplicium expectantes. Sed ipsi tam furioso annisu estuabant ad querendum alium, quod obliti sunt illorum, et dei clemencia non humana industria manus sacrilegas evaserunt. In crastino, id est die dominico, quendam valentem de patria, eo quod amicus fuit ecclesie, occiderunt et ejus caput super collistrigium suspenderunt. Eodem die venerunt (fol. 133 b) homines de villa in monasterium cum maximo strepitu et tumultu petentes sibi reddi cartas et munimenta que eorum commoditates aut privilegia concernebant, addentes quod nisi hoc facerent festinanter, tota maledicta comitiva rediret, monachos occideret et monasterium extirparet. Monachi igitur metu mortis ducti, scrutatis evidenciis, cartas et munimenta ad aulam gilde illorum in crastino detulerunt; presentibus ibi aldermanno majoribus ville et similiter tota multitudine villanorum. Que postquam receperint petierunt a Suppriori tunc temporis presidenti, a sacrista et aliis confratribus ibi existentibus scripta fieri quorum sententia talis foret, videlicet, cum provisor gauderet sua abbatia, tunc conventus cum ipso concederent eis, non solum libertates antiquas, sed eciam novas quas ipsi in posterum petere decrevissent, addentes quod vellent habere nobiliora jocalia monasterii in sua custodia quousque predicta condicio impleretur. Quod si ipsam impleri non contingeret, contradicente conventu, de predictis jocalibus suam facerent voluntatem. Frater vero provisoris, quidam dives de villa, obligavit se et omnia bona sua quod provisor gaudens suo beneficio omnes eorum petitiones perficeret juxta vota. Conventus igitur necessitate coactus tradidit eorum custodie calicem magnum de auro purissimo, similiter et crucem de ligno domini auro et gemmis nobiliter decoratam ad valorem ccc marcarum; hec enim fecerunt eo quod crediderunt provisorem in proximo suo gaudere beneficio. Sic credere moti erant eo quod maledicta comitiva de essexia, inter alias suas petitiones, exegit a rege london quod provisor extraheretur de carcere et sicut abbas suo monasterio redderetur. Quod rex metu mortis ductus annuit, sed statim postquam manum superiorem super rebelles obtinuit, non solum illud verum etiam omnia alia que invitus concesserat, revocavit. Postea vero predicti homines, suum errorem cognoscentes et regiam manum timentes, restituerunt monasterio predicta jocalia in crastino sancti dionisii, cartas et munimenta reduxerunt ad monasterium statim post natale, licet malivola voluntate. Postea vero predicta villa, propter suas transgressiones, posita fuit de consilio totius parliamenti extra proteccionem regiam, et condempnata in duobus millibus marcis quarum mille libras rex haberet pro offensa eorum contra regiam majestatem, et quingentas marcas ecclesia haberet pro suis injuriis et offensis, ut clare patere poterit respicere (fol. 134) volenti litteram regis patentem.

EXCHEQUER Q.R. INQUISITIONS. IN P.R.O.

SERIES I., FILE 1167, 4–5 RIC. II.

Inquisitio capta apud Gippewicum viij die Augusti Anno regni Regis Ricardi secundi quinto coram Willelmo Berard esceatore domini Regis in Comitatu Suffolcie virtute cujusdam brevis domini Regis eidem Willelmo directi et huic inquisitioni consuti per sacramentum Johannis Dextero etc. qui dicunt super sacramentum suum quod Thomas Sampson qui pro quibusdam proditionibus et feloniis per ipsum contra ligeanciam suam perpetratis morti adjudicatus est habuit die quo dictas proditiones et felonias fecit bona et catalla in dicto comitatu Suffolcie videlicet in primis apud Kersey in dicto comitatu.

vj stottos	*pretium*	xxx. s.
iiij boves	,,	xl. s.
v boviculos	,,	xv. s.
iij pullanos	,,	x. s.
viij porcellos	,,	viij. s.
xx ancas	,,	iij. s. iiij. d.
ij quarteria frumenti in granario	,,	x. s.
ij ,, brasii	,,	viij. s.
xvj acras frumenti	,,	xl. s.

viij acras drageti	pretium	xj. s. viij. d.
xxiiij acras pisi et avene	„	xxxij. s.
ij carectatas feni	„	iiij. s.
j tumbrellum cum j cartebonke	„	ij. s.
vetus meremium	„	ij. s.

Item dicunt quod idem Thomas habuit eodem die apud Herkested in eodem comitatu.

In camera sua iij lectos cum linthiaminibus et aliis necessariis	pretium	liij. s. iiij. d.
ij peluvia cum lavatore	„	
iij ollas eneas et alia vasa enea	„	xxx. s.
j discum argenti cum vj cocleariis argenti	„	xij. s.
ij mappas cum ij manutergiis	„	iij. s. iiij. d.
ij duodena vasa de peutre	„	vj. s. viij. d.
ij ollas de peutre ij selers de peutre	„	xvj. d.
ij plumba	„	x. s.
vasa utensilia lignea	„	vj. s. viij. d.
vj boves	„	lx. s.
viij stottos	„	xl. s.
viij vaccas	„	xl. s.
ij tauros	„	vj. s. viij. d.
ij boviculos	„	vj. s.
vj vitulos	„	vj. s.
ccc multones oves matrices et agnos	„	xv. li.
vj porcos	„	vj. s.
vj ancas	„	xij. d.
x capones	„	xx. d.
xviij acras frumenti	„	xlv. s.
xvij „ siliginis	„	xxxiiij. s.
xxiij „ ordei	„	lvij. s. vj. d.
xxvj „ pisi et avene	„	xxxiij. s. viij. d.
viij carectatas feni	„	xvj. s.
ij carectas unde j ferri	„	xiij. s. iiij. d.
ij tumbrella	„	iij. s. iiij. d.
ij carucas cum toto apparatu	„	ij. s.

Item dicunt quod idem Thomas habuit eodem die apud Freston.

iiij stottos	pretium	xx. s.
ij boves	„	xx. s

xv vaccas cum j tauro - -	*pretium*	iiij. *li.*
c hoggastres - - - -	,,	lxxv. *s.*
ij acras frumenti - - -	,,	v. *s.*
v ,, siliginis - - -	,,	x. *s.*
xxij ,, pisi et avene - -	,,	xxix. *s.* iiij. *d.*
ij carectatas feni - - -	,,	iiij. *s.*
j carectam debilem - - -	,,	ij. *s.* vj. *d.*
j carucam cum apparatu - -	,,	xij. *d.*

Item dicunt quod idem Thomas habuit eodem die octavam partem cujusdam navis vocate Waynpayn de Herewich *pretium* liij. *s.* iiij. *d.*

In cujus rei testimonium huic inquisitioni predicti jurati sigilla apposuerunt. Datum die et anno supradicto.

Summa particularum de Kersey   x. *li.* xvj. *s.*
,,   ,,   Herkested   xxxix. *li.* xvj. *s.* vj. *d.*
,,   ,,   Freston   xv. *li.*   ij. *d.*

The Escheator's Roll tells us that the above were held by "Lora," wife of Thomas Sampson, "ad opus Regis."

GENERAL INDEX.

N.B. *Names of Places are in Italics.*
The Poll Tax lists are indexed for Surnames only.

Abington, 43
Abot, 93
Achelard, 113
Acke, 83
Adam, 68, 81
Adgor, 95, 100 (2), 101 (3)
Agge, Rob., 133
Akk, 119
Alayn, 99, 100, 113
Alcombury, 107
Aldech, 116
Alderyd, 98
Aldham, 21
Aleyn, 88, 102, 103
Aleynesson, Ric., 135
Algi, 73
Algood, 87, 88
Alisander, 69, 70
Ally, 86, 87 (2)
Alman, 116 (2)
Alred, W., 130
Alston, 69, 70, 112
Alysawe, 77
Amy, 83 (2)
Anable, 73 (4), 74
Andrew, 80, 81 (2), 107
Andrew, Jo., 45
Andrew, Sim., 45
Anelye, 118
Angold, 73 (2), 76
Anneys, W., 131
Antingham, Manor of, 33
Apelthweit, 95 (4)
Apelthweyt, Rog., 129
Aquile, Edm., 134
Archere, 115
Archers, employed in riots, 32, 58
Ariford, 80
Armiger, *see* Trades and Callings
Arnald, 119 (2)
Arnington, 45
Arnold, 95 (2), 106

Artificers, 2, 67
Ashfield, 109, 110
Ashfield, Robert de, 64
Aslak, Thos., 30
Asscheman, 77
Assh, W., 130
Astone, Andrew, 8
Atered, 117
Atte Brigge, 73, 88, 97 (3)
Attebrook, Jo., 24
Atte Chaumbre, Jo., 131
Atte Church, 79 (2), 103 (2), 104 (2), 108
Atte Church, Thos., 30
Atte Cross, 98, 114, 128
Atte Crouch, 75, 76
Atte Dale, 83
Atte Fen, 73, 91, 92, 98
Atte Ford, 102
Atte Grene, 75, 83, 97, 101, 102
Atte Hach, 83 (3)
Atte Hagwe, 108
Atte Hall, 78 (2)
Atte Hawe, 81, 82 (2)
Atte Heath, W., 23
Atte Hell, 81, 82, 84, 98, 113, 118
Atte Heth, 75, 76
Atte Hooe, Nich., 134
Atte Hyll, 81, 84, 93, 97 (2), 98, 113, 118, *see also* Atte Hell
Atte Hyll, Jo., 33
Atte Lee, 98
Attemer, 71
Atte Moor, 84
Atte Ook, Thos., 133
Atte See, 116 (2)
Atte Well, 79 (2)
Atte Wode, 101
Attwyk, Ralph, 14
Aubrey, Jo., 65
Aubry, 69, 77, 89, 110 (2)
Aunsel, 88
Aylemer, 92, 118

10—2

GENERAL INDEX.

Aylnot, 68
Ayloch, 68 (2)
Aylsham, 34

Baa, 103 (3)
Babraham, 44 (2)
Backe, 99
Bacon, Nich., 62
Bacon, Sir Rog., 3, 26, 28, 30, 32, 33, 132; Trial of, 39
Baconsthorpe, 26
Baday, 94
Badele, 90
Badynhale, 102
Bakoun, 109
Baldry, 104 (4), 105
Baldwene, 79 (2), 111
Balle, Jo., 3, 54, 55
Balsham, 46
Bambonn, 87
Banyngham, 96 (2)
Banyngham, W., 129
Barat, 72, 103, 104, 111
Barat, Geof., 130
Barat, Jo., 130
Barbour, 86, 90
Barbour, Jo., 128
Barbour, Rob., 53
Barbour, Sim., 12
Bardolf, 94
Bare, 76
Bareleg, 78
Barenton, 43
Barfot, Gilb., 128
Barker, 76, 78 (4), 85, 97 (2), 100, 113, 118 (2)
Barker, Rob., 131
Barking, 23
Barningham, 37
Barnwell Priory, attack on, 53; Prior of, 53
Baron, 69, 78, 93, 119
Barr, Thos., 46
Barrow, 67
Barton Mills, 38; Court Rolls of, 64
Barwe, 82
Basely, 105 (2)
Bassat, 117
Bassingbourn, 44
Bataille, Rob., 131
Batalye, Rog., 134
Bateman, 101
Bateman, W., 45, 138
Batisford, 73
Battisford, Jo., 22, 127
Bauleie, 96 (3)
Bawdsey, 24, 25
Baxtere, 86 (3), 104 (2), 109, 113
Bayly, 76, 107, 108
Baylye, Hen., 134
Bayn, 111 (2)

Beccles, 24
Beconn, 88
Bedell, W., 51
Bedingfield, Jas. de, 3, 21, 22, 26, 130 (2)
Bedingfield, Sir P. de, 21
Bedoun, 91
Belamy, 83
Bele, 68, 72 (2), 112, 118 (2)
Belhous, 99
Benacre, 116
Bencold, 118
Benet, 78 (2), 87 (2), 98, 113
Beneth, 75, 100
Benington, 78
Benne, 105, 106 (2)
Bentley, 3, 22, 127
Benton, 111 (2)
Berard, W., 143
Berche, 102
Berd, 82
Bere, 109 (2)
Bereiweie, 96 (2)
Berew, 102
Berewyke, 36
Bergholt, 23
Beri, 96
Bernard, 75, 87
Bernard, W., 128
Bernerewe, 71
Berney, Tho., 120
Berningham, 88
Berton, 85, 87, 88
Bessingham, 37
Bessingham, Jo. de, 37
Beste, 100
Bethwold, 90
Bette, 107, 111
Bettes, 73, 118 (2), 119
Bettes, Hen., 28
Bettes, Jo., 131
Betteson, 104 (2), 105
Beverle, Jo., 128
Billokby, 131
Billyngford, 120
Binham, 27, 34, 35
Birton, Thos., 137
Bischop, 114
Bixton, Walt. de, 30
Blackborne, Hundred of, 102
Black Death, effects of, 1, 3, 64, 74
Blake, 95
Blankgren, Ric., 50
Blankgren, Rog., 50
Blankpayn, Jo., 52, 138
Blauncpayn, 103 (2), 104
Blaxhale, 99, 100
Blechepayl, 92
Blek, 83
Blithing, Hundred of, 115
Blofield, Thos. de, 133

Blok, 77
Blower, 101
Blower, Hen., 134
Bocher, 86, 93
Bogeys, 75, 76 (2)
Bokele, 115
Bokelerplayer, Jo., 36
Bokenham, 26, 132
Bol, 102
Boldiro, 96
Bole, 69 (2), 70, 96 (2), 100 (3), 105
Bole, Rog., 133
Bolynge, 116
Bond, 83, 96 (4), 116 (2)
Bonecold, 103, 113
Boneyr, 112
Bonys, 78 (2)
Boor, 94
Borel, 78, 87
Bosard, 111 (2)
Bosmere, Hundred of, 23
Boteler, 109, 111
Boteler, Jo., 131
Botonn, 105, 106
Bottisham, 42
Bouel, 95
Bouneud, 83
Boure, 99
Bourgh, Jo. de, 126
Bowel, 113
Boyboy, 105
Boydon, 103
Boydyn, 74 (2), 75, 84
Boyler, 77
Boyo, 90
Boys, 68
Boys, Rog. de, 24
Bradley, 81
Bradwell, 24
Braham, 115
Bramfield, 23
Brandon Ferry, 28
Branncestre, 135
Bras, 108
Brastrete, 91
Bray, Ad., 12, 129
Brecete, 95 (4)
Bregge, 101
Brend, 77 (2), 84
Brese, 76, 79 (2)
Brethenham, 80, 86
Brethenham, Clem., 25
Breton, 92, 93, 103
Brettham, 135
Brewes, Jo. de, 31, 38
Brewster, 96, 110
Bricete, 76 (2)
Brid, 87
Brigg, 97
Brigge, atte, 73, 88, 97 (3)
Brigham, 133, 134
Brockley, 67, 71

Brok, 117 (4)
Brokleygh, 69, 70 (2)
Bron, 99
Bronewyn, 88
Bronger, 131
Broun, 98, 112, 118
Brounfield, Edm., 15, 16, 19, 20
Browe..., 100
Brown, 95
Brownyng, 86, 112 (2)
Browster, 96
Brung, Jo., 133
Brungor, 97 (2)
Brustal, 68
Bryd, 109
Brynkele, Jo., 14
Brythren, 85
Bucher, Hug., 134
Bucklesham, 22
Buk, 79
Buk, Jo., 48
Bulbrok, 84, 85
Bulcamp, 117
Bullok, 76, 80, 82, 83, 87, 88
Bumsted, Thos. de, 132, 133
Bunnynge, 82 (2)
Buntyfeld, 83
Buntyng, 106, 119
Burell, W., 120
Burgeys, 105, 108
Burgeys, Thos., 134
Burgh, 119
Burghard, 115
Burkyn, 116
Burnham, 35
Burs, 100
Burwell, 42, 45
Bury St Edmunds, 7, 11, 34, 57, 127; Alderman of, 127; Fined for Riots, 21, 143; Guildhall Meeting at, 20; Riots at, 19
Bury St Edmunds, *Abbey of*, Almoner of, 7; Attacks on, 16, 19, 141; Number of Monks in, 16; Prior of, *see* Cambridge, Jo. de; Provisor appointed to, 15; Violence in Chapter House, 15, 138
Busch, 112
Busschop, 77
Buttre, 80
Buxhall, 92
Buxlow, 115
Buxton, 27, 131
Byl, 90
Byllyng, 118 (2)
Byschop, 117

Cage, 84 (4), 85, 111
Caistor, 33
Cake, 87, 88, 97, 102 (3)
Cakebred, 93, 103
Cakestrete, 91

Caketon, 94
Calcher, 86
Calf, 68, 73 (2), 102 (2), 103
Calfawe, 82
Calle, 68
Calve, 68
Calwere, Thos., 131
Cambridge, 38, 44; *Bridge Street*, 55;
  Carmelite Monastery at, 51; *Corpus Christi Coll*. attacked, 51;
  Estenhall in, 53; *le Pety Cure in*, 52; Mayor of, 42, 53; Mayor
  of, his trial, 53; Riots at, 49;
  St Giles, 50; *St Mary's* attacked,
  51; *St Mary's*, Chest in, 51, 52
Cambridge University, Chan. of, 14;
  Charters of, burnt, 50, 52
Cambridge, Jo. de, 11, 17; his flight,
  17, 139; murder of, 18, 140
Cambridgeshire, Sheriff of, 44
Campaignoun, Ric., 128
Candlesby, Hug., 52, 53
Canon, 78 (2), 93, 94 (2)
Canterbury, Archbishop of, murdered, 42
Caperoun, 95
Capgrave, Jo., his account of events
  in Norfolk, 37; his account of
  events at Cambridge, 55
Capons, 95
Cappe, 113
Cardinal of St Angelo, 23
Cardoun, 101
Carleton, Ph. de, 132
Carpenter, 76
Carpon, 74
Carrow Priory, 32, 34
Carter, 70, 71, 78, 79, 82, 90, 93,
  99, 101, 102, 103, 109, 112
Castel, 86
Castleacre, 31
Caston, 134
Castre, 131
Catelyn, 87
Caunseler, 78, 81 (2)
Cavendish, 10, 11, 14
Cavendish, Jo. de, 11, 12, 14, 18;
  murder of, 13, 126, 141
Cavenham, 83, 84, 86
Cawynham, 71
Chachevache, Jo., 26, 132
Chadenhalk, 87
Chaloner, 90, 118
Chapeleyn, 72
Chapman, 72, 85 (3), 88, 113 (2),
  see Schapman
Charlys, 93
Chaumber, 114
Chaumbre, Jo. atte, 131
Chaundeler, 90, 113
Chaunteler, 93
Chawseler, 74

Chelisworth, 113
Chene, 99
Chese, 90, 91
Chestey, 81
Chetebere, 78
Chevington, 67, 70
Chief Constable, 21, 33, 131
Child, W., 131
Childerhous, 90, 115
Childreston, 85 (3), 86, 87, 88
Childrous, 91
Chippenham, 44
Choke, 78
Chosele, Nic., 135
Christemasse, 82, 100, 106
Church, atte, 30, 79 (2), 103 (2),
  104 (2), 108
Church Property, attacks on, 34
Chyld, 71
Chynchere, 112
Cisterne, 117
Clakke, Jo., 16
Clare, 62
Clark, *see* Clerk
Claver, 85, 106
Claydon, Hundred of, 23
Clement, 72, 76 (2), 89, 91, 102 (2),
  109, 110, 118
Clement, Rad., 129
Clenewall, 77
Cler, 100
Clere, 72, 83
Clere, W., 33
Clericus, 115
Clerk, 75 (3), 77, 81, 85 (2), 90, 93,
  94, 105 (2), 106, 111
Clog, Thos., 133, 134
Clubbe, 90
Clubs of Working Classes, 2, 57;
  funds of, 65
Clymme, Ad., 49
Clytermere, 104
Cobat, Jo., 22
Cobbe, 92, 94, 98
Cobbe, Geof., 44
Cobbe, W., 44, 47
Cobold, 96
Cock, 112
Codynham, 100
Cok, 113
Cok, W., 128
Coke, 106
Cokedon, 81
Cokeman, 75, 98 (2)
Coker, 92
Cokerel, 75, 92, 93, 95, 96 (2),
  99, 100
Cokewald, 106
Coldhacle, 90, 100 (2)
Cole, 88, 102, 103
Cole, Jo., 131
Cole, —, 60

GENERAL INDEX. 151

Colermaker, 114
Colisson, Jo., 128
Colkyrke, 73
Colle, Geof., 134
Colman, 102, 111
Colman, Thos., 37
Colman, Walt., 19
Colyn, Thos., 36
Combe, W., 46
Combes, 99, 129
Coneynhton, 87
Coo, 91
Cook, 89, 90, 93, 97(5), 102(2), 108, 109
Cook, Geof., 129
Cook, Jo., 32
Cook, Ric., 131
Cook, Simon, 28
Cope, 95
Copinger, 92
Coppedok, 128
Copping, 104(3)
Copping, Hervey, 33
Copping, Jo., 33
Coray, 114
Corby, Rob. de, 42
Cordde, 91, 92
Cordwainer, *see* Schordwaner
Cornerd, Thos., 3, 12
Cornish, Hen., 36
Corper, 98(2)
Coselere, Walt., 24
Cosford, Hundred of, 111
Costard, 93
Costyn, 87, 88, 111
Cosyn, 119
Cote, 86, 87
Cottenham, 43, 52
Cotton, 86(2), 87(2)
Counte, 96
Couper, 71, 76, 82, 86, 93, 95(3), 107, 113, 118
Couper, W., 32
Court Rolls destroyed, 21, 23, 24, 32, 33, 34, 37, 46, 49, 62
Coventry, 32
Coventry, Jo., 28, 36
Coyfe, 111
Crane, 91(2), 100, 105, 106, 118(2)
Crane, Thos., 128
Crane, W., 129
Craneworth, 133
Cratfield, 130
Crembyl, 112
Cres, 103
Cressener, 69, 70
Cretyng, 94(2)
Creyk, Jo., 134
Crinyte, 102
Crofford, 116(2)
Cros, 92
Cross, atte, 98, 114, 128

Crouch, atte, 75, 76
Crowes, 110
Crows, 109
Croydon, 44
Cubith, *see* Kybit
Cukhok, 113
Culford, 116
Cullyng, Ric., 131
Culpho, 23
Cur..., 102
Cursun, W., 120
Curteys, Jo., 33
Customs, Manorial, 65
Cut, 116
Cuttyng, 95(2)
Cytlyng, 113

Dagworth, 97, 129
Dale, 83, 100, 107
Dalkys, 99(2), 100
Dallyng, 116(2)
Damysfelde, 113
Dane, 76(2)
Danyel, 82
Dapys, 114
Dasach, 116
Dauntre, W., 136
Dawe, 76
Dawes, 88
Dawes, Jo., 131
Dawys, 102
Daye, 106
Dayoa, 119
Dedmor, 133
Deke, 68
Dekne, 68
Demayne, Jo., 134
Den, 114
Denarstone, 113
Dengayn, Jo., 137
Denham, Geof., 18, 19
Denington, 21
Densi, 96(3)
Depdale, 136
Dereham, 134
Derhawe, 116(3)
Desing, Hen., 128
Deth, 84
Dexter, 90, 113
Dexter, Jo., 143
Deye, 68(2), 71(2), 75(2), 79, 81, 84, 90, 100, 103, 115, 117
Deye, Jo., 48
Deynissone, 105
Dicere, 71
Dilham, 29, 132
Ditton Valence, 44
Dobbys, 113
Dockyng, 73
Dockyng, W. de, 135
Doke, 105
Dokes, 119

Dokeswurth, 137
Dolyngham, 84
Domynyk, Simon, 14
Donewych, 82
Donne, 72, 105, 119
Donnison, 115
Donyton, 84
Doo, W., 131
Doraunt, 68, 80, 81
Dotemay, 119
Dounesby, Geo. de, 57, 127
Dowe, 79 (2)
Doye, 100
Drake, 112
Drake, W., 133
Dranton, 90
Draper, 118, 134
Drinkeston, 128
Drinkeston, 118
Driwer, 77
Dromer, 115
Droughte, 103
Dullingham, 45
Dun, 72 (2), 77
Dunch, 94
Dunken, 95, 97
Dye, 83
Dygge, 108
Dyke, 85 (2)
Dyx, Thos., 134

East Dereham, 36, 133
East Rudham, 134
Eccles, Reg. de, murder of, 30, 132
Edryck, 72 (2)
Edward, 92 (3), 105, 109
Edwardstone, 3, 12
Eldesen, 107, 108
Elfred, 105
Elmham, 87 (2)
Elmham, W., 126
Elmswell, 114 (2)
Elmswell, 14
Elvedon, 86, 87
Ely, Prior of, 33, 46; Sacrist of, 47
Ely, riots at, 47
Elyman, 87
Elys, W., 32
England, state of, temp. Ric. II., 3
English, Hen., 44
Ereswell, 85
Eston, 89, 91, 101
Eston, Jo., 128
Eston, W., 129
Estryle, 119
Eton, 86
Euges, Marg. de, 32
Euston, 103
Everard, 85
Eversden, 48
Eyk, 25, 128

Eyr, Peter le, 43

Falis, 71
Falledew, 111, 114
Fancebroun, 93 (2)
Fastolf, Alex., 132
Fastolf, Hug., 24, 32
Fastolf, Jo., 33, 132
Faus, 111
Fayrchild, 84 (2)
Fectere, 96
Fede, 107
Fedeler, Jo., 46
Felbrigg, 37
Felmingham, 26, 28, 39, 132
Felthorp, 30
Feltwell, 31
Felyrs, 88
Feu, atte, 73, 91, 92, 98
Fenhowe, 86, 88
Fenkele, 102
Fenkele, W., 129
Fenman, 119
Fermer, 96, 98, 101
Ferour, 91
Ferr, 68
Filmond, Ric., 27, 28, 51, 131
Finborough Magna, 91, 129
Fisher, 87, 88, 107, 118
Flecher, 90
Fleded, 116
Fleg, 84
Flempton, 67, 71, 72
Flempton, 79 (2)
Fletcher, Rob., 36, 135
Fletcher, Thos., 23
Flory, Rob., 134
Folcreed, Simon, 131
Folke, 93, 115
Folkmere, 105, 106 (2)
Fool, 117 (2)
Foot, 92, 93
Forbishour, Thos., 51, 54
Ford, 107, 118
Ford, atte, 102
Fordham, 13
Foreigner, a, leader in riots, 24
Foreigners attacked by rioters, 32, 61, 63, 135
Fornham All Saints 67, 72
Forth, 108
Fot, 71
Fouke, 70, 75
Foul, 81
Fouldon, 87
Frame, 74, 75
Frary, 118 (2)
Fraul, 93
Fraunces, W., 22, 128
Fraunceys, 86, 118 (2), 119
Fraw, 96
Freman, 70

GENERAL INDEX.   153

Fremond, 86
French Admiral, 21
Frenchman, 95
Frend, 89, 91 (2), 99 (2)
Frend, Ad., 129
Frenssh, 110
Frere, 119
Freshingfield, 130
Freston, 144
Freston, Jo. de, 30
Freton, 93, 98 (2)
Frie, 90
Froissart, Jo., 27, 29, 31
Frost, 73 (2), 90
Fryote, 82
Fulhond, 75, 76
Fuller, 71, 75, 86, 106, 114 (2), 115
Furbesshor, 89
Fut, 113
Fynch, 119
Fyncham, Jo., 121
Fysshe, 77

Galon, Edm., 48
Galyon, Ad., 133
Gamen, Kath., 13
Gandawe, 77
Gandawys, 106 (2)
Gannuld, 97
Gardener, 69, 70, 77, 88, 99, 101 (2)
Gardener, Jo., 129
Garlek, 114
Garveys, Rob., 32
Gastoun, 111
Gautron, 68
Gaysle, 99
Gazeley, 44
Ged, 87
Geffrey, 95
Geg, 108
Gekes, 75
Geldore, W., 31
Gennote, 86, 87 (2)
Gentil, 92
Gentilhomme, Jo., 27, 28, 131
Gerard, 101 (2), 102 (2), 103 (3)
Gerard, Jo., 22
Gerard, W., 21
Gernon, 104, 109
Geulond, 111
Gibonn, Jo., 44, 51
Gilbert, 87
Gilbert, Thos., 128
Gilbonn, 85, 86
Gilden Morden, 44, 137
Gipping Newton, 97, 129
Gislingham, 21, 129
Gissing, *see* Gyssing
Glanvill, Geo., 25
Glanvill, Mat., 25
Glanvill, W., 129
Glanvill, 99, 101

Glesne, 100
Gobbe, 99
Gobelet, 97
Gobet, 76 (2)
Goche, 72, 86
Godard, 105, 118
Godfrey, 77 (4), 78, 80, 113
Godhall, 75
Godwene, 80
Goldford, 78
Goldwyn, 87
Goldyng, 77 (4), 101, 102
Goldyng, Jo., 129
Goney, 101
Goode, Ad., 131
Goodwyn, 118 (2), 119
Goos, 77, 105
Gos, 76
Gosford, Jo., 7
Gosse, 72
Gosselene, 101 (2)
Gowene, 111
Goye, 111
Goyer, 113
Grafton's Chron., 10
Grantchester, Jas., 50
Grantchester, Thos., 50
Graunt, Edm., 128
Gravele, Rob. de, 31
Green Wax, Rolls destroyed, 49
Gregory, 86, 88
Grene, 92, 96, 119
Grene, atte, 75, 83, 97, 101, 102
Grenefeld, 103
Grenegres, 102 (2)
Greyne, 85 (2), 112
Greyston, Jo., 42, 57
Grom, 69
Gundel, 86, 88
Gundre, 100
Gunne, 99
Gunneld, Jo., 46; Nich., 46
Gunnild, 102
Gunnyld, 118
Guntre, 90
Gunyld, W., 131
Gurnay, 95
Gurney, Edm., 35, 135, 136
Gybon, Laur., 134
Gyle, 83 (2), 85
Gylles, 118
Gylley, 119
Gyrling, 100
Gyssing, Thos. de, 3, 26, 40, 132
Gyssok, 113
Gyste, 95

Hach, atte, 83 (3)
Hadenham, 44
Hadleigh, 111
Hagwe, atte, 108
Hakebeche, Rob., 120

GENERAL INDEX.

Hakoun, 92
Haldene, 117
Hales, Jo., 120
Hales, Rob. de, murdered, 42
Hales, Stephen, 31, 120
Halesworth, Thos., 16, 18, 19
Halle, 98
Halle, atte, 78 (2)
Halsted, 87 (2), 88 (2)
Hamond, 68, 71, 87, 98 (4), 102 (2), 113
Hamond, Jo., 129
Hampton, 97
Hanchach, Ann, 44
Hanchach, Jo., 44, 45, 51, 136, 137, 138
Hanlyn, 82
Hanworth, 37
Harald, Jo., 131
Hardhefd, 97
Hardy, 87
Hare, 92, 105
Hardfot, 71
Harg..., 88
Hargham, 118
Hargrave, 67, 73
Harksted, 22, 144
Harleston, 45, 98
Harleston, Rog., 43, 52, 138
Harlyng, 105
Harre, 93
Harsyk, Jo., 120
Hartismere, Hundred of, 114
Hary, 78
Hascard, 104
Haselden, Thos., 44, 45, 136, 137
Hashard, 100
Hassele, 96
Hastyng, W., 120
Haukyn, 82, 83
Hawe, atte, 81 (3), 82 (2)
Hawsted, 67, 74
Hayl, 112
Haynford, 33
Heath, W. atte, 23
Hebyl, 75
Hecham, 36, 135
Hegeman, 68
Hegsete, 98
Heigham, 30
Heigham Potter, 131
Helgey, Gil., 44
Hell, 98, 101, 108 (2)
Hell, atte, 81, 82, 98, *see also* Atte Hyll
Hemgrave, *see* Hengrave
Hemmyng, 112
Hemyng, Edm., 32
Hemysby, 72
Hengham, Thos. de, 37
Hengrave, 67, 75
Hengrave, 76

Hensted, Hundred of, 33
Herist, 83
Herkested, see Harksted
Herlyng, 134
Herlyng, Jo. de, 133
Hermer, 77 (3), 81 (2)
Herringswell, 21
Hers, 119
Herst, 113
Hert, 89
Hervy, 79, 90
Heryngwell, 82 (2)
Hessete, 96
Heth, atte, 75, 76
Hethe, 81 (4), 82, 119
Hevingham, 120
Hevy, 98
Hewes, 111
Heydón, 31
Heydone, 113
Heyham, 93
Heyr, 105
Heyr, the, 79
Heyward, 75 (2), 82
Hibele, 69 (2)
Hill, *see* Atte Hyll
Hillesone, 106
Hinderclay, 105
Hobert, W., 131
Hog, 106, 107
Hog, Jas., 46
Hok, 96
Hoketon, 73 (2)
Holboy, 110 (2)
Holdernesse, 82
Holgate, 115
Holkam, Jo. de, 35, 135, 136
Holland, 24
Hollesley, 24, 25
Hollesley, Jo., 131
Holm, 68, 87
Holm, 135 (2)
Holmbulke, 136
Holt, 35
Holterelyn, 90
Homite, 109
Hoo, 71, 90 (2), 91 (2), 96 (2), 102
Hoo, 133
Hooc, 99
Hooe, atte, 134
Hoòt, 87, 99
Hoppere, 75
Hopton, 82
Hore, 69, 70 (2)
Horn, 73, 104
Horning, 131
Horningsheath Mag., 67, 76
Horningsheath Parva, 67, 77
Horold, 81
Horsecroft, 80 (2)
Hosbond, 94
Hosier, Simon, 51, 54

GENERAL INDEX.

Hotost, 101
Hotot, 89, 91, 95, 102 (3)
Houtot, see Hotot
Howard, 82
Hoxne, archers of, 58, 130
Hoxne, Hundred of, 21, 130
Hubert, 89
Hulet, 88
Hunstanton, 36, 135
Hunt, 104, 105
Huntingfield, Jo., 128
Huntingdon, 128
Hurt, 75
Husk, 92
Hyll, *see* Atte Hyll
Hyne, le, 87 (3), 88
Hynks, W., 131

Ibry, W., 133
Icklingham, 38
Ickworth, 78 (2)
Ickworth, 67, 78
Ide, 71, 75
Iken, 119
Ikesworth, Jo., 36
Iklington, 46
Ilbert, 104
Illeye, Ric., 120
Indictments, Antient, 7, 126-136
Indyben, Rog., 128
Ingold, 108
Ingrode, Step., 134
Inquisition, Escheator's, 143
Ipswich, assizes at, 64; *Carmelites'
   House in*, 16; riots at, 22; St
   Stephen's, Rector of, 22
Iryng, Gilb., 129
Isbel, Thos., 131
Isleham, 44
Iteryngham, 121
Ixning, Thos., 46
Ixworth, parson of, 16
Ixworth Thorp, 106

Jackysone, 100
Jade, 103 (6)
Jakelyn, 107 (2)
Jay, 93, 109
Jebbys, 117 (2)
Jent, 76
Jerveys, Thos., 131
Jery, 100
Jour, 91
Joy, 93
Joyze, 118
Judy, 105
Julle, 81 (2), 83
Jurymen, Lists of, 128, 129, 131, 134
Justise, 113

Katerineson, 94

Kegyl, 100
Kelfynch, 85, 87
Kellyng, Aug., 44
Kempe, Jo., 45
Keneld, 101
Keneman, 108
Keniston, 134
Kenman, Thos., 35, 135
Kenne, 109
Kennygale, 79
Kent, 74, 87, 90, 93, 102 (2)
Kent, 60
Kentford, 109
Ker, 101
Kersey, 143
Kertlyng, 74, 75
Kes, 75
Kessingland, 115
Ketel, W., 121
Keteryngham, 90
Ketleston, 34
Ketyl, 68
Kik, Jo., 32
Kirkley Road, 32
Kirkowe, 87
Knattishall, 104
Knighton, Hen., 6, 10
Knot, 119
Knyt, 104
Knyth, 77, 82, 103
Koo, le, 80 (2)
Koune, 118
Kybit, William, 28, 32, 38
Kymberly, W. de, 34
Kynch, 77
Kyneyston, 68
Kyng, 97 (3), 101 (2)
Kyng, Jo., 129
Kyppyng, 74 (2), 81
Kytebote, 87

Labourers, 2, 67
Lacford, 77 (2)
Lackford, 67, 79
Lacy, 97, 101
Lacy, Nich., 128
Lacy, W., 32
Ladde, Jo., 132
Lakenheath, 13, 17, 21, 126, 141
Lakenheath, Edm. de, 21, 22, 130
Lakenheath, Jo. de, execution of, 19
Lamber, 83
Lamberd, 84 (2)
Lambyn, 108
Lancaster, Duchy of, Steward of, 35; Registers of, 31, 44
Lancaster, Duke of, his supposed connection with rising, 60; unpopularity of, 59
Lane, 68, 71, 96
Lane, In the, 81

GENERAL INDEX.

Langemere, 87, 88, 92, 93
Langeton, 107
Langford, 31
Langham, 107
Langham, 76, 107 (2)
Langham, Step. de, 61
Langlyf, 90, 91 (2)
Langlyf, W., 129
Lanwade, 85
Lardy, 87
Lark, The river, 38
Larke, 95
Larlyng, 118
Lavenham, 11, 46
Lawney, 81 (2)
Leaders of Rising, see Rioters
Lee, 98
Leg, 90 (2)
Leg, Jo., 6
Legat, 93
Legt, 87
Leman, 102
Lemmer, 94
Lenedey, 104 (2)
Lenegor, 91, 92
Leneve, 103, 104
Lenote, 108
Lenyng, 119
Lerling, 96 (2)
Letyl, 98, 99
Levyrmere, 93
Lewote, 77
Leycester, Ric. de, 47, 48
Lilye, 98
Lincolnshire, messenger from, at Bury, 57, 127
Linton, 44, 48, 136
Lister, 86
Lister, Edm., 53
Lister, Geof., 26, 27, 28, 31, 32, 35, 37, 132; slain by the Bishop, 27, 39
Lister, Jo., 27, 35, 52
Lister, Thos., 52, 54
Lister, W., 27
Liston, 9, 10
Litster, Jekke, 38, 39
Litster, Thos., 47
Littlehawe, Manor of, 64; Nativi of, 64; Customs of, 65
Littleport, 33, 46
Lityngton, 137
Loche, 117, 118
Lof, 119
Loksmith, 86
Loksmyth, Rog., 135
Lomb, Thos., 33
Lomyner, Hen., 30
London, 42, 43
Longcham, Jo. de, 133
Long Melford, 9, 14
Lose, 119

Love, 119
Lowys, 100
Lowestoft, 24
Lucas, 103 (2)
Lucas, Rod., 36, 133
Lyly, 68 (4)
Lymghook, 117, 118, 119
Lyncoln, Thos., 46
Lyng, 70
Lyng, 134
Lynn, 28, 35, 38, 39, 121, 135; *Bokenham's place in*, 36; *Cokrowe in*, 36
Lyonn, 113
Lyons, Ric., 10

Mabbesson, 104
Mabylonn, 111
Macworth, Ric., 44
Madour, Jo., 37
Maisterman, Ric., 137
Malkyn, 100
Malle, 115
Malt, W., 45
Man, 88 (2), 99, 105, 109
Manning, 86, 97, 104
Mannyng, Mar., 133
Manser, 91, 96
Manton, Walt., 25
Manuscript Authorities, Antient Indictments, 7, 126–136; Assize Rolls, 7, 41, 64, 136–138; Cottonian MS., 8, 138, 139; L.T.R. Enrolled Accts., 120, 123; Subsidy Rolls, Lay, 67
Manysbody, 100
Maraille, 116
Marchal, 109, 110 (3)
Marchand, 89
Margret, W., 45
Mariot, 88
Markys, 97
Marl..., 95
Marleford, 25
Marscal, 113
Marsh, W., 24
Marshall, Jo., 34
Martyn, 70, 71, 87, 95, 99, 119 (4)
Martyn, Ad., 29, 132
Martyn, Jo., 137
Martyn, Ric., 52, 53
Martyn, S., 13
Mason, 72, 73, 107, 110
Masselyn, 95
Massote, 68
Massyn, 95
Massyngham, Jo. de, 134; Nich. de, 28
Massyon, 118
Mateshall, Vicar of, 132, 133
Mauger, 101, 102
Mauncer, 113

GENERAL INDEX. 157

Mawpas, Nich., 36
Mayhew, 69 (2), 70 (2), 71, 72
Maykyn, 107
Mayner, 88 (2)
Maynere, Ric., 134
Mayster, 71, 79, 80, 81 (3)
Medwe, 113, 115
Mekke, 88
Meleway, 101
Melforth, 114 (2)
Melk, 71
Melle, 114 (2)
Meller, 70, 71, 82 (2), 83, 85, 89, 91, 95, 100, 108 (2), 109, 111–114
Melton, 22, 127, 128
Members of Parliament attacked, 22, 23, 29, 30, 32, 52, 63
Mendham, 131
Menewood, 84, 85 (2)
Mentyl, 111
Mere, 98
Merel, 81
Mery, 71
Meryel, 68 (5)
Mesham, 93
Messager, 86, 88, 89
Metfield, W. de, 28
Methwold, 28
Methwold, Jo. de, 31
Mettingham Castle, 24, 57, 61
Mey, 101, 119
Michel, Geof., 46
Michel, Jo., 46, 131
Middleton, 117
Mildenhall, 13, 14, 17, 18, 25, 34, 85, 126, 139, 140; *Heath*, 18, 19; Vicar of, 14
Mildman, 88
Milicent, Jo., 134
Miller, Mat., 14
Millere, 87 (3)
Mincin, 116
Mitte, 113
Monchesey, Th., 3, 12
Montenay, Jo. de, 26, 40, 132
Monteney, Thos. de, 133
Moor, 94
Moor, atte, 84
Morel, 118
Moriel, 102
Morieux, Thos., 7, 31, 126
Morlee, W. de, 31
Morley, 87, 88 (2)
Morley, Thos. de, 38
Mors, 75
Moryel, 74, 75
Mot, 99, 100
Motonn, 96 (3)
Motonn, Jo., 129
Mounpelers, 94
Mountys, 117
Mower, 75, 79

Mud, 68
Muggard, 112
Mulberye, 86
Multon, 96
Mundeford, 84
Mundegome, 98
Munk, 115
Murwell, 83
Mushold Heath, 27, 29, 132; meeting at, 28
Mustardar, 86, 88
Mutford, Hundred of, 115
Mylys, 93

Naunton, 93
Navys, 82
Neb, 85, 86
Needham, 23
Neel, 93, 96
Neeys, 112
Neith, 84
Nel, 112
Neng, 70
Netherstrete, 96
Neteshird, 33
Neue, 91, 92, 114, 115
Neuman, 98, 101, 119
Neuton, 97
Neve, 90, 91, 106
Newelle, Thos. de, 133
Newhawe, 77
Newhous, 116
Newman, 97, see Neuman
Newmarket, 14, 17
Nicole, 71, 73, 118
Noble, 77
Noon, Jo., 134
Noon, Rob., 134
Noreys, Jo., 52
Norfolk, Countess of, 24
Norfolke, 75
Norman, 68 (2), 80, 81, 82, 84
North, W., 43
Northern, 86
Northern, Jo., 25
North Walsham, 37, 131; date of encounter at, 37; encounter at, 39
Northumberland, 4
Norwich, 27, 31, 38, 39, 121; riots at, 28–30
Norwich, Archdeacon of, 30
Norwich, Bishop of, 34, 36, 38, 55, 67, 135; fined by the king, 61
Norwich, Jo. de, 58
Norys, Geof., 134
Note, 104
Nottinghamshire, 54
Nottynge, 71
Nowton, 67, 80
Nugge, 110
Nysc, 119

GENERAL INDEX.

Odam, 87
Ode, 102 (2)
Okele, 83
Old, Jo., 128
Old Newton, 95, 128, 129
Oliground, 117
Onehouse, 98
Ook, atte, 133
Organisation of movement, 57
Ormer, 96
Orwell, 44
Osbern, 71, 82 (2), 92, 97, 102
Osbern, Jo., 127
Osborn, 119
Osburn, 71 (2)
Osbun, 110 (3)
Ossegut, 119
Otysdole, 107
Overstrand, 37
Oxeford, Jo., 62

Pachat, 93, 94
Padenhale, 101, 102
Padinak, W., 134
Page, 71, 74 (2), 78, 79 (2), 81, 82 (2), 86
Page, Jo., 131
Pakenham, 98, 99, 106
Pakenham, Hen., 121
Pakkeman, 103 (2), 104
Pakynham, *see* Pakenham
Palmer, Jo., 134
Palmere, 96
Pampeswurth, 136
Panton, Ralf., 135
Papworth, 44
Parfay, Geof., 12, 129
Parham, Rector of, 25
Park, 78
Parker, 118
Parmater, 86
Parmeter, 88
Partre, 90, 91
Partrich, 85
Parys, 74, 85, 111
Pascale, 80
Pattemere, 110
Payn, 72 (2), 73 (2), 93-95, 111
Payn, Thos., 128
Paynot, Thos., 36
Pedder, Jo., 13
Pedebef, 112
Peke, 71
Pelle, 112
Penne, 86, 88 (2)
Penrith, 3
Penyman, 88
Peper, Jo., 48, 136
Perdon, 119
Perot, 119
Perrers, Alice, 10
Pers, Edm., 134

Pers, Ric., 134
Personnesman, 106
Pese, 113
Petel, 114
Petrisburg, 86
Peyntor, 100
Peytevyn, 82 (2)
Peyton, 72
Pinchebek, —, 36, 119
Pirie, 92
Place, 87
Plant, 91
Plat, 95
Playford, 87
Plays, Jo., 24
Plomesgate, Hundred of, 119
Plumbe, 90
Plumer, Robt., 46
Pole, Jo. de, 13, 126
Poll Tax (1377), 6; Enrolled acct. of, 6, 120
Poll Tax (1381), amount collected by, 5; clerical, 7; collection of, 4; Enrolled accts. of, 6; first returns of, 6; second commission of, 6
Poll Tax lists (1381), vii; analysis of, 67
Pope, 72, 109
Pope, Ad., 35
Population of England (Clerical) in 1381, 123
Population of England (Lay) in 1377, 121; in 1381, 121
Population of Wales (Clerical) in 1381, 124
Poreth, 119
Port, 82
Porter, 110 (2), 111, 113
Poter, Jo., 13, 126
Potte, 90
Powel, Rog., 25
Powgwene, 74
Poyt, 104
Prat, 87
Prat, Walt., 36
Prentys, 100, 108, 114
Prest, 76
Preston, 112 (2)
Prillay, 117
Priour, Jo., 128
Proude, 101
Prycke, 68
Pucool, 107
Puddy, 100
Pulrose, 77
Pulter, Ad., 30, 132
Pumpyn, 70, 71 (2)
Purs, 85 (2), 86, 87
Purston, 79
Puttok, 115
Pye, 77, 78, 84, 93

GENERAL INDEX

Pykbon, 115
Pykerel, Jo., 34
Pykering, God., 131
Pykering, Jo., 131
Pykrel, 87
Pylgrey, 84 (2)
Pyn, 94 (2)
Pynchebek, 36, 119
Pypere, 75, 77, 112
Pyteman, 88

Quarel, 116
Quy, 45
Qwenel, Geof.,134
Qwte, 76; *see* Whyte
Qwyntenoye, Jo., 33
Qwyte, 76, 100
Qwytewyng, 101
Qwytyng, 100

Ramsey, 46
Ramsey, Abbot of, 47
Rande, 85
Randekyn, 117
Randesson, 46
Randolf, 90
Raneld, 100 (2)
Raph, 84
Rash, 104
Rasol, 106
Ratlesden, 88
Raych, 107, 108
Reach, 43
Rebat, 111 (2), 112
Rebel forces, composition of, 62; numbers of, 61
Reche, 89
Rede, 67, 69
Rede, 108, 119 (2)
Redere, 87, 106
Redmedowe, Edm., 53
Redyng, Ben. de, 131
Redynhale, 71
Ree, 119
Reed, 90, 118
Reed, Jo., 120, 121
Ressh, Ric., 24
Resshebrok, *see* Rushbrooke
Reve, 85, 89, 95, 119
Revenhal, 85
Reymond, 88
Reyner, 112
Reyner, Geof., 135
Reynham, Edm. de, 36, 120
Reynold, 94, 106, 111
Reynolds, Jo., 24
Reysonn, 116
Ricard, 82
Richard II., his arms displayed by rioters, 58; his authority claimed by rioters, 31, 42, 45, 47, 53, 132, 137; his position in 1381,

58; his supposed connection with rising, 59
Riche, 73, 97
Rigge, 99
Ringsfield, 24
Rioters, Leaders of, in Camb., 41, 44; in Norf., 26; in Suffolk, 9, 11, 21, 22, 32; Provincial, in connection with London, 42, 43; tactics of, previous to outbreak, 27, 41, 57
Risby, 67, 82
Rising in East Anglia, organisation of, 57; unopposed, 57, 58; *see* Rioters
Robeld, 90 (2)
Roberdeson, Sim., 134
Rockingham, 42
Rogers, Jo., 45
Roggere, 73, 103
Rogges, Ad., 21
Rogyn, 109 (2)
Rokwood, 69, 70
Rokwood, Jo., 12
Rolf, 79, 88
Rolle, 104
Rome, 92 (2), 100
Rome, journey to, 15
Rond, Ric., 13
Rondham, 86
Rook, 104
Rose, 77, 96 (3), 101, 113
Rougham (Norf.), 31
Rouly, 92
Rous, W., 21, 130, 131
Rowe, 102, 103
Royse, Hen., 29, 132
Rudham, 77
Rumbald, 108
Rungeton, 77
Runting, 103
Rushbrooke, 93, 118, 119
Rushbrooke, W., 68
Russell, Jo., 51, 54
Russin, 71
Rust, 107, 108
Rust, Rob., 135
Ryche, 73, 97
Rychond, W., 136
Ryngedale, 77
Ryssengles, Jo., 131

Sadiller, 86
Saffrey, Jo., 43, 45
St Benedict de Hulm, Abbot of, 30
St Benedict de Hulm, Abbey of, 33; night attack on, 34
St John of Jerusalem, Priory of, 44, 45
Salle, Sir Rob., 30, 31; death of, 29, 132
Saltebek, 107

GENERAL INDEX.

Salter, 93, 94, 112, 113
Sampson, 110 (2), 112
Sampson, Lora, 145
Sampson, Thos., 22, 23, 28, 127; inquisition of, 143
Sannty, 81
Sare, 72
Sarle, 89, 90
Sawer, 102
Saxham, 78
Saxham Mag., 67, 80
Saxham Parva, 67, 81
Sayer, 111
Sayham, 78
Saylour, 72 (2)
Sayvill, Thos., 6
Scales, — de, 31; *see* Skales and Schales
Sceth, 38; *see* Skeet
Schabayle, 78
Schales, 96; *see* Scales
Schalo..., 118
Schapman, 73, 114; *see* Chapman
Schayl, 113
Schene, 97 (2)
Schere, 116
Scherwy..., 68
Scherwynd, 91
Schitte, 101
Schompayn, 79
Schordwaner, 79
Schort, Rob., 128
Schot, 68, 80, 81; *see* Scot
Schypman, 107, 108
Schyth, 100 (2)
Scot, 98, 108; *see* Schot
Sculton, 69
Sebourgh, 76
Sefoul, Geo., 120
Sel, 109
Seman, 110
Semer, 112
Senker, 90
Senlowes, 92
Serjaunt, 80 (2)
Serjiantes de payes, 87
Servants, 2, 67
Setard, 105, 106 (2)
Sewale, 101
Sextayn, 114
Seygge, 92
Seynsbury, Jo., 32
Shakerys, 89, 91
Shaldrye, 98
Shapestre, 105
Shardelow, Jo. de, 64
Sharnebourne, 135
Shelland, 98, 128
Shengay, 45, 138
Shepherd, 70, 79 (2), 80–83, 93, 94, 96, 98, 101, 104, 105 (3), 106 (2), 108, 110, 118, 119

Sherman, Hen., 28
Shethe, Jo., 47
Ship called 'Waynpayn,' 145
Shipman, *see* Schypman
Shirle, Jo., 54, 57
Shitte, 94 (2), 102
Shortnekke, 69 (3), 70
Shudy Camps, 44
Skales, Rog., 126, 129; *see* Scales
Skalman, 112
Skarlet, 86
Skeet, Thos., 28, 38
Skeyman, 93
Skoyt, 115
Skrevenor, W., 25
Skulton, 90
Skut, 93
Skynner, 86, 87, 88, 108, 112
Slade, 82
Slautere, 68, 82
Sloutere, 112
Sly, 86 (3), 88 (2)
Small, 119
Smalbon, 93, 94
Smalwode, 71
Smith, Ad., 32
Smyth, 68 (2), 69 (2), 70, 73 (2), 74–77, 82 (2), 83 (2), 84 (2), 86 (3), 88, 89 (2), 91 (2), 92, 93, 95, 99, 103 (2), 105, 107, 109, 113 (2), 115, 119 (2)
Smyth, Hen., 135
Smyth, Jo., 16, 131, 135
Smyth, Ric., 131
Smyth, W., 133, 134 (2)
Snellyng, 100
Snettisham, 135
Snowyth, 108
Snowwhyte, 118
Snyterton, Sim. de, 36
Soham, 44
Somerton, 13, 126
Somerton, 69, 70
Somerton, Ralph, 11
Sondes Castle, 33
Soneman, 69, 70
Sopere, 85, 86, 88
Sorell, 91, 99
Sorrell, Jo., 129
Soterly, 24
Sothewynd, Thos., 128
Soun, 117
Sourale, 69
Soutere, 68, 86 (2), 87, 99, 105, 117, 119
Soutere, Rob., 65
Southgate, Geof., 24
Southous, Edm. de, 133
Southous, Ric. de, 133
Southrepps, 37
Spak, 71
Spanye, Jo., 36, 61, 135

GENERAL INDEX.

Spark, 68
Sparwe, 91, 107, 108, 112, 114 (3), 115
Sped, 71
Spenser, 82, 107, 118
Spenser, Hen., 61; *see* Norwich, Bishop of
Spetylman, 92, 93 (2)
Spicor, 119
Spot, 90, 91, 100
Spring, 93
Sprot, 113
Sprouton, 97
Stalpy, 92
Stambourne, 109
Stampyn, Rob., 134
Stanford, Hen., 32
Stannford, Jo., 43
Stansfield, 12; parson of, 16
Stanton, 90, 100 (2), 104
Starre, Marg., 52
Statutes of Labourers, 1, 2
Staverton, Jo., 128
Stede, 94 (2)
Steeple Morden, 44, 137
Sterde, 100
Sterme, 80 (2)
Stoke, 95
Stoke juxta Clare, 21, 22
Stone, Jo. de, 135
Stonham, 71, 75
Stonton, 101; *see* Stanton
Storych, 73
Stow juxta Anglesey, 43
Stowe, Hundred of, 89
Stowlangtoft, 109
Stowmarket, 89, 129
Stradbrook, 131
Stratford, Roger, parson of, 23
Straw, Jack, 60
Strongehobbe, Rob., 132
Strotel, 94
Stuntney, 46
Styward, 69
Succlyng, 87 (3)
Sudbery, 96 (2)
Sudbury, 9, 10, 11, 12, 25, 36, 133; All *Saints*, 129
Suffolk, Archdeacon of, 23
Suffolk, Earl of, 18, 25
Suklyng, Ric., 130
Sulman, W., 131
Sumper, 83
Suthrey, 31, 34
Sutton, 46
Sutton, Jo. de, 23
Sutton, Marg. de, 23
Sveyn, 119
Svyn, 119
Swaffham, 42
Swaffham, Little, 45
Swaffham, Thos. de, 43, 45

Swage, 88
Swalwe, 101
Swon, le, 88
Sygo, 86 (3), 87, 89
Symond, 86 (2), 88 (3), 118, 119
Syre, 98

Taillor, *see* Taylor
Talbot, 99
Talihowr, 96
Talmache, Jo., 3, 11
Talmache, Ric., 3, 22, 127
Tangham, 115
Tankard, 74
Tavell, Rob., 11, 12, 44, 47, 49; death of, 46
Taylor, 73, 78 (2), 83, 84, 86 (4), 93, 95, 104, 106, 112 (2)
Taylor, Geof., 128
Taylor, Jo., 37
Taylor, Ph., 134
Tendryng, W. de, 67
Teppyng, 111
Teversham, Jo. de, 134
Tewe, Robt., 31
Thashere, *see* Thatcher
Thatcher, 79, 87 (2), 89, 109
Thedham, 91, 111
Thelich, 96
Thetford, 129
Thetford, Mayor of, 12
Thingo, Hundred of, analysis of Poll Taxes in, 67
Thommyson, 79
Thorndon, 86
Thorney, 101, 129
Thorpe Market, 35, 37, 39
Thresher, 88, 96
Threin, 110
Thurgor, 73
Thurlow parva, 43
Thurmood, 83 (2), 84, 92
Thursford, parson of, 35
Thurston, 88
Thurston, parson of, 65
Thurston, 64
Thwaite, 114
Thyth, 119
Tipping, 96
Tofeld, 85
Toffay, 107
Toke, 96
Tollote, 87
Toly, 105
Topham, 120, 122
Torel, Thos., 43, 138
Tornor, 71
Tostock, 90, 91
Totyngton, Walt. de, 19, 141
Toune, 84
Tower, Keeper of Victuals at the, 51
Tracy, 78

P.

GENERAL INDEX.

Trades and Callings[1]:
  Agricola, 68 (3), 69 (5), 71, 72 (4), 73, 75, 76, 77, 80, 81 (7), 83 (3), 85 (21), 91 (13), 92 (10), 93 (9), 94 (8), 95 (15), 96 (11), 97 (15), 98 (2), 102 (5), 103 (4), 104 (3), 105 (3), 106 (5), 107 (4), 108 (5), 109, 110 (4), 111 (2), 112, 113 (9), 114 (4), 118 (19); *see also* Cultor
  Architect, 107
  Armiger, 69, 76, 78, 81, 89, 92 (2), 95 (2), 96, 106, 109; *see also* Chivaler and Generosa

  Barker, 73
  Basket-maker, 90
  Bercarius, 69, 103 (4), 106, 108, 109 (2), 110 (3), 111 (2), 118; *see also* Pastor
  Bercher, 111
  Bocher, 68, 106
  Brasiator, 69 (2), 85 (7), 90 (2), 105, 109 (3), 112, 114 (3)
  Browster, 71, 73 (2), 74, 78, 81, 96

  Capellanus, 109
  Carnifex, 90, 93 (2), 97 (2)
  Carpenter, 69 (2), 71, 75, 76 (2), 83, 84 (3), 89 (2), 90 (2), 93 (3), 97, 101, 102, 108 (3), 111 (2), 112 (2), 113 (2), 114, 116, 118 (4)
  Carucarius, 69, 70, 107, 113
  Carucarum tentator, 110
  Carucator, 96 (3), 105, 106, 114, 116
  Celarer, 89
  Chinchere, 89, 90 (2), 96, 112
  Chivaler, 107; *see* Armiger
  Cissor, 89, 90 (2), 92 (2), 93 (3), 96, 97, 108 (2), 111, 112 (3), 113, 116, 118 (3); *see also* Tailor
  Claud (?), 1, 112
  Colermaker, 89, 90
  Cordwainer, 79; *see* Sutor
  Corn-loder, 108 (2)
  Cooperator, 90, 105, 106, 109
  Coopertor, 96, 118
  Corsour, 110
  Cultor, 99 (20), 115 (4), 116 (6), 117 (7); *see also* Agricola

  Day, 106
  Draper, 68, 76

  Faber, 69, 73 (2), 75 (2), 92 (2),

Trades and Callings (*continued*):
  93, 95 (2), 96, 109, 113, 118; *see* Smith
  Firmarius, 89, 117 (2)
  Flecher, 89
  Fleicer, 95
  Fouller, 90
  Fuller, 71, 90, 95 (2), 106, 107, 111 (2), 112 (4), 113 (2)

  Generosa, 89; *see also* Armiger
  Gleente?, 90

  Haberdasher, 90
  Hoxster, 90

  Launter, 113

  Meller, 96, 108
  Mercator, 111 (2), 112, 113
  Mercer (?), 103
  Mersonarius, 106
  Messor, 68, 111
  Meter, 103
  Molendinarius, 90, 109, 111

  Paner-maker, 92 (3)
  Pannarius, 85 (3), 112 (10), 113 (4)
  Parve tenure, 111 (2), 112
  Pastor, 96 (3), 107 (4); *see* Shepherd
  Pedder, 69, 96
  Pelliparius, 90, 93, 95
  Piscator, 95, 116 (10)
  Pistor, 89, 90 (2), 104

  Redere, 106

  Sacrista, 96
  Serjiaunts de Payes, 87 (2)
  Shepherd, 70; *see also* Bercarius
  Sherewoman, 90
  Sherman, 69
  Skrevenor, 109
  Smith, 68, 82, *see* Faber
  Spinner, 94 (6), 105 (2), 106 (5), 107 (5), 108 (3), 109, 117 (2)
  Spinster, 90 (2)
  Sutor, 68, 89 (4), 90, 95 (2), 105 (2), 107, 113, 114 (4), 118

  Tachere, 82
  Tailor, 68, 73, 74, 79, 81 (2), 84, 105, 106 (2), *see* Cissor
  Tannator, 90
  Tegulator, 90
  Thasher, 79
  Thatcher, 110

---

[1] This index of Trades and Callings refers only to the Poll Tax lists. The numbers in brackets give the number of persons to whom the term is applied, husband and wife being reckoned as one. The general classifications Artificers, Labourers, and Servants are not here included.

GENERAL INDEX. 163

Trades and Callings (*continued*):
  Textator, 92 (2)
  Textor, 93 (3), 95, 97, 107, 111 (4), 113 (3)
  Tinctor, 89, 112 (2), 113 (2)
  Triturator, 96 (3), 105 (2), 107, 108 (2), 109 (2)
  Turner, 68, 118

  Vannator, 70

  Webbe, 79
  Webber, 96 (3), 101 (2), 114, 118
  Webster, 68, 69, 71, 75, 81, 83, 104, 105 (2), 108 (3)
  Wright, 82
Trenchmere, 76
Trim..., 68
Trist, 98
Trot, 100
Trunch, Jo. de, 28, 32, 38
Trust, 98
Truton, 92
Tryker, 100 (2)
Tudenham, 70
Tuddenham, 82
Turgy, 104 (2)
Turnay, 86
Turnour, 68, 99
Turry, 117
Tweyt, 114
Tyby, 75, 88
Tyd, 87
Tyle, 71
Tyler, 94, 101, 109 (2), 118, 119
Tyler, Wat, 9, 10, 14, 34, 35, 59
Tymworth, 88 (2)
Tymworth, Jo., 15
Tyncewyk, 79
Tynton, 93 (2), 98 (2)
Tyteshall, Jo., 53

Ufford, W. de, 126, 131

Va, 119
Vaus, 98 (2), 111
Verdon, 82 (2), 83
Vicory, W., 136
Vynte, Jo., 128

Wade, 72, 110, 113 (2)
Waketon, 97
Walcard, 73 (2), 83
Waler, 109
Walhous, 72 (2)
Walkelynge, 74 (2), 75
Walpool, Jo. de, 135
Walsham, 69, 70, 85, 87 (2), 96
Walsham, Ralph de, 14
Walsingham, Edm. de, 48, 138
Walsingham, Thos. de, 2, 9, 27, 31; his account of rebel defeat, 37

Walsingham Parva, 28, 35
Walspryng, 69
Waltesheff, Ric., 46
Walton, 24, 136
Wangeforth, 96
Warde, 68, 73 (2), 74, 75 (2), 81, 107, 108
Warner, 68 (2)
Waryn, 86, 101, 111
Wastel, 75, 119
Watlesfield, 21
Wattes, Jo., 28
Watton, 88
Wattys, 85
Wauton, 103 (2)
Waynpayn, a ship called, 145
Wayte, 87
Webbe, 79
Webbe, Jo., 136, 137
Webber, 101 (2), 128
Webster, 83, 86 (3), 115, 117, 118
Wechingham, W. de, 33
Wekys, 90
Wel, atte, 79 (2)
Wele, 75
Welham, 80 (2)
Welhous, 72
Welyngham, 83 (2), 84
Weneis, 96
Wenlok, W., 121
Wente, 100
Wentworth, 47
Wepsted, 76 (2)
Wergowns, 96
Wescard, 119
West, 72 (2), 76, 117
Westbron, Rob., 16
Westbronn, 96 (4)
Westbronn, Jo., 129
Westcretyng, 94
West Dereham, 34
West Lexham, 35
Westley, 67, 83
West Wratting, 46
Wetherde, 110
Wetherden, 91
Wetherden, 95, 129
Weyne, 119
Whederyld, 101
Whelwryghte, 113
Whepsted, 67, 84
Whetewong, Jo., 36
Whyte, *see* Qwyte
Whyte, Jo., 46
Whytewing, *see* Qwytewyng
Whytman, 85
Whytyng, *see* Qwytyng
Wickmere, 37
Wiclif, Jo., 3
Wigmore, W., 51
Wilbraham, 42, 45
Wilde, 90, 91

GENERAL INDEX.

Willingham, 48
Wimpole, 44, 45
Wingfeld, W. de, 126
Winterton, 33
Wirlingworth, Elias, 131
Wlvard, 101
Wode, 83 (2), 91, 92, 96, 107, 108
Wode, atte, 101
Wodecok, 73, 96 (3)
Wodyer, 112
Wokilwode, 134
Wolfreston, Rog. de, 23
Wolleman, 112
Wolrich, Thos., 131
Woodbarningham, 37
Wooditton, 41
Wordwell, 110
Worsted, 28
Wotton, 69
Wrawe, John (of Ringsfield), 24
Wrawe, John (of Sudbury), 9–12, 17–19, 32, 36, 37, 129, 133; execution of, 25; his authority in Cambridgeshire, 41, 48; his authority in Norfolk, 36
Wroo, 108
Wroo, Thos., 41
Wrotham, 25
Wroxham, 32
Wryght, 69, 71, 73, 75, 82, 88 (2), 93, 98, 100, 111, 112
Wryte, see Wryght

Wryth, see Wryght
Wulward, 111
Wyard, 115
Wyfford, 68
Wygg, 119
Wyghton, 31
Wyhot, 106
Wykes, 109
Wylde, 85, 88, 118
Wylkok, 88
Wylymot, Sim., 135
Wymbyl, 107, 108
Wymdyssh, 119
Wymondham, 38, 134
Wympol, Nich., 53
Wyng, 89, 99, 100
Wynyeve, 76, 106, 107
Wyse, 105
Wysman, 69 (2), 70, 76
Wysman, John, 128
Wyth, 110
Wytlok, 109 (2)
Wytnesham, Walt., 128
Wytyng, 119

Yarmouth, 33, 36, 39; charter destroyed, 32; riots at, 32
Yaxham, 133
Yongwone, 83

Zouch, Hugo le, 138
Zyngge, Ric. le, 128

THE END.

CAMBRIDGE: PRINTED BY J. AND C. F. CLAY, AT THE UNIVERSITY PRESS.

www.ingramcontent.com/pod-product-compliance
Lightning Source LLC
Chambersburg PA
CBHW031451160426
43195CB00010BB/936